"*Shadows in the Jungle* [is] a tale that is always gripping if frequently gruesome . . . provides a much-needed remedy to the relative obscurity of the feats of these soldiers. Employing a gritty, up-close style that gives the narrative the feel of a novel, Alexander combines, to great effect, personal testimonies of Scouts he interviewed with official accounts of their deeds. . . . All Americans can be proud of the Alamo Scouts; *Shadows in the Jungle* shows us exactly why."

—*ARMY Magazine*

Praise for Larry Alexander's National Bestseller
Biggest Brother
The Life of Major Dick Winters,
the Man Who Led the Band of Brothers

"Excellent. . . . Anyone who has read *Band of Brothers* will want to read this."   —*ARMY Magazine*

"A great job . . . extremely readable."   —*The Topeka Capital-Journal*

"[A] straightforward study of the best sort of small-unit leader."
—*Publishers Weekly*

Includes a Sneak Peek of Larry Alexander's

In the Footsteps of the Band of Brothers

Coming in hardcover from NAL Caliber in May 2010

Also by Larry Alexander

Biggest Brother: The Life of Major Dick Winters,
the Man Who Led the Band of Brothers

In the Footsteps of the Band of Brothers:
A Return to Easy Company's Battlefields with Sergeant Forrest Guth
(Coming in May 2010)

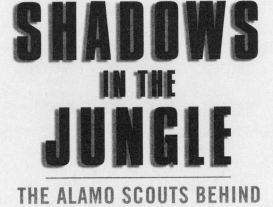

SHADOWS
IN THE
JUNGLE

THE ALAMO SCOUTS BEHIND
JAPANESE LINES IN WORLD WAR II

LARRY ALEXANDER

NAL
CALIBER

NAL Caliber
Published by New American Library, a division of
Penguin Group (USA) Inc., 375 Hudson Street,
New York, New York 10014, USA
Penguin Group (Canada), 90 Eglinton Avenue East, Suite 700, Toronto,
Ontario M4P 2Y3, Canada (a division of Pearson Penguin Canada Inc.)
Penguin Books Ltd., 80 Strand, London WC2R 0RL, England
Penguin Ireland, 25 St. Stephen's Green, Dublin 2,
Ireland (a division of Penguin Books Ltd.)
Penguin Group (Australia), 250 Camberwell Road, Camberwell, Victoria 3124,
Australia (a division of Pearson Australia Group Pty. Ltd.)
Penguin Books India Pvt. Ltd., 11 Community Centre, Panchsheel Park,
New Delhi - 110 017, India
Penguin Group (NZ), 67 Apollo Drive, Rosedale, North Shore 0632,
New Zealand (a division of Pearson New Zealand Ltd.)
Penguin Books (South Africa) (Pty.) Ltd., 24 Sturdee Avenue,
Rosebank, Johannesburg 2196, South Africa

Penguin Books Ltd., Registered Offices:
80 Strand, London WC2R 0RL, England

Published by NAL Caliber, an imprint of New American Library, a division of Penguin Group (USA) Inc.
Previously published in an NAL Caliber Hardcover edition.

First NAL Caliber Trade Paperback Printing, February 2010
10 9 8 7 6 5 4 3 2

NAL CALIBER and the "C" logo are trademarks of Penguin Group (USA) Inc.

NAL Caliber Trade Paperback ISBN: 978-0-451-22913-7

The Library of Congress has cataloged the hardcover edition of this title as follows:

Alexander, Larry, 1951–
    Shadows in the jungle: the Alamo Scouts behind Japanese lines in World War II/Larry Alexander.
        p.   cm.
    Includes bibliographical references.
    ISBN 978-0-451-22593-1
1. World War, 1939–1945—Campaigns—Pacific Area.   2. United States. Army. Army, 6th. Special
Reconnaissance Unit.   3. World War, 1939–1945—Regimental histories—United States.   4. World War,
1939–1945—Reconnaissance operations.   5. World War, 1939–1945—Military intelligence—United
States.   I. Title.
    D767.A66   2009
    940.54'2599–dc22   2008024558

Set in Bodini Oldface
Designed by Ginger Legato

Printed in the United States of America

PUBLISHER'S NOTE
While the author has made every effort to provide accurate telephone numbers and Internet addresses at the time of publication, neither the publisher nor the author assumes any responsibility for errors, or for changes that occur after publication. Further, publisher does not have any control over and does not assume any responsibility for author or third-party Web sites or their content.

This book is respectfully dedicated to the Alamo Scouts, unsung heroes of the war in the southwest Pacific.

CONTENTS

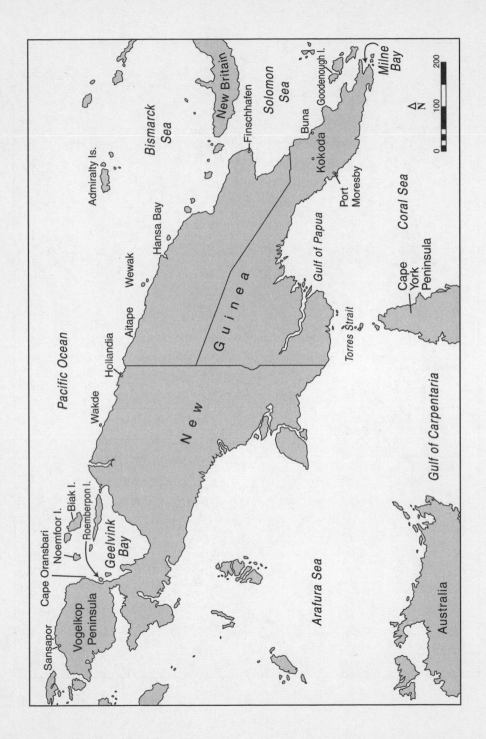

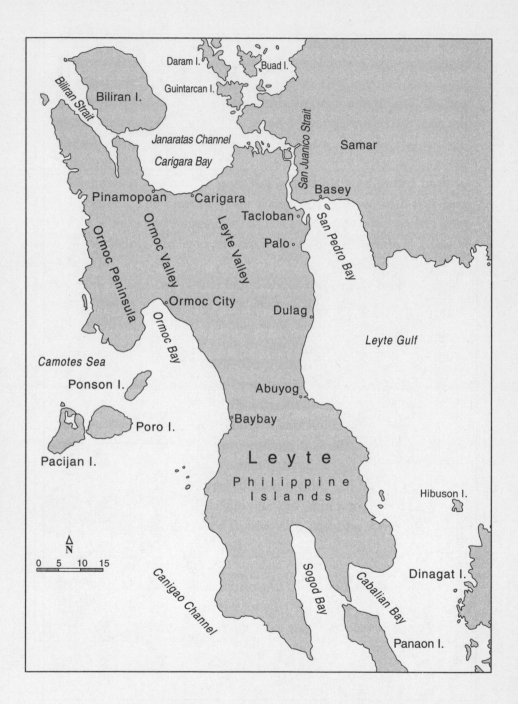

Daram I.

Buad I.

Guintarcan I.

Biliran Strait

Biliran I.

Janaratas Channel

Carigara Bay

Samar

San Juanico Strait

Basey

Pinamopoan

Carigara

Tacloban

Palo

San Pedro Bay

Ormoc Valley

Leyte Valley

Ormoc Peninsula

Ormoc City

Dulag

Leyte Gulf

Ormoc Bay

Camotes Sea

Ponson I.

Abuyog

Poro I.

Baybay

Pacijan I.

L e y t e

P h i l i p p i n e
I s l a n d s

Hibuson I.

N

0   5   10   15

Canigao Channel

Sogod Bay

Caballian Bay

Dinagat I.

Panaon I.

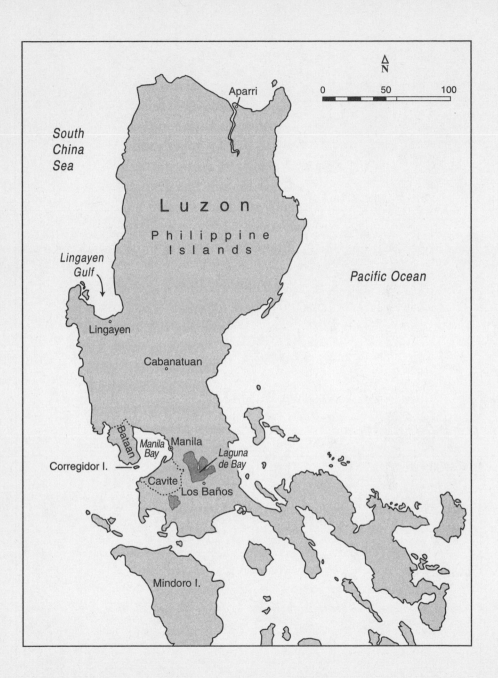

South
China
Sea

Aparri

Δ
N

0   50   100

L u z o n

P h i l i p p i n e
I s l a n d s

Pacific Ocean

Lingayen
Gulf

Lingayen

Cabanatuan

Bataan

Manila
Bay

Manila

Laguna
de Bay

Corregidor I.

Cavite

Los Baños

Mindoro I.

SHADOWS
IN THE
JUNGLE

The Best of the Best

In late December 2006, an eighty-five-year-old man left his favorite restaurant and headed for his parked car. He had just enjoyed his dinner of crispy-fried filet of sole, half of which he had eaten and the other half of which the restaurant staff had dutifully wrapped "to go."

When the elderly man, aided by a cane, arrived at his car, he slipped the key into the passenger-side door lock, opened the door, and placed his doggy bag on the seat. Then he closed the door.

That was when the mugger struck, a hard blow on the right side of the man's head that broke his glasses' frame and cut him above the eye. Somewhat softened by the bill of his baseball-style cap, the blow nonetheless staggered the elderly man. He felt himself falling, but was able to catch himself by bracing his arms on the cane.

Blood clouded the vision in the man's right eye, but from his left he saw his attacker's feet on the sidewalk before him, and in one swift motion he brought the cane up between them. The mugger yelped as the cane connected with his testicles, and he stumbled back. With the advantage now on his side, the old man reversed the cane and, using the curved handle, swung it like a baseball bat against each of the mugger's shins. The cane connected with a resounding crack and the mugger hit the pavement like a felled ox. The old man swung the cane again, this time taking aim on his attacker's knees, and heard the pop of wood striking bone. He delivered another blow to the man's crotch.

By now the mugger was rolling on the ground, howling in pain, his arms shielding his head in anticipation of being hit there. Instead, the elderly man brought the cane down two more times, once to each side of the rib cage, cracking bones with each swing. He then leaned back against his car and waited for the police.

When a female officer arrived, having been called by a witness walking her dog, she took in the scene. Paramedics were tending to a young, tough-looking man writhing in agony on the sidewalk, while at the ambulance another medical worker was bandaging the forehead of the elderly man with the cane. The officer walked up to the victim-turned-victor.

"You did this?" she asked in disbelief, pointing to the thoroughly whipped thug.

"No," he replied. "My cane did."

The police officer was obviously surprised, but had she known the old man, her reaction might have been different. For, sixty-two years earlier, the man, a World War II veteran, had been an Alamo Scout, a decorated member of the U.S. Army's smallest elite fighting force, trained not just in the skills of jungle survival, intelligence gathering, and reconnaissance, but to respond automatically and with deadly force when attacked.

The mugger, although he may never know it, had been fortunate.

★　★　★

It was just after eight a.m. on Wednesday, October 10, 2007, when the taxi rolled up to the main entrance of the Renaissance Hotel in Denver, Colorado. After paying off the cabby, I entered the hotel lobby, where the first thing that greeted my eyes was a table festooned with a red, white, and blue banner proclaiming ALAMO SCOUTS ASSOCIATION.

I smiled. I had arrived.

A little over a year earlier, I had been somewhat in the same shoes as the police officer who responded to the mugging. Like her and many other Americans, I knew little or nothing about the Alamo Scouts. I had come across their name once or twice over the years in the course of my reading but was not really aware of who they were and what they had done.

Now, I had traveled nearly two thousand miles to meet them and get their stories down on tape, for they were to be the subject of my next book.

After the release of *Biggest Brother*, an account of the famed World War II paratrooper Dick Winters, in 2005, I wasn't sure there'd be a "next book." I had not written *Biggest Brother* as a means of securing a second career as an author. Instead, I had done it as a tribute to the life of a man whose story I felt Americans needed to know.

However, after a while, my passion as a writer began to get the best of me and I sought a subject for a second book, fueled perhaps by the many e-mails and phone calls from readers who enjoyed not just *Biggest Brother* but my style of storytelling, and encouraged me to write again. So how could I not? Besides, I've had a lifelong fascination with books and had dreamed of being an author ever since I was twelve years old and my grandparents bought me my first typewriter.

So I began searching for a topic that, if not new and untouched, had at least not been plowed over in countless previous books.

That's how I stumbled across the Alamo Scouts Web site. This site, at www.alamoscouts.org, contains a wealth of information on the unit, and includes photos and personal stories, and the more I read, the more I was in awe of these men and their deeds.

The site led me to the only book devoted to the unit, *Silent Warriors of World War II: The Alamo Scouts Behind the Japanese Lines*, by Lance Q. Zedric, published in 1995. Zedric had begun the book as a college thesis, and had the good fortune to link up with the surviving Scouts and preserve many of their stories.

After looking over the Web site and the book, I contacted Russ Blaise, the executive director of the Alamo Scouts Association and the son of the late William F. Blaise, a Scout with the Sumner Team. Russ was more than agreeable to the idea of a new book about his father's unit, and with his valuable assistance, and the support of Zedric, who is now the Alamo Scouts' official historian, I was off and running.

With Russ's invaluable help, I began making contact with surviving Alamo Scouts, conducting both telephone and face-to-face interviews and obtaining much-needed documents and notes. The work went smoothly, not just in putting together the story of the Scouts but in finding the trivia and detail I needed to help bring those stories to life. But something was missing, and it proved to be the personal touch. I needed to actually meet some of these men.

Getting together with Jack Geiger of the Lutz Team proved easy. He lives in New Jersey and we were able to meet personally on two occasions, and his assistance proved vital in putting together the story of his team and its men.

But I needed more of that one on one, which is what drew me to Denver to attend the Alamo Scouts reunion and meet the men I had been researching and reading about for the past year.

★   ★   ★

The Alamo Scouts were conceived by Maj. Gen. Walter Krueger in late 1943, in response to a desire by his commander—Gen. Douglas MacArthur—for a reliable reconnaissance unit whose information he could depend on for its accuracy. Suspicious and vain, MacArthur distrusted the Office of Strategic Services for his intelligence, because of the OSS's close ties to the Joint Chiefs of Staff, whom MacArthur viewed with extreme skepticism and disdain.

The Scouts were an all-volunteer organization formed under the leadership of Col. Frederick Bradshaw. He laid out a six-week training program that was intense and rugged, designed to weed out all but the best candidates. Men were dismissed not just if they failed to make the grade physically but also based on their personalities. Bullies, loudmouths, and individualists didn't last. The men had to like each other and trust one another, because their lives depended on mutual trust and teamwork. They also needed good survival instincts and keen senses. In once instance, Scouts located a Japanese camp by following the scent of a can of sardines opened by an enemy soldier.

For those who graduated from the Alamo Scout Training Camp, life off the line was as good as Krueger could make it. They had first-class accommodations insofar as food, tentage, and other amenities, such as shower facilities, refrigerators, and radios, could be obtained. Hotel Alamo, the men dubbed their camp.

Bradshaw, through Krueger, also made sure the men had the very best in equipment and weaponry. Whatever a man wanted, he was given.

But it was in the field where the Alamo Scouts proved their worth. Working in teams of six or seven men, they operated miles behind enemy lines on missions that sometimes lasted up to seventy days. Moving silently among the Japanese in their camouflage uniforms and painted hands and faces, and communicating mostly by hand signals, they collected data on possible invasion beaches, tides and currents, troop numbers and locations, enemy morale, defensive positions, the availability of roads and fresh water, and other much-needed information. And while their main mission was to collect intelligence and not fight the enemy, they were sometimes called upon to perform raider duties, such as destroying enemy supply depots, and rescuing civilian hostages and prisoners of war from the Japanese.

Between December 27, 1943, and September 2, 1945, 325 officers and men would graduate from the Alamo Scout Training Camp, but only 138 would be assigned to one of the twelve Alamo Scout teams. Yet the Scouts, as a unit, never numbered more than 78 men—65 men and 13 officers—on active duty at any one time.

By the war's end, the Alamo Scouts had conducted 108 missions, all of them fraught with danger. Working miles behind enemy lines, they are credited with killing more than five hundred Japanese soldiers and taking about sixty prisoners, and while they suffered a dozen or more men wounded, no Scout was killed in combat.

In the course of their work, the Scouts were awarded forty-four Silver Stars, two with Oak Leaf clusters; thirty-three Bronze Stars, eleven with Oak Leaf clusters; and four Soldier's Medals. Three men were recommended for the Distinguished Service Cross and two teams, under Lts. William Nellist and Thomas Rounsaville, won Presidential Unit Citations for their part in the POW rescue at Cabanatuan in January 1945.

After the war, the Pentagon ordered that the missions of the Alamo Scouts be classified, and the Scouts were basically told to go home, resume their lives, and shut up. That, along with the fact that the unit was deactivated without fanfare, ceremony, or any degree of recognition, left a bitter taste in the mouths of many of the men who so proudly wore the Alamo Scout patch.

Around 1988, most of their missions were declassified, and the rest were done so a few years later and finally the veterans, now men into their sixties, received the coveted Special Forces shoulder tab.

By the time I caught up with them in Denver, they were all old men, gray-haired and, in some cases, in poor health. Indeed, only seven Scouts were slated to attend the reunion, and only five actually showed up.

Just as it was difficult for me to imagine the Dick Winters I know today as the twenty-three-year-old paratrooper who jumped out of airplanes in 1944, so too was it hard for me to picture these aging men as the soldiers who crept so close to the Japanese that an enemy soldier actually pissed on one of them without seeing him. But the youthful gleam in their eyes as they spoke to me about those days told me differently.

I wasn't completely comfortable with the idea of meeting the Alamo Scouts there in Denver. Although they knew I was coming, I felt less like a visitor and more like an intruder to these men who played such a key role in General MacArthur's victories and who, now in their twilight years, were gathering to share their memories and relive the days of their youth with their comrades.

I fretted needlessly.

The first Scout I caught up with was Terry Santos, who declined to join a team back in 1944 and returned to his original unit after Alamo Scout training. Terry was lead scout on the Los Baños internment camp raid, helping to free over two thousand civilian prisoners, and he won a Silver Star for knocking out three Japanese machine-gun emplacements.

Still spry at eighty-six, Terry was talkative and outgoing. He seemed to have a drive that made him the obvious leader of the group at the reunion, taking charge of meetings and allocating responsibility for activities.

Wilbur Littlefield, one of the surviving team leaders, soon arrived from Los Angeles. I had interviewed him on the phone and now had the chance to meet him and talk further. He made me feel at ease and seemed to enjoy reliving his experiences with me.

Aubrey "Lee" Hall was there, too. As a temporary member of the team led by John Dove, he took part in a perilous mission in New Guinea. I had interviewed Lee on the phone prior to meeting him, and I had the chance to continue our discussions in Denver.

Likewise, Bob Buschur and Conrad Vineyard, two Scouts who never had the chance to serve on teams, were most helpful, as were the families of the deceased Alamo Scouts Irv Ray, Harold Hard, Bill Nellist, John McGowen, William McCommons, and Zeke McConnell.

I went away from Denver not just with a wealth of information and a further appreciation of what these men did but with a group of new friends.

Only about a tenth of the 325 men who qualified as Alamo Scouts are known to remain. Many have passed on, some taking their untold stories with them. It is because of this, plus their decades of government-enforced silence, that so few people are familiar with their names and deeds.

Making those names and deeds known is the goal of this book.

★   ★   ★

With the exception of the Scouts' role in the famous prisoner-of-war rescue at Cabanatuan, where five hundred Allied POWs were saved from certain death by a small force of 6th Army Rangers, the missions related in this book appear not based on their significance or level of excitement but solely on the amount of information available. Teams like the one led by Lt. Robert "Red" Sumner loom large in this work, not because Sumner did anything the other Scout teams did not do, but due to the wonderful memoirs left behind by Sumner and made available to me by Russ Blaise, Lance Zedric, and Ann Sumner.

Likewise, interviews and memoirs by other Scouts, some deceased and some still living, make the missions of the Dove, Nellist, Rounsaville, Lutz, Littlefield, and McGowen teams appear most often throughout this text.

That is not intended to negate the work of the other five teams.

The work of the Alamo Scouts—all of them, including those who were not on teams, such as Terry Santos, whose story also appears in these pages—deserves the recognition and honor so long denied it. Their contribution toward American success in the southwest Pacific has never been fully acknowledged.

Again, that is a goal of this book.

★   ★   ★

Today, the surviving Alamo Scouts stay in close contact and gather once a year for a reunion. And while their numbers, sadly, are constantly diminishing, the spirit of camaraderie that I saw in 2007 does not fade.

In wartime, these men depended on each other with their lives. Their souls were forged together in ties stronger than family. This will continue so long as one Alamo Scout remains.

For just as surely as Dick Winters and the men of Easy Company were forever bound together, the Alamo Scouts, too, are a Band of Brothers.

CHAPTER 1

Hollandia: "Looks Like We Walk Home."

Dove Team: New Guinea Coast, Midnight, June 6–7, 1944

"We're there," the skipper of PT-363 said in a hushed voice as he slowed the eighty-foot Elco, nicknamed by her crew the *Aces Avenger*, to a complete stop.

Lt. John Dove nodded, gazing toward the dark mass eight hundred yards away that was the coast of New Guinea.

"Fine," he said. "We'll get off."

"Water's pretty rough tonight, Jack," the PT commander cautioned. "You sure you want to try it?"

"We're going," Dove said, his usual boyish sense of humor giving way to an all-business attitude. He turned, left the boat's cockpit, and headed toward the stern, where his six team members waited, sitting on the deck between a torpedo tube and the 20mm antiaircraft gun.

Compared to the PT boat crewmen in their blue dungarees, Jack Dove and his men looked frighteningly fierce. Their uniforms were camouflage, topped off with a soft baseball cap in place of a helmet, which could make noise or reflect a stray beam of light. Their faces and hands were smeared with grease paint. The men carried either M1 carbines or Thompson submachine guns, and each was armed with a

.45-caliber automatic pistol. In addition, each soldier toted binoculars, one hundred rounds of ammo, a knife, two canteens, three days' rations—a peanut-raisin mix—packed in small rubber bags, flares, and compasses.

Dove and his men were members of America's smallest elite fighting force, the 6th U.S. Army Special Reconnaissance Unit, nicknamed the "Alamo Scouts." The name Alamo was derived from their attachment to Maj. Gen. Walter Krueger's 6th Army, code-named the Alamo Force in honor of Krueger's hometown of San Antonio, Texas, where the famous Spanish mission stands as a monument to the Americans who died there 108 years earlier.

The Scouts had been gleaned from hundreds of volunteers and trained for one purpose: to infiltrate Japanese lines, gather intelligence, and get the hell out in one piece.

"We believe the Japs are pulling back from in front of our lines at Hollandia, westward toward Wakde," Dove had been told by one of Krueger's G2 intelligence officers earlier that day. "We're going to put you ashore near the Taorum River just west of the village of Armopa, about midway between Hollandia and Wakde. We want you to confirm that the Japs are pulling back, estimate troop strength if possible, as well as their overall condition, meaning are they capable of regrouping and launching a counterattack."

Dove, a six-foot-tall, ruggedly handsome two-hundred-pounder who looked like a college all-American football star, nodded. A long way from his home at 153 West Norton Avenue in Hollywood, Dove was a deeply religious man who did not drink or smoke, and often led his men in the singing of hymns. This would be his team's first mission, and as he contemplated the possibility of going into battle, he prayed for himself, his men, and even the Japanese.

"If you don't want me to kill the enemy, Lord, don't let me see him," he invoked.

Rejoining his team on the 363's stern, Dove looked to the two sailors standing by the inflated ten-man rubber boat.

"Get that over the side," he said. "Let's load up. Quickly."

The sailors lowered the rubber boat into the wave-tossed water and held on tightly to the mooring ropes. The Scouts loaded themselves and their equipment, which included a heavy SCR-300 radio, into the bouncing dinghy.

Dove was last. Before stepping down into the rubber boat he turned to the one Scout who was not going ashore. Staff Sgt. Vern M. Miller of Jerome, Iowa, would remain on the PT as the contact man, monitoring the team's progress via radio and arranging for its eventual pickup. The contact man was always a member of another Scout team. Miller was one of Lt. Woodrow E. Hobbs's men.

Miller extended a hand.

"We'll see you in two days, Jack. Good luck."

Dove shook the hand, unfazed by Sergeant Miller's use of his first name. Unlike larger army units, such familiarity between ranks was common among the small, elite Scouts.

Dove climbed into the rubber boat, seating himself at the rear in order to man the steering paddle. Once he settled, the mooring ropes were released and the Scouts pushed off from the *Aces Avenger*'s plywood hull and began rowing across the dark sea toward land.

Despite the load carried by the rubber boat, the ride was a rough one as the surf tossed it relentlessly. The oars bit into the water as the men struggled to push the boat toward shore, riding up and down the ocean swells.

As the men fought the sea, Dove's mind was on the mission and the six soldiers accompanying him into action for the first time.

Just in front of Dove and straining with the oars sat T/5 James Roby of North Hollywood, and Pfc. Irvin J. Ray, who at age nineteen was the team's baby. Generally a quiet and unassuming young man, he had tousled dark hair and hailed from Oakland Beach, Rhode Island. Ray had joined the army after his color-blindness disqualified him from the navy. "They like it if you can tell a red running light from a green one, so you know if you're coming or going," he joked. However, his disability sometimes helped him to "see through" camouflage as he noted shapes and was not deceived by colors.

Next came Staff Sgt. John G. Fisher of Jacksonville, Florida, and Pfc. Aubrey L. "Lee" Hall, the team's only experienced Scout. A Texas native, Hall—who later would become the first Alamo Scout to win a battlefield commission and lead his own team—had been temporarily reassigned to Dove from the Barnes Team, which was dissolved when its leader, Lt. William Barnes, had been recalled to his old unit, the 32nd Division. Hall had been on the Barnes Team's lone mission in March.

Ahead of them was a young Dutch and Javanese interpreter supplied by the Dutch East Indies Administration. At the very front of the rubber boat sat T/4 Denny M. Chapman of Kellogg, Idaho, and Pvt. Alton P. Bauer of Melvin, Texas, who, like Ray and Roby, were both manning oars.

All eyes were glued on the dark coastline that loomed closer and closer.

Suddenly Roby whispered, "Sir." He pointed to a small glow emanating from the darkness, about three hundred yards to the right of where the rubber boat was about to reach shore. "Do you see that?"

"I see it," Dove whispered back, watching the point of light grow larger. "Keep going."

Ninety minutes after leaving the *Aces Avenger*, the rubber boat scraped on the sandy bottom with a shushing sound. In an instant, the men were out in the shin-deep water, dragging the heavy boat out of the surf, across the narrow beach and into the field of tall, razor-sharp kunai grass, which grows in profusion on the coastal plains of New Guinea. Kneeling, the men waited quietly, weapons at the ready, for any sound of alarm that might indicate they had been spotted.

Hearing nothing but the cawing of jungle birds, Dove picked up the radio handset and said, "Dove. OK."

"Roger," came Miller's reply.

As Dove reported the team's safe arrival, two Scouts deflated and packed up the rubber boat, its oars, and a full CO_2 cartridge to be used for reinflation, and carefully hid them, noting their location. They then eradicated any signs of their landing as one of the men slung the thirty-five-pound radio onto his back. The team would take turns carrying it.

Dove motioned the team to follow and led them through the tall grass and into the rain forest, where they soon came upon a native coastal trail. Fresh footprints in the soft ground showed the trail was well-used. Dove turned west, moving toward the Taorum River.

He'd not gone a hundred yards when he stuck a hand in the air. The team froze in mid-stride.

On the ground before them an obviously exhausted Japanese soldier was curled up, fast asleep. Using his clenched fist to indicate "hold," Dove silently crept forward. As he moved, careful where he placed each foot lest he snap a twig, Dove slid his knife from its sheath with his right hand and removed his cap with his left. Steeling his nerves, he sprang forward. Shoving the cap into the sleeping soldier's face to muffle his cries, Dove drove the knife into the man's chest. He felt the warm blood against his hand as the hapless soldier squirmed, then went silent.

Dove removed the knife, wiped the blade on the dead man's uniform, searched the corpse for documents, then dragged the body off the trail and into the underbrush.

The team resumed their trek.

After another two hundred yards the men came across two more Japanese huddled around a campfire in a small clearing. This was the glow they had spotted from the rubber boat.

Dove studied the scene briefly. Realizing there was no way to surprise these men, he turned to Bauer, who was next to him. Silently, Dove pointed to his knife and shook his head. Then he pointed to his carbine. Bauer understood. Dove indicated that Bauer was to take the man on the right, and he'd handle the soldier on the left. Both men aimed.

"Now," Dove whispered.

Gunfire crackled in the darkness as both men fired off several rounds. It was impossible to miss, and the two Japanese soldiers died by their campfire.

After searching the bodies, Dove had them dragged into the swampy forest and the fire extinguished. He was just ready to move out again when shots erupted behind him. A Japanese patrol had come upon the team's two-man rear guard, who reacted by cutting loose on the enemy.

The rest of the team quickly joined in and the loud skirmish echoed through the forest. The Japanese Arisakas barked in response to the rapid-firing automatic weapons of the Scouts, muzzle flashes puncturing the inky blackness of the night. Then the enemy soldiers evaporated back into the jungle and a stone silence descended.

"The Japs are moving along this trail in front of us and in back of us," Dove said. "Follow me."

He led the team westward for a short distance, then veered off the trail, moving ten yards into the underbrush. Finding a concealed spot where they could keep an eye on the path, the team hunched down and set up an observation post. The next five hours were spent in absolute silence as the Scouts, trying to ignore the island's insect life that crawled over and around them, counted Japanese soldiers trudging by, some without weapons and all looking tired and hungry, Dove noted.

As the sun hit its apogee in the sky and began its descent, Dove decided to put distance between his team and the bodies they had left in their wake. Avoiding the footpath, he led the team westward, through the tangled muck of the jungle.

★   ★   ★

The Taorum River was a black ribbon in an even blacker night, one of many waterways that flowed down from the twenty-five-mile-long Cyclops mountain range that loomed ten miles inland. The team had spent the afternoon hours slowly, painstakingly wending its way through thick brush and muddy swamps that almost sucked the men's boots from their feet with each step. All along the way, they were surrounded by the smell of decaying foliage, which, as darkness descended, created foxfire that twinkled around them like silent muzzle flashes.

Now it was about ten p.m. and the Scouts, exhausted after nearly twenty-two sleepless hours onshore, knelt in the underbrush on the river's east bank. Waiting in absolute silence, Dove strained his ears for any sound from the opposite side. Hearing none, he turned to Hall and pointed to the other bank.

Hall, holding his weapon and ammo high, waded into the gently flowing water, crossing slowly to avoid any splashing. All eyes remained fixed on the far side. Weapons were pointed and at the ready. When Hall reached the safety of the far bank, Dove sent the next man. Within thirty minutes, the team was across.

Dove knew his men were exhausted, but it was imperative to keep moving. He wanted to at least reach the Mabaf River, another three hours' march away.

★   ★   ★

The trail led through the small village of Kaptisoe, which lay silent in the early-morning darkness. But the quiet was deceiving. Japanese troops, about forty of them from what Dove could determine, occupied the collection of thatched-roof nipa huts. Even now he saw shadows walking the grounds between the huts, possibly sentries making their rounds.

The trek from the Taorum River had been relatively short, just a couple of miles, but rugged thanks to the thick vegetation, mangrove swamps, and steeply ridged terrain. It had taken the better part of three hours. Along the way the team had seen numerous Japanese soldiers. Some were sleeping in clumps, fatigued beyond measure, while others lay dead of starvation or exhaustion brought on by illness. The Dove Team bypassed the sleeping men without rousing them. The dead were searched, then left where they had fallen, to be claimed by the jungle, their families back home left to wonder.

For the past thirty minutes, Dove had been scrutinizing Kaptisoe, trying to think of a way around it, but with neck-deep swamps on both sides, doubtless inhabited by some of New Guinea's fierce crocodiles, his only course of action soon became clear. Gathering his team in a close huddle, he said in a hushed voice, "Going through the swamps is out. They might hear us and we'd be caught out there like sitting ducks. So we're going to walk straight through. Nips have been moving along this trail all day and night. With luck, in the dark, those fellas will assume we're just more of their buddies."

"And if they spot us?" Fisher asked.

"We open fire and run like mad," Dove replied. "Follow me."

Rising, Dove led his men into the village, walking among the darkened huts and sleeping enemy.

Nerves taut, they had gone only partway when a Japanese soldier emerged from the nearby shadows. He saw the strange dark shapes of men walking through the village, and halted. Though the soldier was smiling, Dove could see fear creeping across his countenance. Taking four steps toward the man, Dove swung up his carbine and squeezed off two quick rounds into the man's face. The impact of the .30-caliber slugs smacked the soldier backward and he hit the ground hard.

"Fire!" Dove said, and the team's weapons were instantly in action, the flat, rapid crack of carbines blending with the sharp *brrraaapp, brrraaapp* of the Thompsons.

A Japanese guard came running out from a hut and was swept off his feet as a hail of lead ripped through him, creating a bloody mist with each impact.

"Go! Go!" Dove shouted as he and his men, spraying bullets in all directions, ran along the trail, through the village, and into the gloom of the forest beyond.

The team raced on for several hundred yards, through woods and swamp, tripping over underbrush yet somehow keeping their feet, until Dove finally called a halt. He led them a few steps off the trail, where they sat to catch their breath.

"Jesus, that was fun," the youthful Ray puffed. "Friggin' O.K. Corral."

The boy's analogy—he loved cowboy movies—brought a chuckle from the men. Then Dove said, "This is home for the night. Settle in and get some sleep, but any man who snores gets a boot. And don't forget those quinine pills, I don't want anyone coming down with malaria. We'll stand guard in two-hour shifts, two men each." He pointed at Ray. "Wyatt Earp and I will take the first watch."

⋆ ⋆ ⋆

As Dove sat quietly in the dark, listening to the jungle sounds mingled with the soft, easy breathing of his men, a sensation of scents came to his nostrils: the dank, moldering odor of the swamp and the fragrance of jungle flowers. Then a new smell came to him, that of sweating human bodies. Putting up a hand to signal Ray to remain silent, they sat still as a trio of natives walked along the path, passing not three feet from the sleeping Americans. Dove listened to their steps recede.

"Think they spotted us?" Ray asked nervously.

"I don't know," Dove said. "But we smelled them, so they must've smelled us."

The answer to Ray's question came the next morning, when one of Dove's men shook him awake.

"Someone's coming," Dove was told in a harsh whisper.

Dove was instantly alert as a lone native drew near. From the man's gaze and the wary manner of his approach, Dove was certain he knew exactly where the GIs were. Some yards away, the native stopped and began to speak.

"He says he's a friend, that he hates the Japs," the interpreter said. "He is inviting us to follow him to his village."

The man gestured at the Americans.

"Water," he said. "Ka ka."

"They have fresh water and food," the interpreter said.

Dove turned to the native. Then in pidgin English, which, as a Scout, he had been required to learn, he said, "Bring em me long place kanaka."

The native nodded at Dove's request to be led to the village, and the team followed him through the underbrush. After being introduced to a man their native guide said was the lulai, or chieftain, the team was greeted by gleeful children and overly friendly men who kept pounding them on the shoulder in their enthusiasm. They were also welcomed by smiling, bare-breasted women.

"I've been out in the jungle too long," Bauer said, reacting to the women.

"At least you know it still works," Ray quipped. "Out here you start to wonder."

Offered platters of food, the team spent the morning relaxing and munching on fresh fruit. Through the interpreter, they were able to learn that the Japanese in the sector were poorly armed, and that many were sick and hungry, confirming what Dove and his men had observed.

With the information the natives gave him, coupled with what he and his team had seen, Dove felt satisfied that his mission was accomplished. The Japanese in this sector were definitely pulling back. More important, they were not a cohesive force, but rather a sick, badly armed rabble. They would be launching no organized counterattacks.

That conclusion reached, Dove called for the radio. After some doing, he finally made contact with an army scout plane, which relayed his request for a pickup that night back to 6th Army HQ at Hollandia.

"We're heading back," he told the men. "Hot showers and clean beds tomorrow."

Just then the interpreter approached with some of the native men.

"They are inviting you to go hunting with them," he said.

"Hunting?" Hall said.

"Yes," their native friend said in pidgin English. "Killim e Jap-man."

Turning to his men, Dove said, "They want us to go Jap hunting with them."

Their mission done, the team chomping at the bit for some action, they followed the hunting party into the jungle. The Americans had no success but the natives flushed one unfortunate soldier. He fled in panic as the natives chased him, caught him, and clubbed the screaming man to death.

"Jesus Christ," Chapman said, simultaneously awed and repelled.

"Beats the hell out of any hunting I ever saw back in Rhode Island," Ray added.

Following this macabre expedition, Dove and the team took leave of the village and struck off toward the coast. All were eager to get back to their base camp, nicknamed "Hotel Alamo" due to all the luxuries the Scouts' S-4 supply officer and expert scrounger, 1st Lt. Mayo S. Stuntz, had provided for the men's comfort.

As darkness settled in and the Dove Team approached the pickup point, the heavens opened up and a heavy storm broke. Parts of New Guinea average as much as one hundred inches of rain a year, and to the drenched Scouts it felt as though all one hundred inches were coming down on their heads. Brisk winds kicked up the water off the beach, turning the sea into a witch's cauldron of churning spray. The team assembled for their departure until Dove, after conversing by radio with Miller, reluctantly agreed to a twenty-four-hour postponement.

The men spent a wet, miserable night on the beach, and their mood was not improved by the coming daylight and the return of the hot sun and sweltering humidity. As the men waited, Dove heard some natives approaching from the east and stopped them for information. They told Dove that a small group of Japanese soldiers was heading in his direction.

Feeling his men needed a vent for their pent-up anxiety, he said, "Hey, why don't we declare today open season on Japs." The men stared at him.

"Just follow me," he said, and they struck off through the kunai grass and back into the jungle. Finding a spot along the coastal trail where underbrush crowded the path, the men concealed themselves in the thick vegetation and waited. Within half an hour, a trio of Japanese soldiers trudged toward them. Knives in hand, the Scouts sprang from the underbrush as the enemy passed by.

The quiet, deadly work was over in moments. After stripping the bodies of any letters and documents and stashing the corpses in the brush, the team moved to a new ambush site, where two more enemy soldiers quietly died.

Looking for a third ambush site, Dove spotted four Japanese filling canteens at a small stream. He was signaling the team to fan out when one of the enemy soldiers, perhaps having heard a slight sound, looked up.

In the excitement of the moment, only one command came to Dove's mind.

"Charge!" he yelled, and the team rushed forward, weapons blazing.

Above the rattle of the gunfire, Ray's voice boomed, "That's what we get for having a lieutenant from Hollywood!"

By the time the sun sank below the horizon and the men returned to the beach, Dove and his team had conducted five ambushes and killed twenty Japanese. This, in addition to the eight they had dispatched since landing, put their total at twenty-eight enemy dead for the mission so far. Plus, they had collected two jungle packs of documents.

As the night deepened, another storm began blowing in from the Pacific. Still, the *Aces Avenger* arrived around midnight and the Scouts reinflated the rubber boat with the CO_2 tank.

"It's pretty rough out here, Jack," Miller's voice crackled over the radio. "Waves are about ten feet. Are you sure you don't want to try again tomorrow night?"

"Negative," Dove replied. "My boys and I are wet, tired, and ready for some hot chow. Stand by. Some of us are heading out now."

Not wanting to overload the rubber boat, Dove, Fisher, and Chapman remained onshore while Ray, Bauer, Roby, Hall, and the interpreter went ahead with the captured documents. Rowing away from shore was damned near impossible. The waves seemed to push the boat back several yards for every few they edged forward. The eight-hundred-yard trip took nearly two hours, but the rubber boat and its exhausted rowers finally nudged up to the 363's pitching hull. The interpreter crawled on board first, followed by Roby and Hall. Ray handed the captured documents to a sailor on deck and said, "We're going back for the rest."

With that, he and Bauer were off. The trip to shore was no easier, and halfway to the coast a wave upended the rubber boat and dropped Bauer and Ray into the dark, angry sea. Nearly pulled under by the strong current, the two men struggled.

★   ★   ★

Onshore, Dove, unaware of Ray and Bauer's dilemma, paced as he waited. Then Chapman said, "Look."

It was the rubber boat, washing toward shore. Dove waded out to grab it and drag it to the beach.

"Where are the guys?" Fisher asked.

"I don't know," he replied. "Boat must've tipped."

Then he said, "The oars aren't here. They have to wash up. Spread out and find them."

The three men conducted a frantic search along the beach, watching the waves for any signs of the missing paddles. After what seemed like hours, the oars finally appeared.

With the wayward oars returned, Dove ordered, "Get the gear in the boat and let's go. We'll try to find the fellas on the way out."

After throwing their weapons and the heavy radio into the rubber boat, the men pushed off.

The Scouts, drenched with spray, paddled frantically against the stormy sea for ninety arduous minutes, climbing one side of the large waves and sliding down the other, but seemingly getting nowhere. They were still three hundred yards from the PT boat when Dove saw a pinpoint of light on the water.

"There!" he cried, and the rubber boat was rowed in the direction of the light. As he had hoped, it was Ray, who was holding a small jungle flashlight with one hand while clutching onto Bauer with the other. With great effort, the two exhausted men were hauled sputtering into the bobbing craft. But their respite was temporary. Barely were the two on board, gasping from their ordeal, when a large wave hit the small boat head-on, lifting it and dumping everyone into the turbulent water. The wave engulfed the boat so violently that the weapons and radio shredded its rubber skin. Within seconds, everything disappeared into the sea from the torn and rapidly deflating boat.

From the tossing deck of the PT-363, Miller saw the Dove Team's boat flip.

"Goddamn it," he swore. "Get that spare boat inflated. Quick."

A CO_2 tank hissed and the new rubber boat took shape. Roby and Hall grabbed it without a word, lowered it over the side, and climbed

in, followed by Miller. They pushed off and rowed toward their comrades bobbing in the water, sometimes visible as a clump of floating
heads, other times hidden completely by the rolling waves. Twice over
the next forty-five minutes they tried to reach Dove and the others,
and twice they were turned back by the rampaging storm.

Clinging to the wreckage of the rubber boat, Dove saw the hope-
lessness of the rescue attempt. He signaled the others to follow and
turned back toward the dark coastline.

Once safely onshore, drenched and exhausted, Dove took stock
of their bleak situation. With the radio now on the bottom of the
ocean, there would be no more rescue attempts or rendezvous with
PT boats. He and his men would have to walk out, and it was not a
trip he relished. When the rubber boat sank, it took with it all of their
weapons and much of their gear. The vicious current swept away the
knife of every man except Dove. Worse, all of their food supplies were
gone, and only one canteen survived. Two men had even lost their
shoes, although their comrades were able to give them spare socks to
pad their feet.

"Looks like we walk home," Dove said in a matter-of-fact voice.

"How far?" Bauer asked. "Hollandia's thirty miles away."

"We did twenty-six miles back in training with a full pack, so this
will be a piece of cake, right?" Dove said with an air of humor he did
not feel. "Let's go."

Arming themselves with wooden clubs and coconuts, the five
soaked and bedraggled men headed eastward.

★   ★   ★

By the afternoon of June 10, Dove and his men had spent the day
pushing their way through jungle, wading across murky streams and
rivers, hiding from enemy patrols, and passing the bodies of Japanese
who had died in the retreat, their rotting corpses now home for a
myriad of insect life. Hungry and dehydrated, the Scouts' only source
of water was a few sips from the single remaining canteen, which was

replenished during periods of rain. They passed streams but dared not refill the canteen, since they had no halazone tablets with which to purify the water.

Ahead in a clearing, Dove spotted a village and signaled the men to halt. At first glance, the small cluster of nipa huts appeared to be abandoned. Then Dove noticed a grass-thatched lean-to, beneath whose shade lounged two Japanese soldiers.

Gathering his weary men around him, Dove said, "We're going to take these two. They may have weapons and food. We'll move in as close as we can, then rush them."

The fight that followed was short but fierce. With a rush, Dove and his men sprang forward. Two Scouts grabbed the first Japanese soldier and pinned him down as Dove drove his knife into the man. The other fought more determinedly for his life, kicking and flailing at his assailants. The Scouts beat him senseless with coconuts and he sagged to the ground, where Dove finished him quickly.

The bodies yielded up little of use other than a bayonet, two pocketknives, and a little bit of rice. After his men stashed the corpses in the underbrush, Dove distributed both the knives and the rice, then ordered the team to move on.

★   ★   ★

The sun was just starting its climb the next morning as the ragged men, their faces sporting several days' growth of whiskers, and their bodies sporting open sores from fungal infections known to the GIs as jungle rot or the New Guinea Crud, neared the village of Tarfia. Dove left his weary group in a clearing to rest—they'd covered close to twenty miles since they began the hike—and, along with Ray, conducted a two-man reconnaissance. In the lead, Dove came to a clearing. He was just was about to step out of the underbrush and into the open when Ray said aloud, "Don't go out there."

Dove, with one foot in the air, froze. His first reaction was anger that Ray would break the cardinal rule of talking out loud on a mission.

Then he realized the young soldier had possibly saved his life. Strung along the ground where he would have stepped was a wire rigged up as an alarm to warn against infiltrators. The clearing was an ambush—a killing zone—that he had nearly walked into.

"Ray, this is what we're looking for," Dove said, recognizing the U.S. Signal Corps wire used for the alarm.

Stepping over the wire so it would not vibrate, Dove circled the clearing. He reached a small clump of trees and called out, "Hey, Yanks. Everything quiet in there?"

"Yeah," came a cautious reply. "Who are you?"

"I'm Lieutenant Dove. Alamo Scouts. There are two of us. Can we come in?"

"Sure. Come on in. But slowly."

Dove and Ray rose and, with hands visible, calmly advanced.

"You got some water?" Dove asked. A GI handed him a canteen. He passed it to Ray, who drank deeply before handing it back. Dove took a long swig, capped the canteen, and returned it to its owner.

"Thanks," he said. "I've got a Scout team out ahead of you. Can I go and bring them in?"

"Go ahead," the GI said. "We'll watch for you."

By the time Dove returned with his men, the officer in charge of the observation post (OP) had called for a guide from Tarfia, who led the team into the village. There, the native chieftain welcomed them, laying out a feast of assorted fruit and fresh water. The tired, hungry Scouts wolfed down the food, in exchange for which Dove presented the chief with the two pocketknives and bayonet, whose late owners lay along the jungle trail.

After Dove and his men had eaten and rested, the chief arranged for their return. Dugout log canoes with teams of rowers waited. The Americans climbed into the native boats and were soon gliding swiftly along the water, arriving at Demta, well behind American lines, by afternoon.

Using the infantry's radio, Dove reported his location. Sergeant Miller and a PT boat picked them up for the return trip to Hollandia.

"Good to see you, Jack," Miller said as Dove and his men, their uniforms torn and rotting, their faces unshaven and sweat-soaked, climbed on board. "Roby and Hall have been fretting about you guys like a pair of mother hens."

"That sounds like them," Dove said and smiled. "Now let's go home."

CHAPTER 2

"I'll Form My Own Intelligence Unit."

The Southwest Pacific, 1941–1943

In the warm orange glow of the tropical sunset, four PT boats of Motor Torpedo Boat Squadron 3 cast off from a small fishing pier and slipped single-file out of Sisiman Cove on the beleaguered peninsula of Bataan.

At the helm of the lead boat, the bearded Lt. John Bulkeley steered his PT-41 out into the open water of Manila Bay. Behind him, the other three boats took up positions so that, from the air, the little flotilla resembled a baseball diamond, with PT-41 at second base, PT-32 under Lt. Vincent E. Schumacker at first, PT-34 under Bulkeley's executive officer, Lt. Robert B. Kelly, at third, and PT-35 under Lt. Anthony B. Akers at home plate.

After a short cruise, the boats split up, each heading to an assigned rendezvous.

Bulkeley continued on toward the tadpole-shaped island of Corregidor, which loomed darkly before him. As he guided the 41 boat into the pier at the South Dock, his stone-cold green eyes took in the devastation that had been wreaked by the relentless pounding of Japanese bombers.

While the boat was being tied up to the pier, a small party of people emerged from the shore and came forward. Bulkeley was not at all surprised to see that one of them was the U.S. Army's southwest Pacific supreme commander, Gen. Douglas MacArthur.

Bulkeley and MacArthur knew one another, and, in fact, when MacArthur had been informed by President Franklin D. Roosevelt that he was to leave the Philippines and escape to Australia, MacArthur selected Bulkeley to take him out.

Bulkeley wasn't happy with this. Since the war began, he had lost two of his six boats, PT-33 on December 26 and PT-31 on January 19. Both had run hard aground, were damaged, and destroyed to prevent capture.

His remaining boats were aging and long overdue for routine maintenance. However, the demand for their services in running messages and attacking Japanese shipping, plus the shortage of spare parts, prevented that necessity. Also, with the fall of the Philippines inevitable, he had hoped to get his surviving boats to safety somewhere along the coast of China. So MacArthur's summons was not welcomed. Still, he did as ordered and prepared for the voyage. After reinforcing the decks of his boats to carry extra weight, he had each craft load twenty fifty-gallon drums of the high-octane aircraft fuel his PT boats drank so prolifically.

"Hello, Buck," MacArthur said as Bulkeley stepped onto the pier on Wednesday evening, March 11, 1942.

"Good evening, General," Bulkeley replied, saluting.

He was shocked at MacArthur's appearance. The general's face was white, and the corner of his mouth twitched.

"Are we all set?" MacArthur asked.

"Yes, sir, as soon as we get your party aboard and your gear stowed away," Bulkeley answered.

MacArthur's "party" included his wife, Jean; their four-year-old son, Arthur, clutching his favorite toy, "Old Friend," a stuffed rabbit with scraggly whiskers; and the boy's nanny, a Cantonese woman Mac-Arthur dubbed Ah Cheu, but whose given name was Loh Chui.

Also riding with MacArthur would be his chief of staff, Lt. Col. Richard K. Sutherland.

The party boarded, along with four duffel bags of food and one suitcase apiece. In addition, MacArthur had brought along several cases of Coca-Cola as a treat to the delight of the crews, who had not tasted the soda pop for months.

MacArthur was last to board. Stopping first to face the island, he removed his gold-braided cap and was silent. Then, replacing it on his head, he turned to Bulkeley.

"You may cast off whenever ready, Buck," he said, and stepped onto the deck.

"Wind 'em up," Bulkeley said, making a circular motion in the air with his hand. "Cast off."

The trio of twelve-cylinder Packard engines was fired up, and the seventy-seven-foot craft, released from the pier, glided out to sea.

It was eight p.m. by now, and PT-41 rendezvoused with her three sister craft, who had picked up passengers and supplies at other locations, including the navy's head man in the Philippines, Rear Adm. Francis W. Rockwell, who was riding with Kelly on the 34 boat.

The little flotilla picked up a minesweeper, which guided them safely through an American-laid minefield and, avoiding a Japanese destroyer and cruiser said to be in the area, cleared the bay and zoomed out to sea.

Standing in the cockpit beside Bulkeley, MacArthur watched Bataan and Corregidor fade into the darkness. Off in the distance, red and orange flashes illuminated the night sky, accompanied by the fading rumble of artillery, marking the battle lines.

"Before I left, I told General Wainwright that if I get through to Australia, I'll come back as soon as I can with as much as I can," MacArthur said, as much to himself as to Bulkeley. "And as God is my witness, I will."

★ ★ ★

The seeds of Japanese militarism and expansionism, which by 1942 would give them control of one-sixth of the world's surface, began almost from the time Adm. Matthew Perry hoisted anchor and sailed out of Tokyo Bay in 1854, after having opened Japan to Western trade. Within ten years, the old Shogun rule had been abolished and Emperor Mutsuhito established the Meiji Restoration, which embraced Western technology.

In 1878 the military high command was placed outside of parliamentary control, allowing it to function independently of the emperor. Casting their eyes away from the home islands for expansion and the procurement of needed natural resources, Japanese forces launched a surprise attack on China in 1895 and captured Korea.

In 1904, the Japanese got caught up in a war with Czarist Russia, which culminated in 1905 with the Nipponese navy dealing the Russian fleet a crushing loss at the Battle of Tsushima. By the time of World War I, the Japanese, thanks to an alliance with Great Britain, signed in 1902, took over German possessions in the Pacific, keeping many after the conflict as "mandates."

By 1921 Japan was looking again at China, with plans to monopolize trade. This put Japan in conflict with America's "open-door" trade policy, and led to the Washington Naval Treaty, or Five-Power Treaty, limiting the size and number of warships in the American, British, Japanese, French, and Italian navies, with Japan, France, and Italy allowed less than the other two powers. Japan signed the so-called 5-5-3 Treaty, even though it permitted them just 300,000 tons of naval ships, as opposed to the 500,000 tons granted to both England and America, but soon was looking for ways to get around it.

In 1931, citing a series of supposed acts of aggression by China, Japanese forces overran all of Manchuria, annexed it, and created a puppet state called Manchukuo.

Their thirst for conquest still unsated, in 1937 Nippon's military leaders demanded the right to send men across the Lugou Bridge connecting the Japanese-held Fengtai province, south of Beijing, to Chinese territory across the Yongding River.

Dubbed the Marco Polo Bridge after the famous early European explorer who once crossed the ancient span, the Japanese wished to cross it now to search for a deserter. Whether this Japanese deserter actually existed or was concocted by the Japanese as a pretext for invasion, or whether an actual solider was kidnapped by local Communist Chinese to create an incident between Japan and the government of Chiang Kai-shek, remains unknown.

Chinese officials, as expected, refused. The result was that on July 8, Japanese artillery began shelling the Chinese side of the bridge, followed by an attack by the soldiers of Nippon. The resulting Sino-Japanese War would last until Japan's ultimate surrender in 1945.

It wasn't just China that recoiled at Japanese aggression. A year before the Marco Polo Bridge incident, 1936, western Europe, Russia, and America grew alarmed when the Japanese signed their Anti-Comintern Pact with Germany, agreeing not to interfere if the Nazis got into a war with the Soviet Union. And a year later, President Roosevelt, concerned over the treaty with Germany as well as the atrocities and mass murders reportedly committed by Japanese troops in China, called for a quarantine of Japanese assets in America.

International tensions were cranked up another notch a few months later when Japanese planes sank the gunboat USS *Panay* on December 13, 1937, while it was escorting American oil tankers on the Yangtze River. Japan apologized and paid reparations. But the next year, Japan slammed closed America's open-door trade policy and set up what would soon be called the Greater East Asia Co-Prosperity Sphere, a supposed cooperation among Asian nations, which, not surprisingly, the Japanese would control.

Japan stunned the Western world in 1940 when it signed the Tripartite Pact, allying itself with Nazi Germany and Fascist Italy. Roosevelt responded by slapping an embargo on Japanese exports.

Seeing the Western powers, led by America, as a threat to their overseas program of expansion, the Japanese high command concocted an elaborate series of plans to strike at America, Great Britain, and the Dutch, in one bold swoop, starting with the biggest perceived threat, the U.S. Pacific Fleet, now anchored at Pearl Harbor in Hawaii.

From December 7, 1941, when Japanese carrier planes roared in over Oahu, through April 1942, the war had been a succession of Japanese triumphs and Allied humiliations. The world watched in stunned silence as the Western powers, complacent in the belief of their military prowess, were thrown into headlong retreat on a front stretching for thousands of miles from the central Pacific to the East Indies and on into Southeast Asia. Before the Allies could regroup and stand firm, the rising-sun flag would flutter over more than a million square miles.

Within days of Pearl Harbor, Guam, some fifteen hundred miles east of Manila and a stop for the lumbering Pan American Clippers that linked America to the Orient, was gone. The island's tiny garrison of 427 marines and 247 native troops, inadequately armed with World War I weapons, were gobbled up by 5,400 Japanese marines.

Wake Island, another Pan Am stop located twenty-three hundred air miles west of Hawaii, was bombed just hours after the Pearl Harbor attack by Japanese planes based on Kwajalein, 650 miles to the south. The 447 marines and 75 army signal corps and navy men, along with the help of some of the 1,200 civilian workers whom the war had stranded on the atoll, where they had been working on roads and an airstrip, valiantly fought off the Japanese for two weeks as America watched proudly from afar. But it was a doomed defense, and the island fell two days before Christmas.

The British fared no better.

Hong Kong, Britain's China bastion, fell on Christmas Day.

On the same day Pearl Harbor was attacked, December 7 (December 8 west of the international date line), thousands of Japanese of the 25th Army commanded by Lt. Gen. Tomoyuki Yamashita swarmed ashore on the Malay Peninsula at Singora, Pattani, and Kota Bharu, and began rolling south toward the fortress city of Singapore, Britain's crown jewel in Asia. The British had discounted the idea of a land attack, hence most of the city's formidable big guns faced the sea, as if mocking Singapore's defenders.

The British sent their two most powerful ships in all of Asia, the thirty-two-thousand-ton battle cruiser HMS *Repulse* and thirty-five-thousand-ton battleship HMS *Prince of Wales*, out to challenge the invasion. Foolishly, the ships had no air cover, and on December 10, a swarm of Japanese planes sent both to the bottom, along with the new commander in chief of Britain's Far Eastern Fleet, Adm. Sir Tom Phillips, giving proof again, as if proof was needed after Pearl Harbor, of the vulnerability of unprotected capital ships to modern airpower.

Meanwhile, on land, British and colonial troops pulled together hastily and sent to stop the land attack were easily smashed, and the Japanese were soon shouting a victorious "Banzai" just across the narrow isthmus from Singapore, which they now pummeled with artillery.

On February 8, the Japanese opened a thunderous bombardment and crossed the isthmus. A week later, on February 15, Lt. Gen. A. E. Percival surrendered the battered city and its garrison.

As the Union Jack was lowered at Singapore, the Japanese began advancing on the resource-rich islands of the Dutch East Indies. On February 14, seven hundred of the emperor's paratroopers descended on Palembang in Sumatra.

On the high seas, Japanese ships beat up on a combined Allied naval force of five cruisers—one American, one Australian, one British, and two Dutch—plus two Dutch and four U.S. destroyers, all under the command of Dutch Rear Adm. Karel Doorman. In a running series of clashes collectively known as the Battle of the Java Sea, which was complicated by the fact that Doorman could not speak English, forcing all of his orders to be translated before they could be executed, the Allied force was destroyed. Doorman was lost along with his flagship, the *DeRuyter*.

Two surviving cruisers, the Australian HMAS *Perth* and the USS *Houston*, which was reported sunk so many times her crew called her the Galloping Ghost of the Java Coast, made a desperate run for safer waters. On February 28, they were caught and sunk in the Sunda Strait between Java and Sumatra. A few days later, on March 9, the Dutch East Indies were surrendered to the Japanese.

* * *

As bad as the war news was, the one defeat that most rankled America's senior military commander in the Far East, Douglas MacArthur, was the loss of his beloved Philippines.

Hailing from a proud military family—during the Civil War his father had led the Union charge up Missionary Ridge outside Chattanooga in 1863—MacArthur had graduated from West Point in 1903, ranked first in his class. After serving in the Philippines and in Japan as an aide to his father, Maj. Gen. Arthur MacArthur Jr., he rose rapidly in prestige and was promoted to captain in 1911 and attached to the General Staff in 1912.

During World War I, MacArthur commanded the 42nd Division, which he dubbed the Rainbow Division, and proved himself an able combat leader. He was wounded during the war, and afterward became superintendent at West Point. MacArthur returned to the Philippines in 1922 as military commander.

In 1935, after a stint as head of the Joint Chiefs of Staff, first under Herbert Hoover, then Franklin D. Roosevelt, MacArthur returned to the Philippines at the request of President Manuel L. Quezon. The island nation had just been granted semi-independence by the United States, which had taken over control from Spain after the Spanish-American War in 1898, with a promise of full independence on July 4, 1946. Quezon requested that MacArthur create and supervise a new Philippine army.

The vain MacArthur agreed, taking the title of Field Marshal of the Philippine Army, while still remaining on active duty with the U.S. Army. Demanding, and getting, a salary equal to that of Quezon—$18,000 a year—MacArthur established himself in luxury in the penthouse suite of the world-famous Manila Hotel, which waived the $1,500-a-month room rent when MacArthur was named chairman of the Manila Hotel Corporation.

That all came crashing down on December 8, 1941, Philippine time.

Even as American sailors fought the flames that raged along Battleship Row in Pearl Harbor, Japanese bombers of the 11th Imperial Air Fleet were winging toward the U.S. air base at Clark Field on Luzon.

As early as November 27, MacArthur had been warned by his superiors in Washington about the possibility of a Japanese attack. His response was an order that his thirty-five B-17 bombers be shifted from the vulnerable Clark Field south to Mindanao, out of harm's way. But there was no rush ordered for the move, so that by December 7 only half the Flying Fortresses had been relocated.

News of the attack on Pearl Harbor arrived at MacArthur's hotel at three thirty a.m., Manila time, and was confirmed ninety minutes later. Maj. Gen. Lewis Brereton, commander of MacArthur's air force, wanted to launch an immediate strike on the Japanese airfields on Formosa. After waiting several hours for an answer, he was notified by MacArthur's chief of staff, Colonel Sutherland, that he was cleared to launch a photo reconnaissance of Formosa, in preparation for an air strike the next day. As a result, his aircrews went to chow—it was now around noon—and his planes, eighteen B-17s, plus assorted fighters, mostly P-40 Tomahawks and P-39 Air Cobras, were parked and readied to be fueled.

The Japanese weren't waiting.

Fully expecting to be met by U.S. fighters and antiaircraft fire over Clark Field, the Japanese aviators were delighted to find the skies clear and row after row of sitting ducks on the ground. Coming in at twenty-two thousand feet in several V-shaped formations, the bombers unloaded their explosives on the parked planes, while Zero fighters zoomed in for close-up kills.

Saburo Sakai, who would become Japan's leading ace, found the situation "unbelievable" as he chopped up a B-17 with his two nose-mounted 7.7mm Type 97 machine guns. He next attacked a P-40 as it tried to take off, blasting it from the sky.

By the time the planes, with the red rising sun emblazoned on their wings and fuselages, turned north toward Formosa, they had destroyed all eighteen B-17s, along with fifty-three P-40s and thirty other aircraft. Fully one-half of MacArthur's air force was gone within the first hours of the war, and eighty men lay dead.

On December 22, forty-three thousand Japanese soldiers of the 14th Army came ashore on the palm-lined beaches of Lingayen Gulf, 120 miles north of Manila. Seventy miles to the southeast, another force swarmed across the beaches of Lamon Bay. The Japanese commander Lt. Gen. Masaharu Homma, the "Poet General," whose love of Western movies and culture often put him at odds with Imperial Headquarters, planned to envelope the Americans and Filipinos in a massive pincer movement.

Against them, MacArthur could muster only about 25,000 to 30,000 regular troops, U.S. and Filipinos, and 100,000 raw Filipino recruits of questionable quality.

On December 23, MacArthur put into effect War Plan Orange, an antiquated design that called for the withdrawal of his forces to the Bataan Peninsula, there to hold out until help arrived from America. The plan, which MacArthur detested, abandoned Manila. However, with the United States holding Bataan and the island fortress of Corregidor, it still denied the Japanese use of Manila Bay. Unfortunately, the variable War Plan Orange did not take into account a naval disaster like Pearl Harbor.

The withdrawal began, as lines of trucks and troops moved along the dust-choked roads leading to Bataan. On Christmas Day, Maj. Gen. Jonathan M. Wainwright, commander of the Northern Luzon Force, established a defensive line on the Agno River, but the Japanese 48th Division, with tanks and artillery, cracked it quickly. The withdrawal continued.

The prolonged battle that followed was brave, but the result was never in doubt. Without supplies and reinforcements from America, the Philippines were doomed. And no help was coming. MacArthur knew this, and mentioned it to Bulkeley on March 11. He also told Bulkeley that FDR had ordered him to Australia and for Bulkeley to prepare his boats for the trip. MacArthur had been urged to go by submarine, but he opted for Bulkeley, the one naval commander he knew and trusted.

"When do you want to shove off, sir?" Bulkeley had asked.

"I haven't decided yet," MacArthur replied, refusing to be pinned down.

"I need to prepare the boats for the long trip to Mindanao," the young officer insisted.

"Just get them ready, Buck," he was told. "I'll give you the word."

★ ★ ★

Now the word had been given, prompted by the news that General Yamashita, known now as the Tiger of Malaya after his conquest of Singapore, was en route to Luzon with reinforcements.

The flotilla's destination, two days' sailing, was Mindanao, the large, southernmost island of the Philippine archipelago. President Quezon, his vice president, Sergio Osmena, and the cabinet had already reached Mindanao, boarding a B-17 at the Del Monte pineapple plantation for a flight to Australia. MacArthur would rendezvous with a B-17 at the same place, provided he managed to elude the Japanese.

That night, while skimming across the Sibuyan Sea heading for their first stop in the Cuyo Island group, the boats became separated. Kelly's 34 boat was the first to arrive, gliding into a secluded cove as the sky purpled with the hint of the coming dawn. Dropping anchor in water so crystalline clear that the coral bottom was plainly visible, Kelly sent a man to shore with semaphore flags to watch for the others.

Within half an hour, the squadron was reassembled in the cove. As the sailors scanned the sky and the sea for any sign of pursuit, Jean MacArthur and Loh Chui spent the day relaxing in wicker chairs on the forward deck of the 41 boat, while the anguished general paced incessantly. Taking in his surroundings, Bulkeley noted the pristine white sandy beach marred only by four empty huts, probably used seasonally by men who came to the place to gather coconuts. A stray dog trotted along the shore. Bulkeley then turned and watched young Arthur, the general's only child, playing with General Tojo, the squadron's monkey mascot.

"This is a beautiful beach, General," he told MacArthur. "I'd love to let the boy go ashore and enjoy the sand, but if we're spotted, we'll have to get out of here fast."

MacArthur puffed thoughtfully on his pipe, also watching his son, and said, "I understand, Buck. He'll have plenty of time to play when we reach Darwin."

According to the plan, MacArthur was to rendezvous with a submarine here, and continue the trip underwater. He was torn with indecision, between taking the obviously safer but slower route by sub or continuing on the surface with the skipper he trusted.

"We'll be in more open sea," Bulkeley told him. "The ride will be rougher."

MacArthur looked to Admiral Rockwell, who had joined him on the 41 boat to plan the rest of the journey.

"I'm a navy man, but I've never been able to confine myself in the cramped quarters of a submarine, especially under the water," Rockwell said. "I'm staying with the squadron."

MacArthur mulled it over, then concurred.

As darkness approached, the little convoy was getting ready to strike out on the last leg of the voyage. It was decided that the 32 boat was unable to continue. During the previous night, separated and alone, Lieutenant Schumacker had mistaken Bulkeley's boat, coming up from behind, for a Japanese craft, and dumped his spare fuel drums in order to speed up his escape. He now did not have the gas needed to make it to Mindanao. Bulkeley told him to await the submarine and get fuel from it, then head for Iloilo on Panay for repairs and refueling and to later rejoin the squadron. The remaining three boats headed off. (Schumacker, instead, had the sub sink his boat and take him to Australia.)

About six forty-five a.m., fifteen minutes after leaving the cove, a crewman called out, "Sail ho." A Japanese cruiser was spotted on the horizon. On their current course, the boats would cross the cruiser's bow. Hoping the sharp-eyed Japanese lookouts might mistake the PT boats' wakes for white-top waves, Bulkeley spun his steering wheel hard to the right, to run parallel to the enemy warship. As he changed course, Bulkeley turned and saw the slight form of Mrs. MacArthur standing behind him. She looked concerned but not worried.

"My general is asleep," she said, pronouncing it "my gineral," with her Tennessee drawl. She always referred to her husband by using his rank, Southern style, and he in turn called her "Ma'am" or "Mrs. MacArthur," even in private. "Do I need to wake him?"

"No, ma'am," Bulkeley said. "Let him rest."

The ruse worked and the cruiser was soon out of sight, and Bulkeley steered his flotilla back on course.

The seas got rougher after midnight, with lightning flashing in the distance. In the Mindanao Sea, waves of fifteen to twenty feet crashed over the bows, dousing the men on deck. Bulkeley was riding in the wake of Kelly's 34 boat, hoping to make MacArthur's ride a tad smoother.

The night was cold and pitch-black, and Bulkeley was navigating on dead reckoning. Then, in the first streaks of dawn, he could dimly discern the dark outlines of Mindanao and Negros islands.

It was just after six thirty a.m. when the trio of boats now comprising Squadron 3 tied up at the wharf. Mindanao's commander, Brig. Gen. William F. Sharp, was there to meet his boss. MacArthur stepped onto the wooden pier, followed by Bulkeley. The general shook salt water out of his cap, then flipped it onto his head and said to the PT skipper, "Buck, I'm giving every officer and man here the Silver Star for gallantry. You've taken me out of the jaws of death and I won't forget it. If these boats never accomplish anything more and were burned now, they'd have earned their keep a thousand times over. If possible, when I get to Melbourne, I'll get you and your key men out."

With a salute, MacArthur climbed into Sharp's staff car for the trip to the Del Monte plantation.

★   ★   ★

Even as MacArthur's plane took off for Darwin, conditions were deteriorating for the men he left behind on Bataan. Sickness and malnutrition had become worse enemies than the Japanese, and by late

March, one-fourth of the eighty thousand defenders were unfit for combat. And their spirits were not heartened by MacArthur's radio message to them from Australia, urging them to continue the fight. That message, and his flight to Australia, was commemorated in true GI style, in a poem the men called "Dugout Doug":

> In Australia's fresh clime,
> he took out the time
> to send us a message of cheer.
> My heart, he began,
> Goes out to Bataan.
> But the rest of me's
> Staying right here.

MacArthur knew of the poem, and it stung him deeply, but not as deeply as the fall of Bataan on April 9, or the radio message sent to Roosevelt on May 6 from General Wainwright deep inside Malinta Tunnel on Corregidor: "With broken heart, and head bowed in sadness but not in shame, I report to Your Excellency that today I must arrange terms for surrender of the fortified islands of Manila Bay."

To MacArthur, Wainwright radioed, "I have fought for you to the best of my ability from Lingayen Gulf to Bataan to Corregidor. Goodbye, General."

With that, eighty thousand men, including twelve thousand Americans, went into captivity, and MacArthur's humiliation was complete.

But so was his resolve to return, and from March 1942 on, everything MacArthur did, every military plan he made, every offensive action he ordered was made with one purpose in mind: his promised return to the Philippines.

To begin with, in May the Japanese juggernaut had at last been stopped. An invasion force led by carriers and bound for the vital Allied base at Port Moresby, on the southern tip of New Guinea's Papua province, had been met by U.S. forces in the Coral Sea. While the Americans had taken the brunt of the beating, with the carrier *Lexington* sunk and *Yorktown* damaged, in return for the loss of one small enemy carrier, a Japanese invasion force, for the first time in the war, had been turned back.

In July, the Japanese made another stab at Port Moresby, this time by landing troops on the northern coast of Papua at the villages of Gona and Buna, then along the Kokoda Trail, hoping to take the port through the back door. There, amid the jagged heights of the Owen Stanley Mountains, they were met by American and Australian troops. The result was a running six-month battle as the Japanese were pushed back to the coast, culminating in the bloody slugging matches around Gona, Buna, and Buna Government Station, where men fought wearing gas masks to stave off the stench of putrefying flesh.

But this victory did not satisfy MacArthur, who was still sixteen hundred miles from the Philippines and twenty-one hundred miles from Manila. MacArthur blamed his lack of progress on his superiors, writing to an admirer, "Probably no commander in American history has been so poorly supported," and calling it "a national shame."

He disliked the Joint Chiefs of Staff intensely, and they returned the sentiment, especially the volatile Adm. Ernest J. King, the Chief of Naval Operations. King was so forceful in his condemnation of MacArthur at one meeting that the mild-mannered chief of staff, George C. Marshall, uncharacteristically slammed his fist on the table and said, "I will not have any meetings carried on with this hatred."

This mutual dislike and distrust between MacArthur and the Joint Chiefs spilled over to the battlefield. In planning his eventual return to the Philippines, MacArthur first had to retake New Guinea, as well as the Admiralties, Bismarcks, and lesser island groups, and neutralize the Japanese naval base at Rabaul on New Britain. To ensure success in these movements, MacArthur understood that he needed accurate and dependable intelligence concerning enemy troop strengths, defenses, and morale, as well as beach conditions, waves, tides, and underwater obstacles. But where commanders in other theaters of operation used the highly skilled men of the Office of Strategic Services, or OSS, the forerunner of today's CIA, MacArthur refused, suspicious of its ties to the Pentagon.

Instead, to collect his needed information, MacArthur relied on a hodgepodge of sources, such as the Australian Coast Watcher Service, the Allied Intelligence Bureau, the Allied Translator and Interpreter Service, the Allied Geographical Section, and the navy's underwater demolition teams.

However, since these services fell under different commanders in both the army and navy, and interservice suspicion and rivalries ran rampant throughout the officer corps, it proved difficult for MacArthur to get accurate and timely intelligence. Commanders, both American and Allied, were reluctant to share their data.

In the fall of 1943, as plans were being made for the seizure of western New Britain, code-named Operation Dexterity, a group called the 7th Amphibious Force Special Service Unit #1 was formed, under the command of Lt. William B. Coultas.

Nicknamed the "Amphibious Scouts," the small ad hoc force was a joint navy-army operation that would combine the army skills of long-range ground reconnaissance with the navy skills of beach markings, demolition, and hydrologic studies, into a potent intelligence-gathering force.

The Amphibious Scouts were a combined effort between Adm. Daniel E. Barbey and one of MacArthur's top ground commanders, Maj. Gen. Walter E. Krueger, commander of the sixty thousand men who comprised the 6th Army.

A gruff, wiry Texan, Krueger had been selected to spearhead Operation Dexterity. Krueger, whose father, Julius, had fought under Otto von Bismarck in the Franco-Prussian War, was just eight years old when he came to America with his mother in 1889, four years after his father's death. Krueger joined the army in 1898 and served as a private with the 2nd U.S. Volunteer Infantry during the Spanish-American War. His volunteer enlistment ended after four months, and he reenlisted in the regular army, being assigned to the 12th Infantry. He saw action in the Philippines during the Philippine Insurrection, where he was elevated to sergeant. His actions in the taking of the barrio of San Juan de Guimba led to a battlefield commission as a second lieutenant, and he was assigned to the 30th Infantry.

During the First World War, Krueger held a staff position and by

1919 was a lieutenant colonel. Marshall promoted him to brigadier general in 1941 and assigned him to the 3rd Army, which, by the time of its activation in January 1942, had been redesignated the 6th Army. Krueger, who had settled in San Antonio, Texas, dubbed his command with the code name the Alamo Force, in honor of the old Spanish mission in his adopted hometown.

The Alamo Force, comprised of about sixty thousand men, reached Australia in February 1943, and the general was put at the head of the Papua phase of MacArthur's New Guinea operations.

Krueger's hope that the Amphibious Scouts would be the answer to MacArthur's prayers for reliable intelligence was dashed on the group's first mission. The assignment was a ten-day reconnaissance, October 6 to 16, of the Gasmata area near Cape Gloucester in New Britain.

Before the unit's departure, Krueger briefed mission leader Lt. Milton Beckworth of his intelligence, or G2, section, on what to look for, and to report directly back to him upon their return. The information would then be shared with the navy.

The ten-day mission went smoothly, but a communications glitch on the last day meant the PT boats assigned to recover the team failed to arrive. With no way back, the Amphibious Scouts were stranded behind enemy lines. Their rations depleted, and forced to eat what they could scrounge from the jungle, the half-starved men were finally picked up and returned to their base on October 27, eleven days after their initial pickup date.

There was still more disturbing news, especially for Krueger. Beckworth, who was to report to his general as soon as he returned, was instead shanghaied by the navy and taken to Milne Bay at the eastern tip of New Guinea. There, over his protestations, he was held in seclusion and questioned about the mission by Naval Intelligence officers. After the debriefing, he was forced to remain, a virtual prisoner, on a boat anchored offshore. Four days into his ordeal, Beckworth managed to get topside, dove into the water, and swam to shore. Wet and angry, he worked his way back to Krueger's headquarters.

As Krueger listened to Beckworth's story, his face reddened in anger from the neck up, like a rising thermometer.

"To hell with this," Krueger raged. "I'll form my own intelligence unit."

Turning to an aide, he said, "Have Colonel Bradshaw report to my headquarters as soon as possible."

In that moment of anger, the 6th U.S. Army Special Reconnaissance Unit, which would become known as the Alamo Scouts, was born. The unit would play a key role in bringing the campaign in the southwest Pacific to a successful conclusion, and prove itself one of the most potent weapons in American intelligence-gathering history.

CHAPTER 3

Recruitment and Training

"... the highest quality of soldiering."

Seated at his desk at 6th Army G2, Lt. Col. Frederick W. Bradshaw studied the orders he had just received from General Krueger. Dated November 21, 1943, the order read:

1. The Alamo Scouts Training Center (ASTC) is hereby established under the supervision of Headquarters Alamo Force at the earliest practicable date prior to 1 January 1944, and at a location in the vicinity of the present headquarters.
2. The Training Center will train selected volunteers in reconnaissance and raider work. The course will cover a six-week period. Specially selected graduates will be grouped into teams at the disposal of the commanding General, Alamo Force, and will be designated "Alamo Scouts"; the remainder will be returned to their respective commands for similar use by their commanders.
3. Commanders of combat units will be called upon from time to time to furnish personnel for the above training. Personnel

so selected must possess the highest qualifications as to courage, stamina, intelligence and adaptability.

As directed by Krueger, Bradshaw was to set up a rigorous, innova-
tive program gleaned from the training manuals of other elite units,
such as Carlson's Raiders, Merrill's Marauders, the Amphibious Scouts,
the Devil's Brigade, and Darby's Rangers, with a focus on intelligence
gathering, jungle survival, and fighting skills. The new outfit was to be
called the 6th U.S. Army Special Reconnaissance Unit, or Alamo
Scouts, in deference to its parent organization, the 6th Army "Alamo
Force."

Bradshaw was then to put out a call throughout the 6th Army for
volunteers who wished to perform hazardous duty and develop them
into a reconnaissance force capable of infiltrating enemy lines, gathering needed information, and getting out, preferably undetected. He
had the pick of almost any man he wanted under Krueger's command
and free rein to equip them with the best weapons and materials the
U.S. Army could provide. The training camp would also be the unit's
base of operations and could be wherever Bradshaw wanted, provided
it was within easy reach of Krueger, for the general considered this
unit his personal reconnaissance force, and their use in the field was
solely at his discretion.

Bradshaw had served as G2 intelligence officer for the 31st Division until he had been plucked from there by Krueger to serve on his
staff in January 1943. The general liked Bradshaw's clear-sighted intelligence and his quiet but firm leadership abilities.

An attorney from Jackson, Mississippi, prior to the war Bradshaw
had political ambitions on the state level, including an eye on the
governor's office.

Bradshaw had joined the Mississippi National Guard in 1931, serving as a private in Company C of the 155th Infantry. Shortly thereafter,
with his background and abilities, he was commissioned as a second
lieutenant, and began to climb the command ladder. In October 1940,
Bradshaw joined the 31st Division as assistant judge advocate and

within four months was promoted to major and assigned to the general staff as assistant chief of staff for the division. Sent to general staff school, he graduated on December 6, 1941, just as Japan's Pearl Harbor strike force was closing on Oahu.

Now Bradshaw had been assigned to recruit and train an elite, tough team of jungle specialists, and for that he knew he needed an equally elite and tough staff of instructors.

His first selection as executive officer was Maj. John F. Polk, formerly of the 1st Cavalry Division, but he soon lost Polk to 6th Army HQ, where he was made liaison officer.

Bradshaw next turned to Capt. Homer A. Williams as his XO and chief training officer. The Philadelphia native joined the army in 1927 and rose through the ranks, where he developed a widespread reputation as a stern disciplinarian. With a shock of fire-engine-red hair—he was one of several men among the Scouts to be dubbed "Red"—and a gruff demeanor, he was a man to be obeyed. No soldier who served under Williams wanted to be called into his office for a dressing-down, for he handed out punishments long to be remembered.

Williams's job would be to help Bradshaw recruit and interview candidates, implement the training program, and select the men who would eventually comprise the Scout teams.

For his supply officer, Bradshaw needed someone resourceful, so he turned to 1st Lt. Mayo S. Stuntz. Hailing from Vienna, Virginia, Stuntz was a former member of the Naval Amphibious Scouts. Bradshaw met Stuntz while the two worked together for 6th Army G2 and knew the man was a superior scrounger.

Bradshaw called on Stuntz and told him about the Scouts and what he wanted Stuntz to do.

"I want these men to have the best of everything, weapons, food, accommodations, you name it," Bradshaw told Stuntz. "Think you can handle it?"

Stuntz nodded.

"Provided you don't care about where or how I get the stuff," he said.

Bradshaw smiled.

"No questions asked," he replied with a wink.

Capt. Richard "Doc" Canfield of Pittsburgh had seen duty as a frontline medical officer on Guadalcanal and was working with the 52nd Evacuation Hospital in New Caledonia when Bradshaw approached him. Canfield agreed to serve as medical officer, as well as to oversee camp and mess hall cleanliness. He would also be tasked with teaching the Scout candidates advanced jungle first aid. Typical of the tropics, Canfield would also spend a great deal of time trying to prevent or control malaria, dengue fever, dysentery, and the other myriad of afflictions that could knock a man out of action as effectively as a Japanese bullet. Canfield became very popular with the unit as the inventor of "torpedo juice," a concoction of fruit juice and torpedo propellant, guaranteed to loosen the tongues of even the most tight-lipped of men during the debriefing after a mission.

Assisting Canfield would be his team of medics, men like Dominick Cicippio, a Norristown, Pennsylvania, boy who transferred to the Scouts from the 24th Division. Cicippio and the other medics would not accompany Scouts on missions. Instead, they remained in camp, helping tend those who returned injured or were down with illness. They also implemented Canfield's program of camp sanitation and safety, a job that included, Cicippio recalled, inspecting the area each morning for any of the island's ninety varieties of snakes, especially the lethal taipan and the death adder, who might decide to take up residence in the camp overnight.

The post of adjutant was vacant until April 1944, when Bradshaw tapped Lt. Lewis B. Hochstrasser, who had just graduated from the training program and had impressed Bradshaw. A Billings, Montana, native, Hochstrasser had joined the Montana National Guard in 1932 and enlisted in the regular army on January 8, 1941. As adjutant, his duties included payroll and censoring mail, as well as instructing the volunteers in message writing and how to use the army's Intelligence Handbook.

Except for Hochstrasser, Bradshaw's staff was assembled by Thanksgiving 1943. His next task was selecting instructors. For these jobs, Bradshaw turned to former members of the recently disbanded Naval

Amphibious Scouts, men who had already mastered such skills as rubber boat handling, infiltrating enemy lines, scouting and patrolling, and communications and intelligence gathering. These were all talents his candidates would need. Only the best instructors would do.

One of Bradshaw's first choices was Lieutenant Beckworth, the young Naval Amphibious Scout officer who had led the mission to Gasmata in October and had been kidnapped by the navy on his team's return.

As the war progressed and classes of qualified men graduated from the program, some of them were invited to stay on as instructors. One of these was Lt. Sidney Tison, a former member of the Allied Intelligence Bureau who won a Bronze Star in 1943 after he infiltrated Luzon from the submarine *Nautilus*, linked up with Filipino guerrillas, and led a raid on a Japanese installation that killed two hundred enemy soldiers. Another graduate-turned-teacher would be Lt. Henry "Snake" Baker, another Bronze Star winner in the Philippines, who had rigged the fuses of captured Japanese artillery shells in order to blow up three trainloads of enemy soldiers and equipment.

★   ★   ★

Having assembled his staff, Bradshaw turned his attention to the camp itself. According to the orders from Krueger, the location was up to him, provided it be in the vicinity of 6th Army headquarters. Also, because of the highly classified nature of the unit and the nature of its training, the location had to be near water and yet secluded.

At first Bradshaw scouted locations on Goodenough Island, or Morata to the natives, one of three islands in the D'Entrecasteaux Island group, just off the northeast coast of New Guinea. This island had been home to 353 Japanese soldiers of the 5th Sasebo Naval Landing Force, who had arrived there in August 1942 while en route to the fight at Buna, then were stranded when the seven barges carrying them were destroyed by Allied aircraft. Sixty men had been evacuated by submarine, but before the rest could be brought off, they were attacked by U.S. and Australian troops on October 22–23, 1942. Most of the Japanese were rescued by another sub run, but a forty-man rear guard was annihilated.

Overlooked by the eighty-five-hundred-foot Mount Goodenough, the highest point in the Papuan group, the oval-shaped island, twenty miles long and ten miles wide, and comprised of coastal plain and coconut plantations, was thought to be a good place to establish Bradshaw's camp. On closer inspection, however, it was determined that the island's mosquito-infested swamps and rough surf would hinder rather than help the training.

Then Bradshaw was informed that the Naval Amphibious Scouts were disbanding and their camp was available. Located at Kalo Kalo on the west coast of Fergusson Island, just thirty minutes by PT boat from Krueger's headquarters, it was tailor-made for Bradshaw's purposes. It worked well for the former Naval Amphibious Scouts and now Alamo Scouts instructor Milt Beckworth, who would not have to move his gear out of his tent.

Krueger had directed Bradshaw to erect a training facility on an excellence level beyond anything MacArthur or Admiral Barbey, who oversaw the Naval Amphibious Scouts, had established prior. Heeding those instructions, Bradshaw immediately went about having the camp enlarged and upgraded. Within a month of taking over, a theftproof supply room, a dayroom, and a small-arms range were added, and a second boat dock built. A new shower house was erected, as was a 150-man mess hall with cement floor and screened-in kitchen. New tents were acquired for the men: officers would sleep two to a tent, enlisted men six to a tent.

To Bradshaw's amazement, Stuntz, thanks to his "no questions asked" policy, obtained a kerosene-powered Electrolux refrigerator, a radio, electric lights, and a film projector for the regular showing of movies. The permanent latrine, which consisted of two fifty-five-gallon drums buried end to end, even boasted toilet seats.

The men who would live here proudly came to call the place Hotel Alamo.

To teach the men physical combat, Bradshaw brought in Lt. Carl Moyer from the 1st Marine Division. Moyer's program would include ninety minutes of rigorous exercise daily, including running, swimming, calisthenics, hiking, and self-defense techniques, such as judo and karate, as well as instructions on how to use elbows, head smashes, feet, and knees to immobilize an attacker.

The 260-pound Moyer was an imposing figure who easily tossed both men and officers around, almost with sadistic glee. He sported a brown belt in judo, or what he referred to as "man-to-man combat."

One of Moyer's favorite exercises involved the men standing in a circle, facing inward, all blindfolded. An "attacker" would prowl around the circle and, without warning, throw a stranglehold on a soldier. The victim not only had to break the hold but throw the attacker to the ground and finish him off. To keep the trainees sharp, they were told to attack their fellow Scouts, including officers, at any time without warning.

Bradshaw also began bringing in auxiliary or "overhead" personnel for the operational and maintenance work at the camp. Cooks, drivers, bakers, boat handlers, radiomen, and supply clerks were recruited. Since some of these men had combat experience, they often played the role of "aggressor forces" to aid in the training of the Scouts. The overhead personnel enjoyed their duty, not just because of the quality of the food or the camp but because they were allowed to perform their jobs without officers breathing down their necks.

As the camp was being built, Bradshaw turned his attention to the men who would be training there. He decided early that combat veterans would get first preference. He wanted physically fit men of courage, drive, skill, intelligence, and good judgment. Backwoodsmen, or men used to life in the wilderness, were preferred. The candidates would have to be able to swim half a mile in rough surf, and have twenty-twenty vision. Probably most of all, they had to have endurance, to be able to withstand long marches with little or no rest, and prolonged periods behind enemy lines, with a minimum of food.

Training would be an ongoing process, Bradshaw knew. The rigorous program he and his instructors had mapped out guaranteed that all but the fittest would be weeded out over the six-week course. Of those who completed the training, some, but not all, would be retained and assigned to a team, consisting of one officer and six enlisted men. The rest would still graduate as qualified Scouts, but would be returned to their original units, either because they were not selected for a team or at their own or their commanding officer's personal request, to perform reconnaissance duties there. After graduation, a new class would be recruited, and the process repeated, to meet the war's demand.

As the 6th Army advanced across New Guinea and, eventually, the Philippines, the Alamo Scout Training Camp, or ASTC, would move with it. The Fergusson Island camp, for example, would exist until April 8, when it would be moved to Mange Point near Finschhafen, New Guinea. On July 3, the camp would reopen at Cape Kassoe near Hollandia, the former capital of Dutch-owned western New Guinea. There it would remain until after the invasion of the Philippines, when the ASTC training camp would move to Leyte, then to Luzon, first to Calasiao and, finally, to Mabayo on Subic Bay.

But that was all still in the future. For now, the first ASTC opened on December 3, 1943, with class set to begin on December 27.

Orders were sent to every regiment under Krueger's command to furnish headquarters with the names of one hundred prescreened candidates, enlisted men, and junior grade officers, along with a list of criteria they were to meet. The men were to be interviewed by their platoon leaders and/or company commanders. Usually, but not always, they were told that the duty they were being interviewed for was extremely hazardous, and they could refuse if they so desired. Those who made it through that level were next interviewed by regimental and division officers. Following that process, the top one hundred were sent to Bradshaw.[*]

Unless the candidates were at remote outposts, in which case they

---

*Throughout the war there would be a total of nine Alamo Scout classes, although the war would end before the last class graduated. Since the training regimen for all eight changed little, the narration that follows will not be an attempt to tell the story of each class. Instead, it will largely follow the program as a whole, intermingled with personal experiences of individual Scouts, regardless of their class.

were accepted based solely on their commander's recommendation, each man selected was interviewed by either Bradshaw or Williams. Andy Smith, who would later take part in the Alamo Scouts' most famous mission at Cabanatuan, was one of the former. Told he "fit the qualifications," he was sent to the ASTC without an interview.

Those who did go through the interview would be called into a room and told to sit at a table across from his interviewer. On the table, scattered at random, would be about twenty-five items, such as a pack of cigarettes, a lighter, a compass, a pencil, a comb, a watch, a button, and so forth. Throughout the interview, no mention of these items would be made. Instead, the man was asked about his background and where he was from, his prewar occupation, and his family.

He was asked if he liked the outdoors, and how well he worked with others. If the man was an officer or noncommissioned officer, he was asked how he felt about taking advice or even orders from a private. Throughout this, the prospective Scout was being assessed for his intelligence, his common sense, and his ability to work as a member of a team. Those who fell short in any of these categories were sent packing.

To test his motivation, a man would again be briefed on the hazards of the duty and asked why he volunteered. If his answer was a flippant "To kill Japs," or some similar bit of bravado, he was rejected.

At the conclusion of the interview, the man was dismissed. As he rose and headed for the door, Bradshaw or Williams would say, "Stop! Without turning around, there are items lying here on the table. Name as many as you can."

Those who did not recall an adequate number, even to the brand of cigarettes and make of watch, were sent back to their units.

Robert Teeples, then twenty-five and a member of L Company, 128th Regiment of the 32nd "Red Arrow" Division, volunteered after he transferred out of his former unit "in disgust." He had been busted to private for missing pill call, during which men were given bad-tasting Atabrine to stave off malaria, after he returned from the hard fighting at Buna.

Interviewed by Bradshaw, he was asked if he was afraid to die, how far he could swim, and would he be squeamish about killing another human being. Teeples soon became a member of the ASTC's first class.

Jack Geiger of New Jersey joined the army in 1943 and, after basic training, was assigned to the 422nd Regiment of the 106th Division. But before the Golden Lions could ship out for Europe (where the division would be decimated during the Battle of the Bulge and two regiments, including Geiger's 422nd, surrounded and captured), Geiger and a number of other privates were pulled out to serve as replacements bound for the Pacific.

Geiger ended up with the 31st Division at Camp Patrick Henry, Virginia, where the unit prepared for debarkation. He arrived in New Guinea in February 1944 and worked a stint as a jeep driver, ferrying pilots from their barracks to the airfield.

"It was great," he recalled years later. "I didn't have to do all that crazy training with the division."

Eventually he was sent back to his unit, I Company, and it was there that he saw a notice tacked to the company bulletin board calling for volunteers for intelligence work. With no idea what he was in for, he applied. Geiger went through the initial interview with his company officers, packed his gear, and was sent to see Bradshaw. Of the almost one hundred men who went with him, only fifteen were selected for Scout training and sent on to the ASTC at Mange Point. Geiger was one of them, joining the Scouts' third class.

Lt. Wilbur Littlefield, a twenty-one-year-old Californian with the rugged good looks of a young Clark Gable, was on New Britain with the 40th Division, 160th Regiment, when he caught word that a new unit was being formed. A product of Officer Candidate School at Fort Benning, Georgia, all the Los Angeles–born man knew about this unit, he later recalled, was "that they wanted volunteers for a dangerous mission behind Japanese lines." Littlefield, who had yet to see any action, was one of three officers and twenty-six men from his company to volunteer, which guaranteed stiff competition since only one officer and six men from the entire regiment would be selected for further consideration. Littlefield recalled that, "in typical army fashion," the first officer selected by the company "couldn't even read a map."

"I don't know how he ever got his commission," Littlefield said.

Sixth Army G2 was furious that the division commander tried to pawn this man off and sent an officer of their own to make the selection. By coincidence, before the war this officer had been a teacher in the Los Angeles high school Littlefield had attended. The two knew each other and Littlefield got the nod and would be a member of the ASTC's third class.

Born on a farm forty miles northeast of Seattle, Oliver Roesler was a Pacific Northwest lumberman. He had been a University of Washington ROTC student until the war broke out, at which time he threw his books into his school locker and went out to join the service. Roesler had wanted to fly, but the military needed infantrymen more, so he ended up in the 31st Division. He quickly discovered the army was tough, hardly what he had been led to believe "by watching Bob Hope and Dorothy Lamour movies."

Then he heard about men being needed for a new, elite unit. Rumor was that the men selected would perform "two missions behind Jap lines and we'll send you back to the States," so he volunteered and joined the Scouts' third class. Before the war was over, he would do nine missions.

Terry Santos joined the army in his native San Francisco. A feisty young man of nineteen, he craved action, so he volunteered for the 11th Airborne and, later, a reconnaissance and intelligence platoon attached to the Office of Strategic Services. When he reached New Guinea, he heard about the Alamo Scouts and expressed interest. However, he was informed that General MacArthur did not want any men in his theater of operations with ties to the OSS, so Santos quit that unit and was soon accepted for the ASTC, and would join its fourth class in 1944.

Robert Buschur was an Ohio farmer who was with the 40th Division recon platoon in New Britain when he read about the search for volunteers on the company bulletin board and decided to "check it out." Drafted at the age of eighteen, he trained at Fort Riley, Kansas, and, in August 1943, helped mop up Japanese forces on Guadalcanal. Later, he was set to go ashore with his division on New Ireland, waiting with the troops offshore, when the invasion was canceled by MacArthur, who had learned that there were forty thousand Japanese on the island waiting for his men. The island was bypassed, and Buschur and his comrades were sent back, first to Guadalcanal, then on to Cape Glouces-ter, and, finally, New Guinea.

Yearning for action, the twenty-year-old Buschur now acted on the bulletin board announcement and volunteered for the Scouts. He was accepted for the ASTC's third class.

The end of the interviews was not the end of the weeding-out process.

William Blaise, who was one of the few men who had joined the army before Pearl Harbor and would become a member of the ASTC's third class, recalled, "The first night they put us in a big tent and gave us cards, checkers, and different games. They said training would start first thing in the morning. The next morning some of the men were sent back already. The staff was looking for loudmouths and bullies, and where else but in a card game could you find loudmouths and bullies? They sent the blowhards back right away. You had to have men who could live and work together. Same way with the officers. You would look at the teams and you wouldn't know who the officers were."

In the end, less than half of the men interviewed were accepted for training. These soldiers represented a variety of military and eth-nic backgrounds, including infantrymen, artillerymen, tankers, para-troopers, signalmen, and engineers. Most were Caucasian, but a number of others were Filipino, Hispanic, and Native Americans from at least twenty tribes, including Chippewa, Navajo, Apache, Choctaw, Sioux, Pawnee, Cherokee, and Seminole. Of the thirty-eight men in the first graduating class on February 5, 1944, nine would be Native Americans.

On the first day of training, the Scout candidates would gather in the screened-in mess hall, seated on hard wooden benches, while Bradshaw addressed them.

"You will certainly agree that this is the nicest all-around camp that you have attended in this theater," he told the candidates. "It is a good camp because all have worked together to make it so. You are expected to help keep it that way. A part of your training and a thing you will be strictly graded on is the manner in which you conduct yourselves. You may have had the idea that Alamo Scouts is an organization of cutthroats and toughs. We want you to be tough—just as tough as you can make yourselves—but we don't have any place in this organization for a 'tough.' This type of work does not call for bums and tramps. It calls for the highest qualities of soldiering. Self-discipline is one of the first attributes. Be considerate of your fellow soldiers and of temperate disposition. You will be treated as individuals and as men—gentlemen, if you please. You will be expected to respond in a similar manner.

"Remember, you were not asked to come to this training center. It is our understanding that each and every one of you is a volunteer of his own free will and accord. If there is any one of you who has any reservations, mental or otherwise, make yourself known to the Director of Training and you will be released to return to your organization without any questions.

"You will be closely observed during all of the six weeks you are here. If it is found that you are not mentally, temperamentally, or physically fit and up to the standards required; if it is found that you are not giving it all you have; if it is found that you are not sincerely trying—you will be returned. Time is too precious to waste on those who do not fit. There are no disciplinary problems here. Breaches of discipline are quickly disposed of by returning the violator to his unit.

"The officers of the staff are here with the single thought of furnishing you with their best in the way of training. There is no need for you to have the slightest fear of them. They are ordinary human beings, just as you and I are, and they hope you will consider them as such in your contacts with them. Practically all of us started in the army as privates, including myself. Most of us are civilian soldiers doing the simple job of trying to help our country win a war. If you have any suggestions to offer, any real criticism or complaint or anything else you want to get off your chest, we encourage you to discuss it with a member of the staff; or, if you are hesitant to do that, then simply write a note and drop it in the mailbox in the dayroom. You do not even need to sign it. The relationships here are very informal, based as they are on mutual respect and sincere effort.

"At the conclusion of this class, some of you will be selected as Alamo Scouts and retained to execute such reconnaissance missions as the army commander may desire. The majority of you will be returned to your units, where your training will stand you in good stead and where you will be available to your division, regimental, and battalion commanders for their missions. A few of you will not make the grade for one reason or another. In any event, you will be better soldiers for what you have received here and it is hoped that you always carry with you the tradition and esprit de corps of the 'Alamo Scouts.'

"Training begins tomorrow. That is all."

★   ★   ★

Bradshaw was as good as his word. At five thirty a.m. the men were roused, and after a breakfast of powdered scrambled eggs, fried corned beef, fresh fruit, such as mangoes, coconuts, and oranges, and coffee, the day began in earnest.

The men were divided into teams consisting of an officer and six to ten men, depending on the ratio of officers to enlisted men. For the most part they would remain together all through training or until attrition, which often ran as high as 40 percent in the first two weeks, made the team too small to function. At that time they might be combined with another dwindling group. On occasion, Scouts were rotated to different teams in order to get to know other men and officers.

One of the first orders of business was to draw equipment: black swimming trunks, jungle first aid packets—which included morphine syrettes, sulfa drugs, a small bandage, water purification tablets, and assorted tropical ointments—weapons, compass, binoculars, machete, pistol belt, poncho, cartridge pouch, canteen, and trench knife.

The standard uniform was an olive green herringbone or two-piece camouflage fatigues with soft cap and high quarter hobnail shoes with optional leggings. Rank insignia was worn during training but was not to be worn in action. Officers' bars were an invitation for an enemy bullet in the field.

The teams, on average, were equipped with two pairs of binoculars, two map cases, two compasses, and two canteens per man. Each man carried a personal knife (no machetes) and one hundred rounds of ammo—which was found to be too much and was cut back—four flares, two Handi-Talkie radios, and a rubber boat, complete with CO_2 capsule, although some also relied on hand pumps.

A physical examination was next, after which the men were led to the dock area.

"You now have some free swimming time," they were told. "Controlled swimming starts tomorrow. Jump in and have fun."

The men did, but soon learned that nothing in the Scouts would be "free." The water was deep, twenty-eight feet, which meant the men had to paddle around. Those who tired before the "free swim" was over and had to get out or be pulled out were shipped back to their units.

Controlled swimming meant that the men had to paddle from the dock to a point about half a mile out and back. Sometimes they were taken a mile or more out and dumped over the side and told to swim.

"Chow will be ready when you get in," the instructor barked.

On occasion, the men had to swim carrying gear, the rationale being that their boat might capsize and they would have to save their equipment. Another drill involved swimming out to a waiting boat, where they would find their gear. There, they had to put it on, while still in the water, and swim back. Sometimes strings were stretched out across the water, and when a man came to one, he had to swim under it.

Lt. Robert "Red" Sumner recalled his first day of training when he and his team, fully dressed, were taken half a mile out into the bay on an LCVP landing craft. Then, by the half-mile buoy, the ramp was lowered and they were told to get off.

"I gathered my squad and off the ramp we went, jump or dive, and about twenty minutes later we were on the beach, somewhat tired but none the worse," he wrote years later. "From this point on, we were off and running for our six weeks."

One especially memorable, and frightening, drill was on how to avoid enemy fire while in the water. As the swimmers approached a boat or a pier, an instructor stood, brandishing a Tommy gun.

"Duck," he would yell, and the men went down as fast and deep as they could, moving left or right as they dove, for an instant later, the water where their heads had been was peppered with submachine-gun fire.

Teeples recalled one drill where the men dove into the water on one side of the pier, then swam underwater around the front of the pier, to the other side, a distance of sixty or seventy feet.

Littlefield recalled the intense training and how easy it was for a man to get booted out of the ASTC. His tent mate, for example, was a "helluva fine soldier," Littlefield recalled, who was sent back to his unit because he snored loudly, which would never do for someone behind enemy lines.

Bob Buschur worried. He was not a great swimmer, and swimming was an important part of Scout training. During his first time swimming out to the rubber boat, he recalled reaching it and placing his hands on the boat to rest. An instructor on board the boat stepped on Buschur's fingers, forcing the young man to let go.

"You came out here to swim and practice diving, not to rest," he was gruffly told.

By far, the most physically demanding and dangerous part of the water training was learning to handle the ungainly rubber boats. Ten hours a week were devoted to this, including rowing the boats through the hazardous coral spray on the windward side of a cove at Hollandia. To practice nighttime navigation, two men would row a mile out, pick out a landmark on the shore, and fix a compass reading on the mark. Then they were required to cover their heads with a poncho and, using just the compass, row to shore in an attempt to land as close as possible to the mark.

During the first day of training, each team was issued a six- or ten-man rubber boat with oars. Their instructors, Lieutenants Beckworth, Frederick A. Sukup, Daily P. Gambill, and Henry R. Chalko, taught them how to inflate the craft with lung power, pumps, and CO_2 cartridges, how to board and launch them from PT boats and J-boats, and how to maneuver and land in rough surf. They also learned how to conceal and recover boats once onshore.

The men drilled in daylight and at night. The drills were often dangerous and, on one occasion, deadly. At Tami Beach near Hollandia, a rubber boat capsized and two Scout candidates drowned. They would prove to be the unit's only fatalities in two years of active duty.

★   ★   ★

Onshore, training included communications skills in Morse code and radio. Every Scout candidate underwent this training in case the team's appointed radioman was killed or wounded. They were also taught the use of the blinker light and had to be able to send ten words per minute. The Scouts were trained on the SCR-288 walkie-talkie; the SCR-300 radio, which was carried on a man's back; and the SCR-694 radio, which was powered by a hand-cranked electrical generator, and which, with its greater range, came in handy later in the war during extended missions in the Philippines, when the men were living and moving with the guerrilla bands. They also learned to use the Australian ATR-4 radio.

But sometimes communication would involve dealing with natives and the enemy verbally, so members of the Netherlands East Indies Administration taught the men Melanesian pidgin English, a language developed through interisland trade that blended native words with

English. The Scouts would not be fluent in the language, but would at least know how to ask for food, water, and inquire about the location of the enemy troops. In the Philippines, pidgin English was replaced by Tagalog. The Scouts were also taught basic Japanese, particularly key military words they might overhear.

Courses taught included map reading, the use of the compass and how to find one's way through unfamiliar terrain, how to read latitude and longitude to call in airdrops or guide boats in to shore. They learned how to recognize rivers, valleys, and mountains.

For intelligence-gathering skills, the men were schooled in how to plan missions, including how many men to take, how much food and ammo would be needed, the types of weapons best suited, and the length of the mission. They attended classes on Japanese order of battle and how to handle prisoners. They sketched coastlines, beaches, and other terrain features, to clear the way for invasions, and learned to analyze beach gradients, tides, reefs, vegetation, fresh water sources, soil and sand composition, roads and trails.

Classes were also held on how to evaluate enemy morale, physical condition, defenses, both fixed and mobile installations, bivouac areas, bridges, roads, ammo dumps, airfields, lines of communication, and other targets of opportunity.

"When, where, what, why, who covers everything you need to find out on an intelligence operation," Bradshaw told them. "Never forget that and never vary the order."

Methods of concealment were taught, ways to protect themselves by the use of grease paint, mud, grass, and other ways of blending in.

To survive in the harsh environment of the jungle, the men learned basic reconnaissance and patrolling skills, including escape and evasive techniques, taught by Australian 1st Lt. Raymond "Moose" Watson, on detached duty from the Australian New Guinea Administration Police. Earlier in the war, deep behind enemy lines, Watson and another soldier, along with two native police officers, somewhat derogatorily called "police boys," had trekked across northern New Guinea, including unexplored regions, to observe enemy shipping. The Japanese jumped them, and though they escaped, they lost all of their weapons and supplies. The police boys helped the white men to survive by showing them the ways of the jungle.

Now he was teaching the Scouts those same survival techniques and jungle skills, including tracking, which beetles and grubs were edible, and how to tap drinkable water from certain vines.

Doc Canfield discussed medical and sanitary regulations with the men and stressed ways to prevent malaria and other diseases. He instructed them to take five Atabrine tablets with their evening meals each week, Monday through Thursday. He issued mosquito netting, which was to be put up around their beds in the evening and taken down each morning. Swimming was only allowed between seven a.m. and six p.m., the hours when mosquitoes are less active.

"Shirtsleeves must be worn down and trousers tucked into socks or leggings," Canfield said. "Clothes will be boiled when possible, and a fresh uniform will be worn daily."

While the main mission of the Alamo Scouts was to observe rather than fight, they had to be prepared to fight if need be. For that reason, Krueger demanded the men have the best possible weaponry. Any piece a man wanted was obtained for him. Carbines were the most popular, although some men armed themselves with the Thompson submachine gun and a few preferred the M1 Garand rifle.

Requests were also made for the M1A1 carbine with the folding wire stock. Designed specifically for the paratroopers, it was issued only to the airborne units. Yet if an Alamo Scout wanted one, the everresourceful Stuntz could supply it.

Each man also carried a Colt .45-caliber automatic pistol.

Weapons training included the use and maintenance of the Garand, the carbine, the Thompson, the M3 "grease gun," and the Browning Automatic Rifle (BAR), as well as grenades, pistols, knives, garrotes, and clubs. Sniping techniques, with and without a silencer, were also taught. The men worked with the standard Mark II fragmentation grenade, the M15 white phosphorous, or "Willie Peter" grenade, and the AN-M14 incendiary grenade that burns to two thousand degrees and could melt steel.

In one drill, Teeples said, "We had to climb into a foxhole, then place a grenade on the lip of the hole, pull the pin, and duck until it exploded." He also recalled learning to fire a 60mm mortar without a base plate or elevating mechanism. Instead, he placed the mortar against the crotch of a tree, bracing his elbows against the limbs, and, with another Scout assisting, visually aimed and fired it at a barrel anchored out in the water.

The Scouts were instructed on how to make and use snares and booby traps, how to rig explosives and set demolition charges, and were even drilled on the use of enemy weapons. They learned how to move at five- and ten-yard intervals through jungle, to negotiate wire entanglements and avoid booby traps. They were blindfolded and told to move through jungle without being caught.

During this phase, overhead personnel acting as the enemy sniped at the Scouts with live ammo, placing their rounds so close to the trainees that a few Scouts were treated for minor gunshot wounds.

By the fourth week, the men were swimming up to five miles and were given a written examination on what they had learned. By this time, some classes had less than half the men they had started with.

The Scouts also were used as a testing ground for experimental weapons and ideas. Sumner recalled testing silencers for the M1 carbine, the 1903 bolt-action Springfield, and the M3 submachine gun.

"The .30-caliber carbine models got a good testing too, and we found them to be too heavy, the core material unsatisfactory and the silencers generally unacceptable," he wrote. "The mechanisms were steel tubes stuffed with various quantities of steel mesh or wool. Some had exhaust vents, some did not. We found too that the internal packing deflected the round fired or affected the flight of the round, usually skewing it, and we could never be sure of the strike on the target. We were too expert at our marksmanship to miss very often, and not being able to depend on the hit offset any value of the silencer. We did find that at close range—ten feet—it was effective, but if we closed to that distance, why not go all the way and use a knife or machete in a close attack."

The army also tried to inject some medieval warfare into the Scouts' repertoire of weaponry by testing crossbows developed by the Bell Telephone Laboratories. The bows were made of aluminum and steel, and fired bolts or darts of various dimensions with a wide array of barbs and cutting edges. Poison tips could even be used. The weapon came in two styles, a rifle model and a pistol-style bow.

The rifle model proved unwieldy, Sumner recalled, and good for only one shot because the loud clack emitted by resetting the bow was "earth shattering." The pistol-style bow was better, with a maximum range of fifty feet and a killing range of twenty to twenty-five feet, and a resetting mechanism that was easy to use and virtually soundless. Bill Littlefield's team used such a bow near Vanimo in New Guinea in August 1944, killing a Japanese sentry, the bolt passing cleanly through his body.

★   ★   ★

Not every hour was spent in training. During their off-duty time, the Scouts fished, boated, and hunted wild pigs. They also played baseball and volleyball.

The men enjoyed the best of army food. Lieutenant Stuntz traded surplus items, native goods, and war souvenirs (especially the much-sought-after helmets, swords, rifles, and flags) to the navy or air corps, in exchange for fresh meat, eggs, butter, and vegetables. Stuntz also swapped cigars, chewing tobacco, pineapples, and bananas for meat, eggs, potatoes, apples, and oranges.

The first thing Bill Littlefield noticed about the eating arrangements, besides the quality of the food, was the lack of segregation in the mess hall. Officers and enlisted men stood in one chow line, and the first man in line, regardless of rank, was the first one served. Officers and enlisted men did eat at separate tables, however, since the officers used this time to discuss the next day's schedule.

Not only were Bradshaw's men happy with the arrangements at the ASTC, but so were the locals. Understanding the value of good relationships, Bradshaw employed natives as guards, laborers, and in other jobs, in exchange for which the natives received ample food, clothes, and medical care. This latter included an emergency delivery of a set of twins by Doc Canfield, who, even though one infant died, was rewarded with a fine pearl.

On Christmas 1943, the entire camp spent the holiday with the natives. On Christmas Eve, the wife of an Australian missionary to Fergusson Island led natives into the Scout camp, singing carols in English for the benefit of the men so far from home and loved ones. In return, the singers received gifts of tobacco, calico, candy, cigarettes, knives, soap, and matches.

Bare-breasted women and laughing kids presented the Scouts with tubs of flowers and fruits, and even a live chicken. For the finale, four native men gave Bradshaw a roasted goat.

★   ★   ★

During the last two weeks of training, the men put into practice everything they had learned by going out into the jungle. Sometimes one team would hide while another was sent to find them. Other times, natives were used in place of Japanese. Littlefield recalled nighttime exercises, lying in wait for the "enemy," in this case Watson's police boys, only to have a police boy come up from behind, unheard, and tap him on the shoulder.

Bradshaw often bribed the natives, saying they could have cans of food if they found the Scout team. The Scouts soon caught on to this, and buried cans of meat. Once the natives found the cans, they gave up the hunt.

On other occasions, teams of Scouts were sent behind Japanese lines in lightly held areas to watch for movements of enemy troops and supply barges. This gave the men a true sense of what they would face.

Galen "Kit" Kittleson, who would later be a member of the Cabanatuan mission, spent one night sharing a nipa hut with the skeleton of a Japanese soldier who, possibly, had chosen this spot to die of starvation. It was a rainy night, and the roof leaked. Andy Smith, always quick with a joke, had propped up the skeleton, put a cigarette in its mouth and a GI cap on the head.

The next day, Kittleson and his teammates came across an abandoned village, overgrown with foliage as it was slowly being reclaimed by the jungle. The ground was littered with the rotting bodies of several dozen Japanese, killed either by Americans or, more likely, by natives, since several skulls were missing.

Even though training was winding down, the weeding-out process continued, although generally with less frequency.

During one training mission, an "infiltrator" climbed a cliff, entered the camp of a training team, stole a knife, and escaped undetected. When the theft was discovered, the men argued among themselves, blaming each other for the crime, and debated whether to report it when they got back to base. They did not report the missing knife, and the entire team was dismissed. Honesty was a key to accurate intelligence gathering, and Bradshaw would not tolerate anything less.

One last endurance test involved a twenty-six-mile hike through the jungle with full packs. Zeke McConnell and the Littlefield Team recalled passing through a mangrove swamp, where leeches attached themselves to their bodies. Emerging on the other side, McConnell remembered, "We had to strip down and remove the leeches from each other."

★   ★   ★

Yet even successfully completing the training and receiving a diploma from the Alamo Scouts did not guarantee a man would be assigned to an Alamo Scout team.

The final selection was based on projected manpower needs and a secret ballot, during which both officers and men were asked to list, in order of preference, which men they would like to serve with and under. Officers were likewise told to select the men they'd most like to have on their teams. Those who failed to make the cut would still graduate as trained Alamo Scouts, but would be sent back to their original units, where their skills were put to work. So while some men's diplomas read "Retained as an Alamo Scout," others' did not.

One of these latter was Bob Buschur. Buschur missed graduation. Following his final field exercise, he came in from the jungle with malaria. He reported to the medics, who sent him to the field hospital. There, the doctors refused to treat him because he did not have a pass from his commanding officer. He returned to Bradshaw, who saw that the young man was very ill. Bradshaw personally took Buschur back to the hospital and told the commander, "When one of my Alamo Scouts comes in here, I expect him to be treated."

After graduation Bradshaw visited Buschur in the hospital, congratulated him on his achievement, but informed him that he was being returned to his division to ply his skills there.

"That was OK with me," Buschur said in 2007. "I missed my buddies."

For others, the choice of whether they stayed with the Scouts or returned to their original units was either a personal one or predetermined by their commander. Robert Sumner later wrote, "If selected, graduates had the choice of joining a team or returning to their units with their buddies. Often times soldiers felt a deep connection with their unit and wanted to take back what they learned in the Scouts. A few did that, while others were ordered back because their units needed them. In fact, many units had no intention of letting them stay because they didn't want their best men siphoned off. The needs of the army were paramount and dictated how many teams were retained."

A few decided on their own not to remain and join a team. Terry Santos, for example, heard his old unit, the 11th Airborne, was being put on alert for a drop, and asked to go back. There he led a reconnaissance platoon and was lead scout on the Airborne Division's famous rescue mission at Los Baños in the Philippines.

Bob Teeples was one of those graduates retained by the Scouts. He remembered being "mighty proud" of the inscription on his diploma stating that he was "proficient in all subjects."

For all of the Alamo Scout graduates, whether assigned to a team or returned to their original units, the difficult training forged a bond of mutual respect and solidarity between the men.

Wilbur Littlefield, who would be in the ASTC's third class, was in the hospital with dengue fever when he heard he was retained and was told to select his team.

"The guys were all for each other," he recalled. "They were close-knit."

The ASTC graduated its first class on February 5, 1944; four teams under Lts. John R. C. McGowen, William F. Barnes, Michael J. Sombar, and George S. Thompson.

Training was over. Now it was time to go to work.

CHAPTER 4

The First Mission

McGowen Team: Los Negros Island, February 27–28, 1944

Colonel Bradshaw stepped off the PT boat at Finschhafen even before the vessel had been secured to the pier. Striding along the wooden wharf, followed by his XO, Capt. Homer A. Williams, he headed for a jeep that would take him to General Krueger's headquarters.

This was the day Bradshaw had been waiting for. Summoned from his own HQ on Fergusson Island, he had been handed a mission for his newly activated Alamo Scouts.

On February 5, just twenty days earlier, four teams had graduated from the Alamo Scout Training Center: twenty-four highly trained men, all piss and vinegar to prove their mettle. Two of those teams would be joining him at the Finschhafen briefing. Which one would actually undertake the mission, Bradshaw had yet to decide.

One team was led by Lt. John R. C. McGowen, a twenty-five-year-old Texan from Amarillo who, like many of the men in the first graduating class, had come to the Scouts from the 158th Infantry Regiment.

Having graduated with a master's degree from Texas A&M, where he was also enrolled in the ROTC program, McGowen had worked in Panama for the United Fruit Company before the war, joining the army immediately after Pearl Harbor. (His draft board back home evidently was slow to get the message and bombarded his mother with demands that her son report for duty, even after he had been sent to the southwest Pacific.)

A man of perseverance, driven to push himself to his limits and beyond, McGowen volunteered for the Alamo Scouts despite his lack of swimming prowess. The amount of swimming required by the Scouts proved a monumental challenge, but "grit and determination like no one else," his wife Christine later recalled, led him to succeed.

McGowen had a daring, never-say-lose attitude that Bradshaw liked. During training, to keep their reflexes sharp, Scout candidates were encouraged to launch surprise attacks on each other, officers included, at any time of the day or night. McGowen chose to attack Lt. Carl Moyer, the group's rough, tough self-defense instructor, diving at Moyer's feet and taking him down. McGowen's action won everyone's admiration, including Moyer's.

The other team joining Bradshaw at Finschhafen was led by Lt. William Barnes, a twenty-six-year-old graduate of the University of Tennessee who, in 1938–39, had been a member of the school's number-two-ranked football team. Barnes had come to the Scouts from the 32nd Division, where he had been on special assignment to train intelligence and reconnaissance platoons for the 127th Regiment.

The mission Bradshaw had been handed was actually the second one to come the Scouts' way. The first, a four-day reconnaissance of the Marakum area fifteen miles east of Bogadjim on New Guinea's northern coast, had been assigned to McGowen, but then was scrubbed.

This one would not be. The Scouts were to perform a reconnaissance mission on Los Negros Island, a prelude to MacArthur's planned retaking of the Bismarck Archipelago and final isolation of the huge Japanese naval base at Rabaul on New Britain, 390 air miles to the southeast.

★   ★   ★

Part of MacArthur's plan for seizing and neutralizing both the Bismarck Archipelago and the northern coast of Dutch New Guinea as far west as the Sepik River called for Krueger's 6th Army to capture the Admiralty Islands, off the northwest coast of New Guinea.

Earlier in 1944, MacArthur's forces had taken key areas along New Guinea's northern coast from troops of Gen. Hatazo Adachi's 18th Army, sealing off the Vitiaz Strait between New Guinea and New Britain, and blocking Japanese access to the Bismarck Sea.

Farther to the east Adm. William F. Halsey's naval forces, moving up from the Solomons, sailed to within 125 miles of Rabaul. There, Grumman Hellcats and Dauntless dive-bombers from his powerful carrier strike force plastered the Japanese with a series of relentless air attacks.

Orders for MacArthur's planned leap at the Admiralties, code-named Brewer, were cut on November 23, 1943, with D-day tentatively set for April 1.

Initially Dutch, the Admiralty Islands were discovered in 1615 by Capt. William Schouten, but became part of German New Guinea in 1848 when the Netherlands, Germany, and Australia divided up control of New Guinea. In 1918, as Germany was being stripped of her overseas holdings under the Treaty of Versailles following the First World War, the islands passed to Australian control, which was how things stood until the Japanese arrived in early 1942.

The Admiralties consist of 160 islands, with the two principal ones being Manus to the west and Los Negros to the east. The two are separated by a narrow, shallow strait that is navigable only by native canoes and small boats.

The northern coastlines of Manus and Los Negros, combined with the curving shores of the lesser islands, form a U shape. In the middle of this U is Seeadler Harbor, which, at twenty miles long, six miles wide, and 120 feet deep—accessible through a channel that cuts between the islands of Ndrilo and Huawei—is one of the finest anchorages in the Pacific.

Manus, the largest island at forty-nine miles long and sixteen wide, is cut by a rugged mountain range running its length to a height of

2,355 feet. The soil of Manus and Los Negros is a reddish clay, traversed by many fordable streams that are prone to flash flooding. Coastal plains are bounded by mangrove swamps, while the interior of the islands are thick jungle. The entire area sweats under a climate that is hot and humid, and frequent heavy rains turn the clay into a sticky substance the natives call gumbo. In 1944, about thirteen thousand natives, mostly Melanesian with Micronesian blood, inhabited the islands.

★   ★   ★

The first mission selected for the Alamo Scouts was to be a one-week reconnaissance of the western portion of Manus, with a team of Scouts rowing ashore from a submarine. This plan was soon cut back to a four-day patrol of New Guinea's Marakum area, with insertion to be by PT boat. In approving this revision on February 21, Krueger's chief of staff wrote, "This should be a good test for Scouts and should prove of value to them."

Plans changed again three days later, just before the mission was to commence. MacArthur moved Operation Brewer's D-day up five weeks to February 29.

Prompting the change were reports from reconnaissance pilots flying low over Los Negros, who said they spotted no signs of the enemy. Up until this point, debate had raged over how many Japanese inhabited the island. MacArthur's staff guessed 4,050. The 1st Cavalry Division, whose nearly one thousand men were to comprise the initial strike force in the invasion, set to go ashore in the Hyane Harbor area, estimated 4,900, while 5th Air Force intelligence insisted the number was less than 300. Now, however, there was speculation that perhaps the enemy had abandoned Los Negros entirely.

Krueger, always bowing to caution, refused to believe that the Japanese would abandon Los Negros. Nor was he convinced by the fact that U.S. Mitchell bombers, trying to distract enemy attention away from photo reconnaissance planes, drew no hostile fire as they roared over the island at treetop level.

"It doesn't take a genius to fool aerial reconnaissance," Krueger told his G2 intelligence chief, Col. Horton V. White. "I want to know what's there before I send the First Cav in. Let's put a team of Scouts onshore and find out. Get Bradshaw up here."

★ ★ ★

Bradshaw, orders in hand, now struggled over which team to send. As he prepared for the briefing at Finschhafen, he turned to Williams for his thoughts.

"So who goes? Barnes or McGowen? Both are capable."

"Flip a coin," Williams suggested. "If it's heads, McGowen goes. If it's tails, Barnes gets the job. The loser will serve as the contact."

Finding the solution agreeable, Bradshaw fished a coin from his pocket and flipped it. It came up heads.

Within thirty minutes, McGowen and Barnes entered the briefing hut, standing with their commander around a table, which held a map of what both officers recognized as the Admiralties.

"I flipped a coin to see who got this mission," Bradshaw said. "John, you lost, so you're going in." Everyone chuckled. "Bill, you're the contact team."

He turned to Colonel White, who took over the briefing.

"The mission is Los Negros," White began, tapping the map with a finger. "The air force is telling MacArthur that the Japs are abandoning the place, but General Krueger doesn't agree. This is a two-day mission. You'll fly in tomorrow night by PBY, landing as close to shore as the pilot can get you. You'll go the rest of the way by rubber boat, landing on the beach here, at Chapatut Point.

"There are two airfields on the island, a thirty-three-hundred-foot strip just northwest of Lorengau village and a four-thousand-foot airfield at Momote Point. To keep the Nips' heads down, B-25s will attack those fields while you are landing. Once ashore, recon the area to the northeast noting troop strengths and defenses, if any. First Cav, which will go in near Hyane Harbor on the twenty-ninth, needs that info. Then get back to the pickup point by the next morning. During the extraction, the bombers will again hit their airfields. If, for any reason, the Catalina can't get in to pick you up on schedule, it will return again twenty-four hours later, and again twenty-four hours after that, for three days.

"You will carry a walkie-talkie so you and Barnes can coordinate the pickup. As always, avoid contact with the enemy if possible. If there are no questions, get some rest. You leave at oh three thirty."

After the briefing broke up, Krueger called the team members into his tent, shook each man's hand, and wished him luck.

"This is our first mission," Krueger told McGowen. "Our first time at bat. You know how important that is."

"Don't worry, General," McGowen replied. "We'll hit a home run."

★　★　★

Emotions ran high that night as the men prepared for their first assignment, and sleep proved elusive. At three thirty a.m., dressed in their jungle fatigues, faces blackened, they gathered up their gear, which they had checked and rechecked.

McGowen watched his men get ready. He had carefully handpicked these men prior to the ASTC graduation in anticipation of the talent he might need for future missions.

McGowen's number-two man, Tech Sgt. Caesar J. Ramirez, was an able veteran and strong leader whom McGowen felt could take over in case something happened to him in the field. The other team members, all combat tested, were Sgt. Walter A. McDonald, Sgt. John A. Roberts, Pfc. John P. Lagoud, who, at twenty-nine, was the oldest member, and Pvt. Paul V. Gomez.

Besides their personal weapons, each man carried two hand grenades and two days' worth of K rations. One man also had the walkie-talkie, with its range of about twenty-five miles, slung over his shoulder.

The Catalina was waiting onshore and the Scouts climbed aboard. Taking seats on the floor of the PBY, the men sat back and relaxed as the graceful seaplane taxied out into Langemak Bay. Its two twelve-hundred-horsepower Pratt & Whitney Twin Wasp engines roared as the plane bounced across the dark water, building up enough speed to lift its twenty-one-thousand-pound bulk into the sky.

The Scouts sat in the dark for two hours, feeling the vibration of the plane's fuselage and listening to its engines hum. Some men chatted quietly, while others were silent, resting or lost in thought. Here and there, the pinpoint orange light of a cigarette glowed.

As they approached Los Negros, the plane flew into a heavy tropical thunderstorm. The pilot circled the area in an attempt to land, but the seas were too rough. The wind buffeted the plane, which creaked and groaned in response.

"Jesus Christ," said Sgt. Robert W. Teeples, one of the contact team members, looking out at the storm through the PBY's right blister window. "I think the goddamn wings are flapping."

Moments later, something flashed in the sky above the PBY. Teeples did not think it was lightning.

"Did you see that?" asked the sailor at the blister window across from Teeples.

"I thought I imagined it," Teeples said. "What do you make of it?"

"If I didn't know better, I'd say it's the exhaust flash from a Jap plane," the crewman said.

"And you'd be right," the Catalina's radar man said from forward in the plane. "I picked him up about five miles out. Probably a scout plane caught on patrol in the storm and barrel-assing back to base. He was above us, so I doubt he saw us in all this shitty weather. At least I hope not."

It wouldn't have mattered if the Japanese flier had seen them because the PBY pilot decided he could not safely set the big plane down. Banking the Catalina, he returned to Langemak Bay. There the Scouts, disappointed over the delay and waste of good emotions, spent the day aboard the seaplane tender USS *Half Moon*.

There was no storm over the landing area the next day, nor was there much darkness, as a delay in taking off meant the PBY did not arrive over the bay until dawn.

Things went downhill from there.

The Catalina touched down, gliding effortlessly across the water. The pilot throttled back, slowing the plane. Standing by the open hatch, McGowen waited for the aircraft to stop, but it did not.

"We're a half mile from shore and still moving," he said. "God-damn it."

He turned to Barnes. "Bill, go up to the cockpit and see what that idiot is doing."

Barnes did and was right back.

"He said he doesn't want to get closer to shore or stop the plane," Barnes reported. "He said it'll make him a sitting duck."

"But it doesn't matter if we drown or get chopped up by his fucking propellers," McGowen cursed. Then he said to Sergeant Ramirez, "Get that rubber boat into the water."

"We're going to get out of a moving plane?" Ramirez gasped.

"What choice do we have? That fool isn't going to stop."

Loading was precarious, but it was accomplished without anyone or anything falling over the side. As the rubber boat cast off, the PBY pilot pushed open his throttles and the seaplane roared off across the surface of the water and lifted into the sky, its prop wash rocking the Scouts' boat.

"How much does one of them planes cost?" Gomez mused as he watched the Catalina lift off, water cascading from its boatlike underbelly.

"About ninety thousand bucks," McGowen replied. "Why?"

"Just wondered. The way that pilot treats it, you'd think he had to pay for it himself if it got scratched."

As the team began rowing to shore, one of the men noticed another glitch in the plan.

"Hey," McDonald observed. "It's awful quiet onshore. Where the hell are the bombers?"

He was right. There was no distant, heavy *karrrumpp* of bombs falling on the airfields, or the deep, beelike humming of airplane engines. The sky was ominously silent.

"Goddamn flyboys," Lagoud said. "I'll bet someone forgot to wake 'em up."

"Keep rowing," said McGowen, who was not prone to idle chitchat.

It took McGowen's team about thirty minutes to reach the island. Gomez jumped out first, and helped drag the rubber boat across the beach. (Gomez was later angered to learn that MacArthur had awarded the Distinguished Service Cross to a young lieutenant for being the "first man ashore" on Los Negros during the invasion, three days after his own foot had touched the sand.)

The team moved off the beach quickly, deflating the rubber boat and burying it, along with its CO_2 cylinder, near a tree. Assuring themselves they could quickly find it again, they struck out in the direction of the Momote airfield.

★　★　★

What McGowen and his team could not have known was that their arrival had been observed by a lone Japanese soldier patrolling near the beach. He had hurried back to report the Americans' landing and the nervous leader, Col. Yoshio Ezaki, commander of the Admiralty Islands garrison, immediately dispatched patrols to find the Scouts. Then he inadvertently played into the Americans' hands.

Fearing this to be the prelude to an overwhelming invasion, Ezaki began shifting troops to the west, away from the island's eastern shore at Hyane Harbor, where, so far as he knew, they would not be needed.

★　★　★

Considering the overall ruggedness of the Bismarck Archipelago's terrain, the Scouts' trek took them over relatively level ground. Still, in the thick jungle, there were few landmarks to guide the way, so their course was set using their original compass bearing.

McGowen and his men picked their way through the dense foliage for about three hours, then they came upon vines strung tree to tree to tree, about five feet off the ground.

"What do you make of this?" Sergeant Gomez whispered.

"My guess is it's to keep the Japs on the trail in the dark," McGowen said. "I think the general is right. The Nips are still here."

The words were no more than uttered when heavy machine-gun fire opened up in the distance, several short, sharp bursts. The Scouts dropped to the ground and listened in absolute silence. Then another sound reached their ears—aircraft engines, followed by the dull booming of bombs and the *rat-tat-tat* of strafing fighter planes. It was the air strike meant to cover their landing.

"Now the bastards get here," Ramirez said.

"Probably still have their watches set to San Francisco time," Roberts observed.

"Let's keep moving," McGowen said.

Still advancing on their compass heading, McGowen and his team almost literally stumbled into a series of trenches running for some two hundred yards northwest to southeast, and camouflaged by small branches and leaves. The trenches were about two feet wide and two feet deep, and the dark earth indicated that they had been recently dug. In some spots, what looked like three machine-gun revetments had been carved out.

There were also signs of men—a lot of them—in the form of footprints and discarded ration packages.

McGowen was leading his team around the trenches, careful not to disturb anything, when they heard a nearby scream, possibly from a soldier wounded by the bombs. Then another, more soothing voice was heard, as if someone was trying to calm the injured man. Other voices filtered through the trees to the Scouts as well.

At the first scream, McGowen, at the point, put up a hand to indicate "freeze," and the men stopped dead. A few minutes passed in stone silence before McGowen proceeded. He wondered how far away the Japanese were. Then he got his answer. An enemy patrol, more than a dozen men, was moving perpendicular to McGowen's team, not fifteen feet out in front. McGowen's hand shot up and the men converted themselves into statues.

Watching the enemy patrol, which he had no way of knowing was looking for him, McGowen desperately wanted to hit the ground, but he dared not. At this distance, even the slightest movement would have been spotted by the patrol. Sweat poured down his face, burning his eyes, as he watched the patrol pass by so close that he could distinguish the insignias on their dark brown uniforms. Then, oblivious to how near they had come to locating the Americans, the Japanese faded into the underbrush.

McGowen gave the enemy plenty of time to put distance between them and him before moving on. At about one p.m., the team came to a wide, swift-moving creek. McGowen halted the men and had them gather around him.

"Goddamn it," Gomez gasped. "I thought I was gonna shit my pants back there. Any closer and we coulda smelled the breath on those rice bellies."

He took a slug of water from his canteen to calm his nerves.

"Listen up," McGowen said. "The airstrip is just beyond this creek. We know there are Japs there, plenty of them. I don't want to risk crossing and possibly get our asses in a real jam, only to discover what we already know, so we're heading back."

"Suits me," Roberts agreed.

"I think it suits us all," Ramirez injected. "I don't know who said the Japs were gone from this island, but I wish the bastard was here with us."

The Scouts picked their way back through the jungle, eventually coming to a well-used footpath. Hunching down in the foliage, the men watched as Japanese soldiers trudged along the trail in a steady stream. During intermittent breaks in the line, the Scouts crossed the path in ones and twos. During this slow process, Ramirez and Gomez got separated. McGowen waited beyond the path as long as he could, then said, "They can read a compass and they know the rally point. Let's go."

By six p.m. McGowen and his men reached the rendezvous site, where they were soon joined by the absent Ramirez and Gomez. Reunited, the team continued on to a spot about thirty yards from the beach. There McGowen ordered a security perimeter set up and the men settled in for the night.

At daybreak, the team worked quickly, retrieving the rubber boat and inflating it with a CO_2 tank. McGowen tried several times to reach Barnes on the radio, feeling the information he had was too valuable to wait until his pickup. After much difficulty, he finally got through.

"Tell Bradshaw this island is lousy with Japs," McGowen told him.

"Roger," Barnes replied.

About an hour later the distinctive silhouette of the PBY came into view, cruising lower and lower over the water until it touched down. McGowen's men had loaded into the rubber boat and pushed off as soon as they'd spotted the aircraft. As they rowed toward it, it quickly became evident that the same pilot who had brought them there was again at the controls, as the plane slowed but did not stop.

McGowen's team rowed the rubber boat to the side of the slow-moving PBY. Barnes, locking his knees inside the seaplane, reached out through the open hatch and grabbed the dinghy, now bobbing in the choppy water churned up by the PBY's prop wash. Using Barnes's body as a bridge, McGowen's team began crawling into the Catalina.

Despite the dangerously close proximity of the whirling propeller, four men made it aboard safely. Then the plane turned right and the prop blast from the whirring blades swept McGowen's hat from his head, dumping the lieutenant into the roiling water.

Roberts, the last man in the rubber boat, grabbed his commander's arm. He hung on tightly as the two were hauled into the aircraft by Barnes and the rest of the team. Even as the seaplane accelerated for takeoff, McGowen crawled over Barnes and into the plane, followed by Roberts. Barnes opened the rubber boat's air-release valve and let it go.

Sitting on the floor of the Catalina, wet and angry, McGowen glared at the cockpit and swore, "Goddamn that yellow sonofabitch."

The PBY arrived back at Langemak Bay at about nine thirty a.m. Maj. Franklin M. Rawolle, one of Krueger's intelligence officers, was waiting on board the *Half Moon* for the Scouts' return. McGowen repeated that Los Negros was "lousy with Japs."

Rawolle, realizing the impact this information would have on the invasion plans, commandeered a PT boat. Then he and McGowen were off to meet Brig. Gen. William B. Chase, commander of the landing force now aboard a destroyer en route to Los Negros.

Reaching Chase's flagship, McGowen and Rawolle were taken on board and McGowen briefed the general. Chase quickly called for a conference with his unit commanders and his naval gunfire liaison officer. He ordered increased prelanding naval gunfire, especially on the areas the Scouts had highlighted.

MacArthur, meanwhile, refused to believe the report by the McGowen Team, saying the new, untested men were overeager and had exaggerated.

Krueger, on the other hand, had full confidence in McGowen's report and foresaw disaster. In response, he dispatched additional troops to be held offshore as a reserve in case the landing force would, indeed, meet superior numbers.

Operation Brewer went off forty-nine hours later, hitting the beach at Hyane Harbor, which the Japanese had weakened in response to the Scouts' landing. Initially, as MacArthur predicted, the troops met little resistance and the island seemed to be lightly defended. In fact, the fight seemed so easy the general himself paid a brief visit to the front. But the Japanese on the island recovered from their confusion and soon met the Americans head-on, and it was the reserve forces Krueger had sent who made the difference between victory and a bloody repulse.

In tribute to the work done by McGowen and his men, Chase's after-action report declared the significance of the information supplied by the Scouts, in that "subsequent developments proved that the Scouts were . . . correct . . . with estimated total garrison of between 4,000 and 5,000 troops."

The importance of McGowen's mission was more completely revealed later when captured Japanese documents told that the reason the island appeared uninhabited to the air force was because soldiers had been ordered not to give away their positions by firing at enemy planes.

The documents also confirmed that McGowen's team had, in fact, been spotted as they first rowed ashore, and that the Japanese had been actively trying to find them the entire time they were on the island.

Last, the papers stated that Colonel Ezaki, fearing an invasion at Chapatut Point, where the Scouts had been spotted, moved a large portion of his forces away from Hyane Harbor, where the actual landing was set to come ashore. "We were fooled," a Japanese officer wrote in a letter that was among the captured documents.

Despite the evidence of Japanese troop strength, the air force refused to admit its error in so badly misjudging the numbers of enemy troops on the island.

Lt. Gen. George C. Kenney, commander of MacArthur's Allied Air Forces, disputed the worth of the information obtained by the Scouts, saying, "twenty-five enemy in the woods at night" is of no value.

Chase and Krueger knew better. And so did MacArthur. Never again would he question an Alamo Scout report.

* * *

Following the debriefing of the McGowen Team, the Alamo Scouts prepared a list of "lessons learned," one of which was that seaplanes no longer be used to take teams to and from their missions. Planes are vulnerable to weather and easily spotted.

Another recommendation was that the walkie-talkies be replaced by the powerful, albeit heavier, SCR-300 radio.

The recommendations were sent to Krueger, who approved them.

* * *

The same day he did that, March 20, 1944, Krueger traveled to Fergusson Island and the Alamo Scout Training Center. There he presented a Silver Star to each member of the McGowen Team for the reconnaissance of Los Negros.

Krueger announced the pride he felt for "my Scouts," and said their dedication and training made them elite among soldiers.

He was correct.

Over the next eighteen months the Alamo Scouts would perform 108 missions without losing a single man killed or captured in action. More important, techniques they developed are still being employed today by Special Forces and Long Range Surveillance Units.

CHAPTER 5

"God Bless You, Brave Soldiers."

Saidor to Geelvink Bay, Dutch New Guinea, April–June 1944

With the fall of the Admiralty Islands on March 24, General MacArthur's next target on his return to the Philippines was the north coast of Dutch New Guinea at Hollandia, the former provincial capital.

The invasion on April 22, Operation Reckless, coincided with a similar assault 125 air miles to the southeast at Aitape. The goal of the twin assaults was to secure Japanese airfields at Hollandia, Sentani, and Cyclops, and start the process of eliminating the Japanese from the entire northern coast of New Guinea.

The Hollandia area reaches from the sea to the twenty-five-mile-long Cyclops mountain range, which rises up five to ten miles inland, with peaks topping off at seven thousand feet before descending sharply on the southern side toward the Lake Sentai Plain.

MacArthur's assault would constitute a double envelopment, with troops of the 41st Division wading ashore at Humboldt Bay (Operation Letterpress) while men of the 24th Division stormed the beach at Tanahmerah Bay (Operation Noiseless), twenty miles to the west.

The Japanese defenders, led by Gen. Kitazono Toyozo of the 3rd Field Transport Command, were ill prepared. Of Toyozo's fifteen thousand army and navy troops, only about 20 percent were combat-ready.

In addition, in eastern New Guinea, Americans and Australians were still pushing back Japanese forces in the weeks and months following the bloody fights at Buna and Gona.

With all this action going on, the Alamo Scout team leader Lt. Bill Barnes did not have long to wait for his first assignment. Three days after serving on the contact team for McGowen's successful mission to Los Negros, Barnes was climbing into the nose of a B-25 Mitchell bomber for a flight to eastern New Guinea. American forces of the 32nd Division, pushing west, were driving the Japanese back from Saidor toward Madang, where Australians were preparing to spring a trap. Barnes's mission was to scout the area around the Male River, halfway between Saidor and Madang, to make sure that the enemy was not planning a trap of his own. Since he had no photo reconnaissance pictures of the region, Barnes, seated in the bomber's Plexiglas nose, camera in hand, would be taking the needed photos as the Mitchell swooped in low over the beach.

On March 3 Barnes and his team, Sgt. Louis J. Belson, Pfc. Warren J. Boes, Pfc. Aubrey L. "Lee" Hall, Pvt. John O. Pitcairn, and Pfc. Robert W. Teeples, along with their contact team, Lt. Michael J. "Iron Mike" Sombar, and three of his five Scouts, were on board a PT boat bound for the landing beach, fifty yards west of the mouth of the river. Jammed into the cramped wardroom of the boat, seasickness became a memorable malady.

"God," Teeples still recalled sixty-four years later. "I figured landing on a Jap island couldn't be worse than that."

Around four a.m. the PT glided to a halt one hundred yards from shore and both teams loaded into rubber boats. The sea was choppy, and as they closed on the beach, a wave tipped Barnes's boat, dumping its contents. Teeples's finger was broken in the fall. It would cause him considerable pain for the entire four-day mission. The two Scout teams set up a defensive perimeter for the remainder of the night in case the landing had been detected. Just before dawn, Sombar and his men rowed both dinghies to the PT boat while the Barnes Team headed inland.

Everything went smoothly at first. But on March 6, the mission's third day, while moving through a field of tall kunai grass, Boes, the point man, was suddenly face-to-face with a Japanese patrol. The enemy, with only two rifles among them, had been walking along casually, obviously pulling back. Americans were the last thing they expected to encounter. Jolted by the confrontation, Boes opened fire. Two of the Japanese fell and the rest fled into the tall grass.

In the confusion, Boes and Barnes became separated from the rest of the team. Fearing the skirmish had tipped off their location, the two continued on alone, hoping to link up with the others later. They passed through the villages of Kumisanger and Bibi, spotting several Japanese bivouac areas, but no enemy troops.

The rest of the team, now led by Hall, moved west to the Bau Plantation, which was found to be unoccupied. There they rested and chowed down on their standard peanut-raisin mix. While they were leisurely eating, the high-pitched engine scream of diving airplanes shattered the calm day. Several Australian fighters were swooping down out of the sky right at them, machine guns blazing and hundred-pound bombs dropping from the wing racks. Amid the deafening explosions and the dirt and debris kicked up by heavy machine-gun slugs, the team scrambled for cover. Emerging unscathed moments later, they cursed the receding planes.

Almost at the same time Hall and the others were ducking Australian planes, American fighters spotted Barnes and Boes. Coming down in steep dives, the .50-caliber machine guns chattered and bombs fell, one bursting fifty yards from the two hapless GIs. For the second time that day, men of the Barnes Team cursed Allied flyboys.

Barnes and Boes continued to move east to the rendezvous point, where they finally linked up with Hall and the others. The team was soon all back on the PT boat, much to the dismay of the sailors. After four days in the same clothes in the sweltering jungle heat, the men smelled so badly the crewmen held their noses as they came aboard.

The Male River mission of March 3–7 was the first and last for the Barnes Team. Since Alamo Scouts were technically on detached duty, their old units had the ability to recall them. Barnes would soon be ordered to return to the 32nd Division to become an aide to Maj. Gen. William H. Gill, and his men were absorbed by other teams. Teeples, who was shortly promoted to sergeant, would also be recalled by his former unit because of a shortage of experienced NCOs. He would eventually win a battlefield commission to second lieutenant.

* * *

On March 31, 1944, two new Scout teams were formed under Lts. Woodrow E. Hobbs and William G. Reynolds. A few days later, to keep up with 6th Army advances, the ASTC camp was moved from Fergusson Island to Mange Point near Finschhafen, an area of cleared land in a palm grove some five hundred yards across at its narrowest point and eight hundred yards deep. Scout Bob Sumner, who trained there, recalled it "afforded an excellent training area." Natives of the nearby village of Kalo Kalo threw the Scouts a feast. As Bradshaw's adjutant and the Alamo Scouts' first historian, Lewis B. Hochstrasser later wrote, for over an hour drums were heard pounding in the darkness.

"We had heard them before, but never like this," he recalled.

The natives gathered by torchlight and boys ages six to twelve performed a combination dance and song, as the local missionary's wife, named Priscilla, and her two daughters sat cross-legged and sang "The Old Rugged Cross" and "God Bless America."

Concluding, they said, "Good luck and God bless you, brave soldiers."

It was a most touching ceremony.

* * *

Then it was back to work, this time for the Thompson and Reynolds teams. Taking the field for the first time, their job was to perform reconnaissance missions for the 158th Regiment, nicknamed the

"Bushmasters," the same unit to which a number of the Alamo Scouts had once belonged.

Born in Bevier, Missouri, Thompson attended a small school called Central College, where he enrolled in the ROTC program. With the attack on Pearl Harbor, his unit was activated and, amid the national hysteria that followed the Japanese attack on Hawaii, Thompson found himself on the West Coast, attached to a unit patrolling California's Monterey Peninsula against enemy invaders.

Once calmer heads prevailed and a Japanese invasion of the West Coast was deemed unlikely, Thompson was sent overseas and attached to the Bushmasters of the 6th Army. That was where he heard about the need for volunteers for a special unit. Being a strong and proficient swimmer, the idea appealed to him and he applied. Accepted, he graduated in the Alamo Scouts' first class.

George Thompson's team, with Sgts. Theodore "Tiny" Largo and Jack E. Benson, and Pvts. Joshua Sunn, Anthony Ortiz, and Joseph A. Johnson, landed at Tanahmerah Bay, and began patrolling the Tablasoefa area.

Interestingly, Thompson's team included four of the nine Native Americans who graduated from the first class at the ASTC. Private Johnson, nicknamed "the Ghost," was of the Eagle Clan of the White Mountain Apaches in Cibecue, Arizona. Sergeant Largo was a Pima Indian from Phoenix, while Private 1st Class Ortiz of Chamitam, New Mexico, was a San Juan Pueblo Indian and Private Sunn of Laveen, Arizona, was of the Maricopa tribe.

Thompson thought highly of his Native American team members, calling them all "exceptional Scouts." He was particularly fond of Johnson.

"I never went anywhere without him beside me or in front of me," Thompson later wrote. "His eyesight was exceptional, the best I had ever seen on a human. He could distinguish the enemy in dense jungle from several feet and he was absolutely silent. In New Guinea he used to track the natives. He showed them a thing or two about scouting."

On this particular mission, however, the eyesight was not needed. The only soldiers the team spotted were other Americans.

Reynolds's team had a much grimmer experience.

Coming ashore near the village of Demta by Humboldt Bay, the team—Reynolds, Staff Sgt. Leonard J. Scott, Cpls. Winfred E. McAdoo and William R. Watson, and Pvts. William C. Gerstenberger and Lucian A. Jamison—had a rough landing. A high surf tossed them against a thirty-foot cliff, destroying their rubber boat. Saving what gear they could, the team managed to scale the cliff to the top, where, exhausted, they collapsed for the night. Moving into the Dutch coastal village of Moeris Besar, a mile south of Demta, the next day, they came across the bodies of three men, two Dutch and one native. The Dutchmen had each been shot in the stomach and head, while the native had his face beaten to a pulp by a bloody club that lay nearby. Under a hut they discovered a fourth body, that of a naked man. Although the corpse had been half eaten by wild dogs, it was easy to see the man, another native, had been castrated and his left hand cut off. For a long moment, the Scouts gazed at the bodies, the only sound breaking the silence the buzzing of the many insects that were feasting on the gore.

Despite these brutal signs of a Japanese presence, the team saw no enemy soldiers before they turned and headed for home.

★   ★   ★

While Reynolds and Thompson were returning to camp, Iron Mike Sombar and three members of his team were slogging through six miles of jungle and knee-deep swamp toward the village of Goya. Word had been passed to them that the Japanese were holding 107 hostages at the village, all foreign missionaries and nuns.

Moving cautiously through the undergrowth, the men came across two native huts, including one with a saddled horse tied up outside. Knowing no native would own a saddle, Sombar crept closer and saw a Japanese soldier inside, sitting on a bed, changing clothes. Not knowing if the man was alone, the Wyoming, Delaware, native slipped a grenade from his belt, yanked the pin, released the lever, or "spoon," and lobbed it through the window. The explosion shook the hut and

Sombar charged inside. Miraculously, he found the Japanese man dazed and on the floor, but otherwise unharmed. As the man tried to rise, Sombar punched him on the jaw, knocking him over. The Japanese soldier started to rise again, and Sombar leveled his carbine and squeezed off several quick rounds.

Continuing on toward the village, the team came across one of the missionaries, a man sitting on a log, utterly exhausted. He told Sombar the rest were just ahead, and that the Japanese had fled. Sombar, skeptical, assigned Pfc. David M. Milda to escort the missionary back to American lines, and pushed on. (Milda would perform four missions with the Sombar Team in New Guinea before returning to his original unit. He was killed in action on Luzon in 1945.)

Arriving at Goya, the team spotted the missionaries, but, as the first missionary had said, there was no sign of the Japanese.

"Spread out and make sure they're gone," Sombar told his men.

They did, and soon flushed out and captured a Japanese naval officer who had been hiding.

"I won't run away," the officer said in perfect English, a gun pointed at his head.

The missionaries, seventy Dutch, thirteen Americas, three Poles, one Czech, one Australian, and, oddly, nineteen Germans, were overjoyed at the sight of the Americans, and a nun embraced Sombar.

"Oh, it is so good to see a real man again," she said.

Knowing the difficulty of evacuating so many people, some weak from hunger, over the rough terrain with just three Scouts, and convinced the Japanese were gone for good, Sombar decided to leave the freed hostages where they were and head back to Hollekang, where he could send back more help. Taking with them the three Polish missionaries and their prisoner, Sombar's party began trudging back toward American lines. The prisoner was put to the task of carrying the pack of an exhausted missionary. He refused.

"You cannot make me do this," he said defiantly. "You are under the Geneva convention. You can shoot me if you want."

"If you won't carry the pack, you're of no fucking use to me," Sombar said. He nodded to a Scout, who waved two of the missionaries out of the way as he leveled his carbine at the man. "We'll just kill you and leave you here for the flies."

The officer stared at the carbine, then slung the pack onto his back.

By noon Sombar had made contact with men of the 34th Division. That unit sent a detachment, including medics, to the village and brought out the rest of the missionaries. Escorted back to safety, all were set free except for the Germans, who, as enemy civilians, were turned over to U.S. authorities until the war's end.

★　★　★

Throughout April and May and on into June, the Scouts were dispatched on a host of missions, often lasting just one or two days. On April 24, Lt. Henry R. Chalko, an instructor at the ASTC, pulled together a scratch team of men from the Hobbs and now-defunct Barnes teams for a short excursion to Ali Island, a few miles north of Aitape. During the mission, they got into a firefight with a small Japanese force. The skirmish lasted six hours, until the GIs were reinforced by two platoons from the 127th Regiment. When the shooting stopped, there were twenty-three dead Japanese in the brush.

All the while, American forces continued to push westward across New Guinea. In May, Krueger's 6th Army was advancing toward the Wakde-Sarmi area, 140 miles west of Hollandia. Their job was to establish forward air bases in order to launch future attacks on the enemy on the Vogelkop Peninsula on New Guinea's westernmost tip.

On May 3, Sombar's team was sent on a one-day reconnaissance mission to tiny Vandoemoear Island in Sarmi Harbor. This was followed ten days later by a two-day mission to gather data on roads and beaches near Maraena, west of Sarmi.

The Thompson and Reynolds teams, meanwhile, were dispatched to Biak Island to look for suitable beaches for landing craft. They completed this task successfully, but not without coming under attack by a Japanese fighter plane. They escaped the strafing plane without casualties.

On June 17, about two weeks after his one-day excursion to Biak, Thompson and his team boarded the S-47, one of the navy's aging class of submarines, in Seeadler Harbor for a two-week mission to Sansapor, near the Sansapor coconut plantation on the western side of the Vogelkop. Accompanying him and his men was a special team consisting of Maj. Frank Rawolle of 6th Army G2, Lt. (j.g.) Donald Root, and Coxswain Calvin W. Byrd, both formerly with the Naval Amphibious Scouts, and Lt. Col. G. G. Atkinson and Maj. William M. Chance of the 836th Engineer Aviation Battalion. The group also included Sgt. Heinrick Lumingkewas and his brother, Cpl. Alexander Lumingkewas, of the Allied Intelligence Bureau.

Their mission, at least initially, was to pave the way for the invasion of the Vogelkop Peninsula, by landing on Waigeo Island. There they would locate three suitable sites for air and naval bases. However, while en route, the men were notified that aerial reconnaissance showed that Waigeo was unsuitable for either. They were rerouted to the Vogelkop itself, landing on the west coast near Cape Sansapor, to see if two enemy airstrips already in existence could be made to accommodate fighter and light-bomber groups.

Arriving off the coast on June 23, Thompson spent the day gazing through the S-47's periscope at the shoreline three miles away, seeking a likely spot to go ashore. The submarine popped to the surface at midnight, fifteen hundred yards off the coast.

"This will be a quick recon," Thompson said. "We won't need everyone right now."

It was decided that Thompson and three members of his team, Sergeants Chanley and Butler, and Private Moon, along with Sergeant Lumingkewas, would make the first trip, rowing ashore in a six-man rubber boat.

Reaching the mouth of the Wewe River, the team rowed four hundred yards up the waterway before coming ashore and hiding the rubber boat in a stand of heavy undergrowth. They remained there the rest of the night, ever watchful. As dawn began to streak the eastern sky, they moved toward the intended landing area. En route they discovered an abandoned Japanese campsite, but saw no sign of the enemy or any native inhabitants.

The S-47 surfaced that night and the men rowed back to the sub, their initial reconnaissance done. On board, and safely back under the water, the landing party spent two hours briefing the others on what they found, and the entire group readied themselves to go ashore the next night.

The men left the sub at midnight on two rubber boats, and rough surf caused the Americans to land three hundred yards northeast of their intended spot at the Wewe River. They dragged the bulky boats to the river mouth, where they reboarded and rowed inland to near where the group had come in the night before. There they stopped and camped. Early the next morning, while searching the riverbank for a good spot to hide the boats and radios, Chanley and Butler spotted a camouflaged barge. They also saw four Japanese, one of whom seemed to be examining the tracks in the mud the team had left after the first reconnaissance. The two Scouts hustled back to the camp.

"Japs know we're here," Chanley told Thompson. "They found our tracks from the other night."

The quiet of the jungle now was broken by the unmistakable sounds of men moving toward them through the bush. Backtracking quietly into the undergrowth and hunkering down, the Americans held their breath as the Japanese patrol, rifles at the ready, passed by.

The team now split into two groups and spent the next three days reconnoitering. Thompson and his group trekked inland to locate Japanese troops and defenses, while Rawolle and the rest scouted out the most promising landing beaches. Once or twice they heard Japanese off in the distance, but saw none. The two groups reunited on the riverbank on June 29 and retrieved their boats and radios. Rain began to fall, increasing to a downpour, and the Scouts spent six miserable hours soaked to the bone, waiting at the water's edge for their two a.m. pickup. Around ten thirty p.m., as they sat huddled in the wet darkness, they heard the sound of a barge cruising down the river, heading toward the open sea. An hour later, another chugged by.

At one forty-five a.m., on June 30, the fourteenth day of the mission, they reinflated their boats, then rowed downriver and out to sea. As their oars bit quietly into the water, the chugging sound of a motor was heard from somewhere out in the darkness. The men froze and ducked low as a Japanese barge churned past them, just fifteen hundred yards astern of Rawolle's boat. Two more barges passed by within fourteen hundred yards of the bow of the surfaced S-47. As the barges faded into the night, the Scouts continued rowing and nudged up against the sub. After the men had clambered back on board and the rubber boats were stowed away, the S-47 silently dove for the safety of the deep and headed for home. Inside the sleek, pressurized hull, the landing party enjoyed a dinner of steak and brandy.

The information gathered by the team gave Allied planners details of the terrain, as well as troop numbers, locations, and dispositions. The beaches the team had pinpointed proved ideal for landing heavy equipment, although the site where planners thought an air base was being built was actually nothing more than a tilled field. The overall ground proved to be too rough for an airstrip. However, the area would make a fine base for PT boats, as well as a supply dump. The mission was considered a glowing success, and an invasion date of July 31 was set.

★   ★   ★

Lieutenant McGowen, reviewing after-action reports of the Scout missions to date, realized that the teams were being "misused," often because they were sent in where other units had also dispatched patrols. Besides being counter to the reason the Scouts had been formed in the first place, this duplication heightened the possibility of Alamo Scouts and GIs exchanging fire. McGowen also noted how the teams were sometimes called upon by area commanders to conduct combat patrols, which was counter to their training.

McGowen passed his findings along to Maj. Homer Williams, Bradshaw's XO. He, in turn, passed them on to Krueger, and such missions soon ended.

McGowen also informed Williams that the Scouts were having trouble requisitioning the ammunition, weapons, and supplies they needed from other units while they were in the field. When Bradshaw mentioned this to Krueger, the general issued each team a four-by-six-inch Alamo Scout Card, which read:

To whom it may concern:

1. The officer whose signature appears below is the leader of an Alamo Scout Team and is on a specially assigned mission for this headquarters.
2. It is requested that such items of equipment that may be needed by his team for the accomplishment of the mission be made available to him.
3. It is further requested that utmost cooperation be given this personnel in obtaining air/or water transportation.

This small but powerful document, which quickly became known as the Krueger Card, because it bore the general's name, directed anyone under Krueger's command to give the team bearing it any help or material it needed. Ordinarily, this worked like magic, although Lt. Red Sumner recalled it being challenged once in the Philippines. Sumner handed the card to the supply officer of the 158th Regimental Combat Team and requested two hundred to three hundred rifles, plus ammo and grenades, in order to resupply Filipino guerrillas. The officer dismissed the request, and the card, with a "Hell no."

"Fine," Sumner said.

He next visited the regiment's chief of staff, who picked up his field phone and called the S4 officer.

"Goddamn it," he stormed. "Give the guy what he wants."

Sumner got his supplies from the sheepish S4.

★ ★ ★

Throughout their existence, the Scout teams rotated as Krueger's personal bodyguards, taking ten-day shifts. Traveling in a three-jeep convoy, with two MPs and two Scouts in the first jeep, Krueger, his aide, and driver in the second, and the Scout team leader and the rest of the team in the third, they made the rounds of the units under the general's command. If Krueger was on foot, the Scouts formed a protective ring around him, seven paces away.

Bodyguarding was not unwelcomed duty. Krueger was a stern, gruff man, but with a warm heart for his men.

Sumner recalled Krueger's inspection of the lines of the 158th Regimental Combat Team, which, he said, got "a little hairy." Just five hundred yards from the front line, artillery shells zooming overhead, mortars exploding in the nearby jungle, and machine-gun fire clipping the leaves and branches of trees, Krueger walked the infantry line, stopping to talk to individual soldiers.

"When did you last eat, son?" he'd ask. "When did you change clothes last? Have you had any mail lately? Show me your weapon."

The whole time, a wary Sumner envisioned himself being court-martialed if his commanding general was shot dead.

There were also perks to guarding Krueger. Wilbur Littlefield recalled his team escorting the general on Leyte in late November 1944, when Krueger made a point of stopping at a division headquarters at mealtime so his Scouts could enjoy Thanksgiving dinner.

★   ★   ★

Throughout the first half of 1944, MacArthur's forces pushed the Japanese relentlessly westward, clearing the northern coast of New Guinea mile by bloody mile. By May, half of the world's second largest island was under Allied control, and MacArthur next set his sights on Wakde, a small island off the New Guinea coast, which boasted an excellent airfield. His final goal was the bird's-head-like shape of the Vogelkop Peninsula, New Guinea's westernmost land area. But between there and Hollandia, which fell at the end of April, were six hundred miles of coast, defended by the well-fed, well-armed men of the Japanese

2nd Army. Unless the Vogelkop was seized, MacArthur knew its air bases posed a serious threat to his rear as he continued toward the Philippines.

On May 17, MacArthur made his move on Wakde and Sarmi. Ten days later, American troops stormed ashore at Biak, the northernmost and largest of the Schouten Islands at the mouth of Geelvink Bay, New Guinea's largest anchorage. The Biak operation would last until August 20 and cost the Americans about four hundred dead and five missing, along with two thousand wounded and another seventy-two hundred laid low with jungle ailments, such as dengue fever and scrub typhus. The Japanese would lose at least forty-seven hundred killed or missing and two hundred captured.

During all these moves, the Alamo Scouts were ready, but they would be going into action without Colonel Bradshaw at their head. In May, Krueger, satisfied with the job Bradshaw had done in getting the Scouts up and running, promoted him to executive officer of 6th Army Intelligence. Homer Williams, Bradshaw's XO, was promoted to major and took over the Alamo Scouts' day-to-day operations. As his executive officer, Williams chose Maj. Gibson Niles, a New Yorker from Albany who, in April 1944, took part in a deception mission behind Japanese lines. Prior to the Allied landings at Hollandia and Aitape on April 22, Niles had planted an aviator's notebook in an empty rubber boat for the enemy to find. The notebook contained false information on American invasion plans, confirming Japanese suspicions that Hansa Bay, at the mouth of the Sepik River and well east of the real invasion zone, was the target. He also arranged for "supply drops." The ruse worked.

On June 22, the ASTC at Mange Point graduated its third class, four teams led by Lts. Robert S. Sumner, Wilbur F. Littlefield, William B. Lutz, and Arpad Farkas. This addition gave Williams ten teams and sixty-eight highly skilled officers and men under his charge. Four days after the graduation, the ASTC was moved to Cape Kassoe near Humboldt Bay, in order to stay close to the 6th Army HQ.

★   ★   ★

By the end of June, the ever-restless MacArthur was ready for his next move, this time on Noemfoor Island, the westernmost of the Schoutens, which, like Biak seventy-five miles to the east, lay at the entrance to Geelvink Bay.

Code-named Tabletennis, the oval-shaped Noemfoor, fourteen miles long and eleven wide, contained three enemy airfields: the four-thousand-foot-long Namber Airdrome at Roemboi Bay, the five-thousand-foot Kamiri air base on the western coast, and the unfinished five-thousand-foot Kornasoren Airdrome just a short distance to the north.

Much of the island's coastline, especially on the western side, is choked by mangrove swamps. These thick morasses also cover the several small islands that all but block access to Noemfoor's largest inland body of water, Broe Bay, on the northeast coast. The islands' five thousand wartime inhabitants lived mostly along the southern and northern coasts.

The island was headquarters for the Noemfoor Defense Detachment of the 219th Infantry Regiment, 35th Division, along with assorted support troops and construction personnel. These latter included six hundred Formosan laborers and two thousand Javanese slave workers. The troops under Col. Shimizu Suesada numbered about two thousand, although MacArthur's G2 guessed them at thirty-two hundred.

The landing was set for July 2 on Yellow Beach, a strip about eight hundred yards wide just west of the Kamiri airfield. Two teams of Alamo Scouts under John McGowen and Woodrow Hobbs were sent in advance of the strike force, the Cyclone Task Force, which was to depart from Wakde-Sarmi on the night of June 29–30.

The two Texans—McGowen was from Amarillo and Hobbs from Fort Worth—and their men spent June 21–23 onshore, counting Japanese noses, checking defenses, and gauging morale, which, based on the disheveled appearance of the enemy and the fact that many of them were unarmed, they determined was low. They also spotted three tanks, possibly Type 1 models, toting a 47mm gun and two 7.7mm machine guns apiece.

The mission included an examination of Yellow Beach, which they found to be a gradual sandy slope leading up to a wood line forty to sixty feet from the water's edge. During one dark night, the Scouts spent two hours wading offshore in neck-deep water, feeling with their feet for a channel through the coral reef.

Their presence was eventually discovered by the Japanese, but the Scouts remained one step ahead of the enemy and managed to get back aboard their PT boat without a fight. At least not on land. At sea, the PT boat crew had to fend off strafing runs by a fighter plane from Kamiri airfield. The boat managed to elude the plane with minor damage but no injuries.

The information the team brought back was vital to the coming invasion, although they seriously overjudged the Japanese troop strength, guessing it at close to five thousand men.

★   ★   ★

Three days after the invasion, on July 5, Hobbs and two of his men left Woendi Island by PT boat bound for the tiny island of Japen, off the Noemfoor coast. Landing at the village of Ansoes, they quickly located and took custody of the captain of an interisland schooner who had been using his vessel to supply information to the Japanese. The man's schooner had been shot up by American planes and natives had been holding him. Hobbs picked up his prisoner, but as he and his team rowed the rubber boat back to the PT boat, the PT's radar picked up what was thought to be an enemy barge. After a few tense moments, it was discovered that the "barge" was actually a small land mass.

Shortly after returning, Hobbs, along with Staff Sgt. Leonard Scott, Lt. Raymond Watson, an Australian officer attached to the ASTC, Dutch officer Lt. Louis Rapmund, and a native guide, were dispatched on a mission with multiple goals. The first objective was to monitor Japanese barge traffic at Seroei, off the southern coast of Noemfoor. Rowing into the harbor on a rubber boat, they discovered just one heavily damaged barge abandoned on the beach.

Moving next to nearby Naoe Island, they captured a native who had been accused of spying for the enemy. Their mission ended the next day on Koeroedoe Island between Japen and western New Guinea, where they pinpointed Japanese coastal and mountain guns, and mapped out enemy beach and harbor defenses at Manokwari Harbor.

Despite the American advances, Japanese troops, both those in front of the Americans and those bypassed by MacArthur's leapfrogging up the New Guinea coast, continued to receive supplies and reinforcements, mostly brought in by shallow-draft barges. Because of U.S. air superiority, barges could only move at night, and lay hidden by day.

To ferret out these hiding places, commanders turned to the Alamo Scouts.

CHAPTER 6

"... The Entire Shoreline Was Ablaze."

Sumner Team: Geelvink Bay, Dutch New Guinea, July 21–22, 1944

Lt. Robert "Red" Sumner's team had not had an assignment since graduating from the ASTC at Mange Point near Finschhafen on June 22. So he was elated when, on July 10, he was put on alert for deployment to the PT base at Mios Woendi Island. PT boats meant action.

Sumner sent Staff Sgt. Lawrence E. Coleman to draw equipment for the team, then took the men through two days of refreshment drills, including handling of the rubber boat, radio use, jungle survival, and scouting skills, followed by a trip to the shooting range, where weapons were sighted-in.

While most of the team used carbines or Thompsons, Coleman drew for himself one of the newly issued M3 "grease guns," the .45-caliber, stamped metal submachine gun with a folding wire stock. Coleman also requisitioned a 60mm mortar and a BAR, although these, as it turned out, would be left in camp.

Before dawn on July 18, the men hoisted themselves aboard a deuce-and-a-half truck for a quick ride to the airfield at nearby Sentani. There a C-47 transport, its engines thrumming, awaited them.

They had no sooner plopped down on the jump seats that lined each side of the plane than it taxied to the runway and was airborne, banking northeast, over Vitiaz Strait to the open ocean, for the nearly six-hundred-mile flight to Biak Island at the mouth to Geelvink Bay. Around ten thirty a.m., the C-47's wheels touched down at Borokore Airfield, one of three airstrips on Biak's southern coast, along the Japen Strait. Upon debarking from the plane, the team was assigned a squad tent and told to sit tight. A short distance away, a battery of 105mm guns sent harassing rounds at the enemy positions, a few thousand yards inland.

"They shootin' at Japs?" Pfc. Edward Renhols asked, startled at the first salvo.

"They aren't duck hunting," Cpl. William F. Blaise replied.

"Parts of this island are still hot," Sumner explained. "Wander too far into that jungle and you'll end up with your fool head mounted on some Jap officer's trophy wall."

The harassing fire kept up all through the day and into the night, to the discomfort of the Japanese and the Alamo Scouts alike, both of whom were deprived of sleep.

On July 20, Sumner and his men boarded a PT boat for the three-hour trip to the 6th Army HQ and the main PT base on Woendi Island, southwest of Biak. John McGowen, already a legend since he and his men had conducted the first Alamo Scout mission back in February, met the team as their boat tied up to one of the several long piers that jutted out from the sandy beach.

"Hi, Red," McGowen greeted Sumner. "Welcome to Woendi. Looks like I'll be your contact for this mission. I'll help you get your team situated, then we have a briefing with the Ops officer for PT Ron Twenty-one."

Slinging their weapons and gear over their shoulders, the men followed McGowen to their temporary billet. En route, Sumner learned he would be transported by Squadron 21, one of many PT boat units operating out of Woendi Island. Ron 21, led by Lt. Cmdr. Selman S. Bowling, consisted of five boats, PT-128, -131, -132, -320, and -321, all eighty-footers manufactured by the Elco Naval Division of the Electric Boat Company.

As evening came on, the team and three PT skippers were assembled in the briefing shack, seated before Bowling and an officer who served as the PT squadron's operations officer. A map of New Guinea, specifically the eastern shore of the Vogelkop Peninsula, was tacked to a corkboard at the front of the room.

"Smoking lamp is lit," the officer said, intoning the old navy term from the days of sail that denoted when it was safe to smoke because the kegs of gunpowder had been stowed away. Some men fired up cigarettes, some did not.

"We've seen a lot of Jap barge traffic operating here in Cape Oransbari, south of the village of Manokwari," the officer said. "We think there's a staging area near the village, maybe a refueling site and a place from which to transport supplies, rations, and ammo from western New Guinea to enemy garrisons still operating along the coast farther east. Because of the heavy foliage, our recon planes can't see a damned thing, and our boats aren't able to get in close enough to take a look-see either. That's where you Scouts come in. Tonight is dark of the moon. We will drop you just offshore at twenty-three thirty hours. You will recon the area and try to spot the Jap supply base, if indeed there is one. If you find the base, you will pinpoint it so our guys can get at them. Exfiltration will be twenty-four hours later. If for any reason you don't make it back by then, the boats will attempt another pickup at twenty-three thirty for the next two nights if needed. Communication will be by SCR-300 radios. Lieutenant McGowen will be your contact."

"We'll be using three PT boats, the 128, 131, and 132," Bowling injected. "You men will be aboard the 132 boat with Ensign Jones, here." He pointed to a young officer. "The other two boats will stand by beyond the horizon, to provide covering fire if needed."

"Are there any questions?" McGowen asked. Hearing none, he said, "Grab some chow and check your gear. We leave in two hours."

★ ★ ★

The trip across the stretch of water where Geelvink Bay meets the Pacific Ocean was a lonely one. The dark, moonless sky and the inky black ocean made it almost impossible to tell where one ended and the other began.

The three boats roared through the night. The 132 boat, *Sea Bat* to her crew, was at the point with the 128 boat, *Tug Boat Annie*, and 131, *Tarfu*, following to port and starboard.

For most of the trip, Sumner and his team—Coleman, Renhols, Blaise, Pfc. Paul B. Jones (no relation to the PT skipper despite the similarity in their names), Cpl. Robert T. Schermerhorn, and Pfc. Harry D. Weiland—along with Lt. Henry Swart of the Dutch East Indies Army, serving as interpreter, remained belowdecks. There they tried to get some rest despite the bouncing plywood boat's best efforts to prevent that.

Robert Sumner was a natural leader, and he had the well-earned respect of his colleagues. He took stock of a situation quickly and always seemed to make the right decisions. Joining the army right out of college, Sumner took to the strict military discipline and hard physical regimen like a fish to water. He felt he was made for the army to the point that he began to believe that he had always been a soldier since as far back as Julius Caesar.

At about ten thirty that night, five miles off the Vogelkop coast, the *Sea Bat*'s skipper, Ens. Paul H. Jones, who was in command of the three-boat flotilla, engaged his underwater mufflers, funneling the exhaust into the water and thus silencing, as much as possible, the three Packard engines. While *Tug Boat Annie* and *Tarfu* dropped back, Jones closed on the coastline, guided by his radar and what visual landmarks he could discern in the night. Sumner's team, their faces blackened and gear ready, were on deck, rubber boat inflated and set to launch.

Half an hour later, the 132 boat idled a thousand yards offshore. The rubber boat was dropped overboard on *Sea Bat*'s seaward side, held tightly against the hull by two crewmen hanging on to ropes, as the Scouts climbed in. Sumner, from his position in the back of the rubber boat, took a compass bearing and the team shoved off.

In the gentle one-foot swells, the trip was smooth and uneventful, even though a nervous Ensign Jones, lingering offshore, kept picking up strange blips on his radar that he feared might be Japanese destroyers, but were more likely ghost echoes.

Reaching the shore, the men hopped out and dragged the rubber boat across the thirty-yard stretch of beach, into the tree line, then hit the ground and silently waited for any sign that they might have been spotted. For fifteen minutes, none of them moved. Sumner next gently rapped the folding metal stock of his M1A1 carbine against the wooden upper hand guard—his all-clear signal—and the team quickly deflated the rubber boat. The escaping CO_2 hissed loud enough to be heard in Hollandia, several hundred miles to the east, Sumner thought.

As that was done, Renhols flipped on the radio, and after it warmed up, whispered into it, "Red One." This was the code phrase announcing the team had arrived and was proceeding. Had he said, "Red One, recover," it would have meant trouble and stand by to pick them up. McGowen replied with "Mac One," and Renhols switched the radio off.

Out on the water, the 132 boat quietly withdrew to rejoin the other two, out of sight, but ready. The SCR-300 had a fifty-mile range over water, so calling the boats back would not be a problem. McGowen's radio would be switched on for the entire mission.

That done, both the rubber boat and the radio were buried in the soft sandy earth among the eight-to-ten-foot-high scrub, while Sumner and Swart kept a watchful eye for intruders.

Indicating with his hand to "follow me," Sumner led the team inland. After picking their way through fifty yards of sparse jungle, they came to a well-used coastal track. Advancing beyond the trail, they entered a small clearing and Sumner signaled "halt."

"It's oh one hundred," he whispered to the men who gathered around him. "We'll rest here. Coleman, two guards, hourly relief."

At first sleep was difficult. The men were jarred awake by the slightest jungle sound, the rustle of the foliage, the call of a bird or an animal moving through the brush. Eventually, they settled in.

Just before five a.m. Sumner woke the team and, as they had drilled so many times, formed them into a circle about ten yards in diameter. He remained in the middle of the circle to control the movements of the men. They remained there, hunched down in the jungle, eyes and ears tuned to any noise or movement. At the end of fifteen minutes, Sumner gave one tap of the metal folding stock of his carbine, and pointed to his left. At the signal, the entire circle shifted about twenty-five yards and halted again. Fifteen more minutes, and the action was repeated. This last move put the team on the seaward side of the jungle trail.

Sumner consulted his map. He noted a river that flowed into the ocean, about sixty yards north of where he and his team now waited. Even as he studied the map, his mind registered a motor sound coming from the waterway.

Two taps of his carbine stock and the team reassembled. Sumner indicated they were to follow him, and they hurried as quietly as possible toward the gurgling engine noise.

The river, a muddy brown ribbon of slow-moving water, was lined by tall grass. Lying in the grass and moving only their eyes, the team saw a Japanese barge gliding along the waterway, headed toward the sea.

Sumner was not sure why the barge was setting out with daybreak already starting to streak the sky. They generally moved under the cover of darkness. So it was with concern and confusion that he watched the thirty-five-foot-long craft, armed with two light machine guns, chug past their position at about ten miles per hour. The barge entered the sea, then turned and sailed south, between the shoreline and the breakers farther out.

Sumner led the team to the beach to keep visual and audio track of the barge until it was gone completely. He was unable to see what it was carrying, whether it was supplies or men.

★   ★   ★

Daylight in the tropics comes with startling suddenness, and by six fifteen a.m. the thinning darkness suddenly burst into complete daylight as the sun seemed to leap out of the eastern ocean. Sumner and his team were back by the river, resuming their watch. There, in the brush, the men broke out their morning breakfast, a six-ounce Australian date bar, washed down with water from their canteens. They ate in silence, keeping a sharp watch.

As he munched the date bar, Sumner noted that, less than one hundred yards inland of where it met the ocean, the river opened into an estuary with a number of small islands. From his position, Sumner could see large trees overhanging the water, and underneath two of them Japanese barges were moored. While he could see no enemy troops, the familiar smell of cook fires wafted toward him on the morning breeze. Breakfast was being prepared.

Voices in the distance convinced Sumner that more unseen enemy barges were moored elsewhere in the estuary.

"Those trees make for great cover," Blaise whispered. "No wonder our flyboys can't spot anything."

"Yeah," Sumner whispered back. "Half the goddamned Jap navy could be tied up out there and our guys wouldn't see them."

The Scouts watched the area for half an hour while Sumner jotted notes in a notebook. Then he signaled the men to follow and led them south, paralleling the shore, keeping about ten yards inland from the beach.

They had gone about a quarter of a mile when they came upon the ruins of eight native houses on the beach to the team's left. Sumner signaled the team to spread out, and, weapons at the ready, they crept forward into the village. The nipa huts, five on the ground and three mounted on stilts, were empty. But discarded ration cans, cigarette butts, and nails once used to secure communications wire told Sumner that this site had been occupied recently.

"Observation post?" Jones asked.

Sumner nodded.

"From up in one of those huts on stilts, you can see the gulf for twenty miles in all directions," Swart added.

"So why aren't they here watching?" Sumner asked. "Where are they?"

As if in answer, a distant machine gun opened up, firing three separate three-round bursts. The Scouts dove for cover around the huts.

"Where the . . . ?" Coleman asked.

"About eight hundred yards away to the south, I'd say," Sumner replied.

"Good Christ, did they spot us?" Schermerhorn said. "When? How?"

"Just sit tight," Sumner said, and the men lay quietly, waiting, sweat pouring from their bodies with such profusion that Sumner feared the Japanese could smell him and his men from half a mile.

There was no more gunfire.

"Probably a gunner clearing his weapon," Sumner said. "Let's check it out. Weiland, take the point. Schermerhorn, the rear."

The team began moving quietly in the direction of the firing when suddenly Schermerhorn whispered, "Down." Five natives—two men, a woman, and two children—were approaching along the track from the north, coming up behind the team. At Sumner's signal, the Scouts emerged from the undergrowth and surrounded the little group. Sumner imagined the people's terror as seven heavily armed white men, their faces painted, suddenly appeared all around them.

"They're scared to death," Sumner told Swart. "Let's get them off this trail and see what they know."

The men led the small party of natives about sixty yards into the jungle, where Swart began speaking to them in Malay, the language most Dutch New Guinea natives spoke. He first allayed their fears by pointing to the Royal Netherlands East Indies insignia on his cap and the letters on his shoulder flashes, which most New Guinea adults recognized from prewar colonial days. Having reassured them, Swart began asking the natives about the Japanese, some of which Sumner could follow since he had some knowledge of Malay.

Swart broke open a ration kit and gave the woman and the children candy from an opened pack of Charms. The two men asked for tobacco. Sumner told them in his best Malay that he feared giving them tobacco, as the smell of a burning cigarette might be picked up by a wandering Japanese patrol. He was assured that no Japanese were nearby. Still hesitant, especially after hearing the machine gun earlier, he handed over a few cigarettes, and the men lighted up immediately.

As the natives relaxed, so did their tongues. They told Sumner, through Swart, that about sixty Japanese, led by a lieutenant, along with ten to twelve barges, were on the river, manning a supply and staging area. The barges carried food, ammunition, and reinforcements to isolated garrisons farther to the south.

"This man says there is a large gasoline storage tank about twenty feet across and fifteen feet high along with many drums of fuel," Swart said. "There is plenty of ammunition but not much food. There are several small houses scattered about for the troops and a number of mooring sites."

"Are there any Nips around other than the sixty with the barges?" Sumner asked.

Swart translated, then said, "About two hundred. But they're about a kilometer away."

"That's twenty to one," Sumner mused, as he watched the natives chat and draw maps in the dirt, while pointing with sticks and smoking up the team's limited number of cigarettes.

"The Japs have a radio station set up at the supply base," Swart said. "But these fellas don't know who they are in contact with. All they know is there is a loudspeaker and sometimes the Japs play music loudly. I guess trying to spread Japanese culture to the heathens."

"Culture, my ass," Coleman muttered.

The natives said they lived in a nearby village of about twenty inhabitants, who might become alarmed if they were missing too long. The men, Sumner was told, were forced to work for the Japanese as laborers, loading and hauling fuel and ammunition, digging trenches and shelters, and doing other menial tasks. Their pay was the standard island currency, tobacco or maybe rice. Judging by the leanness of these people, Sumner guessed they were underpaid.

Some of the men fished, Swart was told, but their catch was seized by the Japanese, who paid the hapless fishermen about a quarter of the value.

After about an hour, Sumner knew he'd gotten from these people all he was going to. Now what to do with them?

"Think they'll rat us out if we let them go?" Blaise asked Sumner.

"What else can we do?" Sumner replied. "We can't tie them up because once they're found, half the island will know we're here. We'll have to hope they liked their former Dutch rulers better than they like the Japs."

To secure their friendship, Sumner gave the native men twists of tobacco and the woman and children more candy. Swart wrote down their names in an official-looking notebook and told them they would be rewarded for their cooperation after the war. Sumner reiterated that they would be rewarded later.

"Bye'm bye all e givim you good fellow pay," he said in pidgin English.

Then the natives were sent on their way. The team buried all the cigarette butts and food and candy wrappers, obliterated the maps in the dirt, and struck off back to the river for a closer look at the supply base.

Silently, the team reconnoitered the enemy staging area, spotting several more barges. The large fuel tank the natives had mentioned stood three hundred yards away, camouflaged from the air by overhanging tree branches. As they observed, Sumner made notations on his map. They saw no enemy soldiers, but could clearly hear them.

"Wonder what they're talkin' about," Weiland whispered.

"Prob'ly bitchin' about the work and their officers, lousy chow, and crappy duty, just like our guys," Jones replied.

"Pipe down," Sumner said, busily taking notes. "Or we'll end up as Jap chow."

After taking in all they could, the team retreated back along the river toward the beach, near where they had observed the barge that morning. On the way, they found the log canoes the five natives had used to cross the water, which explained how they had approached Sumner's men from the rear. Withdrawing to a spot near the ruined village, the team again dined on date bars, candy, and water.

Nighttime descended over the jungle with typical tropical suddenness. In the darkness, the team slowly made their way to the pickup area. A hundred yards from where the boat lay hidden, Sumner deployed his men in a circle, set up guards, and let them get some much-needed rest. Their nerve endings were rubbed raw, both from the oppressive heat and the tension, and the team could use the break. He roused the men at ten thirty and they stealthily advanced toward the beach. The team halted within sight of where the rubber boat and radio were buried, and dropped to a knee. With all senses alert, they waited several minutes to make sure the Japanese had not discovered the site and set up any ambushes.

Then Sumner said, "Recover the rubber boat. Renhols, Jones, break out the radio and make contact."

The rubber boat was quickly uncovered while Renhols and Jones retrieved the radio. They carried it to a nearby clump of vegetation, which allowed them a clear line of sight to the ocean, and switched the set on.

On schedule, at eleven oh five Renhols said into the handset, "Red One. Stand by."

"Roger," was the immediate response.

"Hot damn, Mac's out there," Sumner thought. "I didn't even hear the boat approach."

Now it was eleven twenty and Sumner said, "Inflate."

The CO_2 tank hissed and the popping sound of the inflating rubber boat sounded like artillery fire in the silent darkness. Sumner knew this was the most critical moment of their recovery. If there were any Japanese in the area, whether looking for them or on routine patrol or just out to take a piss, they'd have heard the pops and be hauling ass in the Scouts' direction.

Within five minutes the rubber boat was inflated and loaded. Sumner looked at Renhols and nodded.

"Red One, launch," Renhols said into the radio.

"Roger," was McGowen's reply.

Renhols swung the radio on his back and joined Jones to form a rear guard as Weiland, Blaise, and Coleman dragged the rubber boat into the surf. Sumner, Swart, and Schermerhorn joined Renhols and Jones as rear guard, with Sumner facing left and Swart right to protect the team's flanks.

Once everyone was on board the rubber boat except the rear

guard, Sumner sent Jones, then Swart, and then Schermerhorn. When they were safely on the boat, he turned, dashed into the surf, and clambered aboard.

"Hit it," he said, and four of the Scouts began rowing with even, rapid strokes.

Sumner retrieved the steering paddle from under the boat's cross member and guided through the lines of breakers. As the men rowed, Swart and Schermerhorn, weapons trained on the beach, covered the retreat. Each also had a paddle, ready to add their muscle to the escape if more speed was needed.

With Coleman at the front, setting the pace, the rubber boat slipped expertly through the breakers without once being in danger of tipping.

Finally making it beyond the coral, Sumner turned to Renhols.

"Give the visual signal," he said.

Renhols laid his oar aside and took his hooded flashlight off his belt. He pointed it straight out to sea and gave the Morse code for *R*—dot, dash, dot.

The radio crackled as McGowen said, "Red One, got you."

The verbal response was used so no eyes onshore would see the PT boat's signal lamp. Beyond the pounding surf of the breakers, the men could hear the low gurgle of the PT boat's muffled engines. Moments later the 132 boat came into view about a hundred yards out and to the right of the rubber boat.

The men rowed around to the seaward side of the *Sea Bat*, thus putting it between them and any hostile fire from shore; ropes were tossed out and the rubber boat was hauled in close, then the team crawled aboard the PT boat. With the help of the *Sea Bat*'s crew, the rubber boat was dragged up onto the deck. As the team stowed their gear, Sumner, McGowen, and the PT skipper, Jones, went below into the *Sea Bat*'s tiny wardroom. The boat captain flipped on the battle lanterns, bathing the room in a red glow. Jones broke out his navigational charts of the area.

"So what do you have?" he asked.

"There's a Jap supply base here," Sumner said, consulting his notes and pointing to the area on the map just inland from the river. "About one hundred yards from the river's mouth, it widens and turns southward. There are several small islands, with about a dozen Nip barges hidden under the trees. There are at least two fuel tanks and the place is manned by about sixty rice crackers under a lieutenant."

As Sumner talked, Jones marked targets and radar bearings. Then he summoned his executive officer.

"I want the other two boat commanders here," he said, and the XO, Ens. Robert M. Muller, vanished.

Within twenty minutes, two more boyishly young naval ensigns were crowded into the wardroom. Jones outlined what Sumner had said.

"The flyboys can't see them or hit them, but we can," he said. "We'll attack at first light and rake the area with everything we've got. I'll be point, and we'll go single-file." He handed the other two men sheets of paper. "I've marked radar reference points, based on landmarks onshore. We'll hit 'em at oh six hundred."

With that, the meeting was over. Since daylight was five hours away, Sumner went into the crew compartment, where his team was sacked out. The small room reeked of jungle mildew and sweat.

"Get all the rest you can, fellas," he told those who were still awake. "We're gonna hit those bastards at daylight, and with all the firepower these boats carry, it's gonna be a helluva show."

With that, he lay down on one of the bunks and was instantly asleep.

★　★　★

What seemed like just a few moments later, a crewman was gently prodding Sumner.

"It's oh five hundred, sir," he said.

Sumner nodded, took a moment to clear his head and remember where he was, then roused his men.

"Come on, guys," he ordered. "Up."

Climbing topside, the team took up position on the starboard side of the superstructure, out of the line of any return fire from shore. This was the navy's show, and they were mere spectators.

With the engines still muffled by the underwater venting, the three boats swung south, keeping about two miles from the dark coastline. All battle stations were manned. On the starlit water, Sumner could barely discern the other two boats, illuminated by the twinkling phosphorescence of the 132's wake.

Sumner and McGowen stood side by side in the cockpit, leaning against the combing of the afterdeck house. Belowdecks Sumner could watch the illuminated radar screen, now unmanned because the operator was also a gunner. The river's mouth was plainly visible on the radar. Jones had the con, a steering wheel similar to that of an automobile, jutting out of the console about waist high. Muller, the XO, was to his right. Both were somewhat protected by a thin steel splinter screen.

At five forty-five a.m., after cruising three or four miles south of the river mouth, the three boats closed in to within a few hundred yards of the shore. Jones took the microphone of his radio and told the other boats, "OK, here we go."

He pointed the boat north and pushed open the throttles. The PT boat leaped forward, skimming across the ocean at twenty miles per hour. The other two boats followed about a hundred yards behind.

As they reached the target area, Jones yelled into his mic, "Commence firing."

Instantly, the 132's bow-mounted 20mm gun opened up, as did the four dual-mounted .50-caliber machine guns located in two gun tubs. The stern-mounted 40mm Bofors was last to join. This cacophony of noise, multiplied by the three boats, tore apart the quiet night. The darkness was lit by colored tracers, leaving a fiery trail as they sought targets inland. Brass shell casings from all the weapons clattered to the wooden deck, striking each other and ringing like the bells of Hell.

The PT boats walked their fire along the coastline. Then rounds from the rearmost boat found a fuel dump, and an angry ball of orange flame and thick black smoke billowed a hundred feet or more into the sky, followed by a deafening explosion. Incendiary rounds from the PT boats added to the deadly pyrotechnic display.

Sumner was speechless, as it seemed as if the entire shoreline was ablaze.

Passing the target area, Jones ordered the boats to do another 180-degree turn.

"We're gonna hit 'em again," he said.

The PTs raced back, pouring another barrage of fire into the area. Now there came a twinkling of light from the shore, followed by waterspouts and a whizzing noise in the air. The enemy was firing back, fortunately with light weapons. The .50 calibers on the PT boats zeroed in on the muzzle flashes, and the Japanese fire diminished. Meanwhile, in the staging area, more balls of flame rose skyward, adding to the inferno already in progress.

"On me," Jones said into the radio, and turned his boat into the mouth of the river, the other two close behind. In the estuary, the PTs raked one shoreline, then the other, as well as the small islands. Fires raged everywhere, both onshore and on the water. Barges were shredded by the heavy fusillade of automatic weapons fire.

The Japanese onshore returned what fire they could, and bullets thunked into the wooden boats. With full daylight now upon them, Jones turned the 132 toward the mouth of the river and led the way out.

Emerging into the open sea, the three PT commanders pushed open the throttles and unmuffled the engines. The Packards roared and the screws bit into the water. The trio of PT boats, bows lifted in the air, spray cascading over their decks, sped away at forty-five miles per hour. As the coastline diminished, so did the volume of return fire, although some heavy-caliber slugs still hissed into the water around the retreating boats.

"Think they're still mad?" Coleman asked, as he watched the waterspouts from the Japanese bullets.

"Let's just say I wouldn't expect no Christmas card from them this year," Jones replied.

After leaving the throttles open for fifteen minutes, the boats finally slowed to about twenty-five miles per hour. Jones picked up his talk-between-ships mic.

"Damage report," he said.

Both the 128 and 131 responded with no damage, no casualties.

"Let's go home," he said, and set course for the three-hour trip to Woendi Island.

Sumner was elated and, based on the grinning faces around him, so were his men. His team's first mission had been a resounding success. They had scouted out an enemy supply base and made possible its crippling, if not its destruction. And they had done it with no injuries.

"Good job, guys," he said, and shook each man's hand.

McGowen, beside Sumner, said, "When we get back, we'll debrief with the Naval Ops guys at Woendi. Then you can radio your report to ASTC at Hollandia. Every mission is a learning experience, and what we do out here is incorporated into training for the new teams." He stuck out a hand. Sumner took it and they shook. "Excellent mission, Bob."

"We had some luck," Sumner said modestly. "I just hope it continues."

He went below to get some rest.

CHAPTER 7

Final Operations in New Guinea

The Lutz and Littlefield Missions, July–September 1944

On July 30, 1944, over seven thousand troops of the U.S. 6th Army came ashore unopposed along a twelve-mile front between Cape Sansapor and Cape Opmarai, on the northwestern coast of the Vogelkop Peninsula, the last major objective in MacArthur's retaking of New Guinea.

Code-named Operation Globetrotter, the island has a rugged, mountainous terrain, cut by numerous rivers, and includes coastal terraces ideal for airfields. Planes from these fields would be able to block Japanese shipping from the East Indies and the Philippines and isolate the fifteen thousand Japanese on the eastern side of the Vogelkop, as well as those still fighting on Biak and Noemfoor islands.

More important, at least to MacArthur, taking the Vogelkop would bring him to within six hundred miles of Mindanao, the southernmost island of the Philippines.

★ ★ ★

Lt. William B. Lutz and his team had been idle for the entire month since their June 22 graduation from the ASTC. A serious-minded man, Lutz was more concerned with getting the job done than in rewards for doing one's duty. In other words, as he informed his men, neither he nor, by extension, they were in the war for glory and medals.

"We're here to win the war as fast as we can, and I'm not going to worry about handing out medals," he told his team. "If any of you have a problem with that, speak up."

No one did, for Lutz was a methodical and thorough officer, and the men felt confidence in his leadership and believed that his decisions were not going to get them killed.

Religious "before it became fashionable," Scout Jack Geiger recalled, Lutz often read Bible passages to his team, who were a mixed bag of men. There was Cpl. Clifford A. Gonyea, who, for reasons none of his surviving teammates recall, was nicknamed "House Wrecker," and Pvt. Robert E. Shullaw, the team's radioman. There was the tall Sgt. Bob Ross, a Jewish man who, when the army cooks served pork— as they often did—called it beef and ate it. Staff Sgt. Oliver Roesler's father was a Pacific Northwest lumberman who also owned a small farm in Washington State, growing raspberries and raising cows and chickens in order to keep his sons "out of mischief." Roesler was a Seventh-Day Adventist, "although," he admitted, "not a very good one." And there was Pfc. Jack Geiger, whom his buddy Ross nicknamed "Handsome Dan."

Ross and Gonyea had served as the contact men for the Hobbs Team on a two-day mission that included reconnoitering Japen, Naoe, and Koeroedoe islands in early July, but aside from that, it was just lying around camp on Woendi Island, playing cards and volleyball and exercising to stay fit.

The men's spirits were raised around July 13 when a message was received to "hold Lutz Team for a mission for 6th Army." The mission, a two-day excursion that came on July 22, was to land about twenty miles east of Sansapor, three hundred miles behind Japanese lines. The enemy had long been operating a barge staging area in Cape Sansapor, running supplies between Sorong and Manokwari to the east.

The team, along with a Dutch youth to serve as interpreter, was to escort Lt. Everett M. Hodges, a 6th Army engineer, onto the shore to map out serviceable roads, fresh water supplies, and bivouac areas in advance of the July 30 invasion. A reconnaissance a week earlier by Alamo Scout Jack Dove said the target area seemed unoccupied by enemy troops.

"He's a good man," Ross told his friend Geiger, referring to Dove. "If he'd seen any Japs, he and his tough bunch of bastards would've killed them, like they did on that Hollandia job back in June. They killed thirty Nips that time."

The trip from Woendi Island by PT boat—there were two of them, one for the Lutz Team and one for Dove's contact team—was long and arduous, and necessitated a stop to refuel at Noemfoor. There, the Scouts swam in the clear Pacific while, onshore, the sound of battle rumbled across the water as GIs mopped up the remaining enemy troops. Around five p.m., with the boats refueled and two hundred miles still to go, the Scouts continued their trip, arriving in the Sansapor–Cape Opmarai area around midnight. The trip had been uneventful, except for around sunset, when a Japanese barge was spotted on the horizon. As the boats' crews and the Scouts anxiously prepared for action, it soon became evident that the barge was actually a large, partially submerged tree. The men were disappointed because, as Ross said, they "didn't get to see a show."

At the landing point, the rubber boat was inflated and lowered into the water. The sea was calm and visibility was good, almost too good, the men thought. After signaling the PT that they were ashore and OK, Lutz told Gonyea and Ross to deflate the rubber boat. The men tensed as the air hissed from the craft. It was then rolled up and hidden, after which the team settled in to get some sleep as best they could as the local insects tried to eat them alive. Up at dawn, the team had coffee and a breakfast of ten-in-one rations, good for either one man for ten days or ten men for one day.

Penetrating four hundred yards inland, the team struck off to the east, paralleling the shoreline. During a rest break, Geiger heard the shuffling sound of footsteps and signaled the team to freeze. Four armed Japanese soldiers were walking along the beach, coming toward Lutz's position. As Geiger watched, three more appeared, following the first group. The Scouts lay silent, watching from the underbrush as the seven men passed by, breathing a sigh of relief only when they were gone from sight. Lutz pointed eastward, and the men headed out. Two hours later they reached the bank of one of the many rivers that flows down from the Vogelkop's mountainous interior. This was the easternmost boundary of their patrol area. As they arrived, a Japanese soldier, bare-chested and dressed in shorts, came walking along the bank. He shouted to an unseen person on the opposite shore, then continued walking. Roesler, at the point, was barely ten feet from the man, and for one chilling moment the Japanese soldier looked right at him. Their eyes seemed to be locked, but because of the tall grass and Roesler's camouflaged uniform and painted face, the soldier failed to see him, and thus lived.

Continuing on, the Scouts crossed a jungle trail marred by the many footprints of passing Japanese. The patrol route next took them up a large hill, where they stopped. This was the end of their patrol area, and they headed back. Approaching the jungle trail again, Roesler, still at point, shot up his arm to signal "freeze." Two unarmed Japanese, evidently stragglers, were walking along the trail, carrying huge packs. The two were not molested and the Scouts continued their westward walk. Stopping for the night to eat some supper and get some sleep—their ten-in-one ration included roast beef, corn, and peas—the men got a rude surprise. Shullaw spotted four Japanese soldiers approaching along a trail Lutz and his team had been unaware of because, Geiger said years later, they had failed to reconnoiter before they stopped to rest—a first-mission mistake that would not be repeated. The Scouts froze to immobility.

After the Japanese had passed, Lutz whispered, "Sweet Jesus, I didn't realize we were still so close to the trail. Roesler, Gonyea, check it out."

Roesler and Gonyea crept toward the trail, found it was less than ten yards away, then hurried back. Gonyea also gestured that four more Japanese were coming, all armed. The Scouts huddled down in the vegetation until the soldiers had passed, then Lutz led the team deeper into the underbrush, to find safer overnight accommodations. Still, as the men lay restlessly on their ponchos, they could hear Japanese soldiers shouting to each other in the distance. To add to their misery, a drenching rain started to fall. The men spent a miserable night, with each man standing watch for an hour and fifteen minutes in the steady downpour.

Good news came with the dawn. Hodges, reviewing his notes, said he had all the information he needed, and the team could return to the pickup point. Arriving at the beach by late morning, they retrieved the radio and rubber boat as another heavy rain began pouring down on them. An attempt to stave off the deluge by erecting a shelter with their ponchos proved futile.

The Scouts observed the beach all day in case more Japanese came by. The men were wet, miserable, and irritable, and any enemy soldier who crossed them that day would not survive. Luckily for the Japanese, none did.

The PT boat arrived on schedule that night, although it hit a log and bent one of its three screws, slowing the trip home. The Scouts, tired and drenched to the bone, sat in the tiny wardroom, enjoying cups of hot cocoa. However, sleep on the PT boat proved just as elusive as on the island. The surf kicked up by the rain squall kept dumping the men on the top bunks onto their buddies in the lower berths.

Back at Woendi, the team found that their tents had been taken over by Red Sumner's men, so they had to move to new quarters elsewhere. Lutz and Jack Dove were flown to Wakde with whatever intelligence had been gleaned at the Vogelkop. Lutz's men joined him a few days later. Camped near the edge of the American perimeter, the men were kept awake by intermittent Japanese machine-gun fire, and jarred by an enemy artillery round that exploded on the nearby beach. By August 8, they were back in the safer environs of Hollandia, where they could quietly recover from the insect bites and crotch itch that afflicted them.

But the respite would not last long.

★   ★   ★

Six days later, on August 14, the Lutz Team was dispatched to the village of Arso, twenty miles inland from the Hollandia invasion area. The Japanese reportedly had established a radio station there, and although the air corps had bombed the place repeatedly, it was uncertain if they had successfully knocked the station out. The Lutz Team was to recon the village, check on the damage, and see if the radio station was still operational. If it was, they were to destroy it, which could prove difficult. Allied G2 estimated two hundred Japanese in the area of Arso.

Planning for a five-day mission, the men packed six days' worth of K rations, clean clothes, several changes of socks to prevent the growth of debilitating fungus on their feet, and as much ammo as they felt they could carry. The men also took rolled-up hammocks to sleep in, rather than lie on the ground. They were warned that the mud was knee-deep in places, and that there was little drinkable water available, so each man took two canteens and plenty of halazone tablets for purification.

Trucked to the beginning of the trail, the team climbed into their packs and set off, hoping to reach the halfway point—the village of Isobo—by dark. They hiked for fifty minutes, then took ten-minute breaks, stopping at noon for lunch near the Tami River. En route they overtook a squad of engineers.

"We're on our way to the Tami River," their leader told Lutz. "We're supposed to set up a defensive position. Can we follow you guys?"

"You may," Lutz said. "But we plan to move quickly."

With that, the Scouts were off, the engineers following, although they were soon lagging behind.

"A defensive position?" Ross wondered aloud. "Who are they kidding? There aren't any damned Japs there."

As if taunting Ross for his flippancy, as they approached the Tami, Lutz waved the men to get down. Two weary-looking men in Japanese military uniforms were approaching. As they drew up, the team rose and quickly took them prisoner. One of the men, in broken English, told the GIs that they were Taiwanese, not Japanese, and that they were part of a labor unit and were on their way to surrender.

"I've heard that story before," Geiger snarled. "They could have Tojo tattooed on their ass cheeks and they'd still say they weren't Japs."

The two men were in pitiful condition, with jungle sores covering their legs, and they stank.

The Scouts waited until the engineers caught up and turned their two prisoners over to them to be sent back, then continued their hike. As they trekked inland, the trail, as promised, became muddier and muddier, and the lifting of each foot became an arduous chore. The muck was so thick and heavy that it pulled off part of the bottom of Ross's hobnailed Australian army boots.

Exhausted from their exertions, the team reached Isobo just after sunset and settled in for the night. The village was empty of inhabitants, although someone had stuck a Japanese skull on a stake. Finding fresh water, the Scouts washed their clothes and themselves while one man stood guard. Nightfall came around seven p.m. and the team strung their hammocks and tried to get some sleep. In the distance they heard the sound of rifle fire—an American Garand. Noises out in the jungle jolted them awake from time to time. The men rotated guard duty, although in the pitch-black, where it was literally impossible to see one's hand a few inches in front of one's face, guard duty seemed pointless.

Somewhat refreshed, the team was back on the trail by eight a.m. and following the bank of a river. After about forty-five minutes, Lutz indicated "freeze." By a bend in the trail about 150 yards ahead was a man in a Japanese uniform, bent over, dipping water from the river.

Gathering his team around him, Lutz said, "Gonyea, Geig, Ross, try to circle around him and take him prisoner."

Just then the man, suddenly aware of a foreign presence, rose and looked as if he was going to run. The team opened fire, spewing lead at the hapless soldier, who dropped and rolled into a depression. After they ceased firing, the team hurried forward and their jaws dropped as they found the man sitting against a tree trunk, trembling violently.

The entire area around him had been chewed up by gunfire and several bullets had passed through his clothes. But he was unharmed.

"If this young man did not believe in God before, I'm sure he does now," Lutz said.

Then a look of irritation spread over Lutz's face when he realized seven men had fired all their weapons at the lone soldier at a range of one hundred yards, and the man was unscathed. Lutz turned to his men.

"When we get back, we are putting in time on the rifle range," he said.

The frightened man began jabbering in Malay, which Ross could speak and understand. The man turned out to be a seventeen-year-old Javanese who had been in New Guinea for ten months as a Japanese laborer. Under questioning by Ross, the boy said there were ten Japanese in Arso and eight rifles.

Thin and sick from malaria, the boy, now nicknamed "Junior," was given K rations and Atabrine tablets, which he downed hungrily. It was also decided Junior would accompany them to Arso.

The heat and humidity of the land was intense and by nightfall the team's water supply had run out, forcing them to drink what water they could scoop from muddy footprints after first dosing it with purifying halazone tablets.

The next day, August 16, the men continued toward Arso, passing the remains of Japanese soldiers, mostly bones and rotting uniforms, lying along the trail, their identities long ago obliterated. Around noon the team stopped for lunch by a stream. Lutz took Ross and Junior ahead to reconnoiter, although the boy grew more frightened the nearer they drew to the village. Creeping through the tall grass for about an hour, the three saw the first house in the village. As they drew closer, Japanese voices could be heard inside the house. Junior told Ross there were two men inside, as well as two at the other end of the village and six at a large hut in the center.

Returning to where the rest of the team waited, Ross and Junior came across more dead Japanese. Ross discovered a stash of papers, which he tucked away, and then, to his amazement, picked up a pair of black oxford shoes.

"These fellas sure carry the strangest things," he said.

He gave the oxfords to Junior, who kept them awhile, then tossed them away.

★　★　★

The team rose at four thirty the next morning and, leaving their packs behind, headed toward Arso. Arriving before dawn in a misty rain, they quietly approached the first house. The team split, with Lutz, Shullaw, Ross, and Junior slinking off one way while Gonyea, Roesler, and Geiger went another.

"When we get there," Lutz had whispered, "Shullaw, you and Ross strangle the Japs and I will finish them with my knife."

That was the plan, but as the team drew closer, the plan changed. The Japanese were awake and, seated inside the oblong, open house, were making breakfast. Worse, they were facing the direction from which the Scouts would have to approach. The only solution would be to rush them. Lying behind a foot-high wall surrounding a well just twenty feet from the house, Lutz, Ross, and Shullaw watched the enemy. A Japanese soldier walked the length of the house, parallel to the trio of Scouts, who were plainly visible behind the low wall, had the man looked in their direction. But he didn't. With his hands, Lutz indicated that Ross was to take the man on the left and he would handle the other. Shullaw was to provide cover. Readying their knives, the men sprang forward, across the clearing, and burst into the house. The man Lutz was to take was working by the fireplace, two knives in his hands. Stunned by the sudden intrusion, the man froze just long enough for Ross to swing his carbine, striking the soldier with the barrel. Then he drove the knife home, first in the heart, then several times to the throat.

Lutz, meanwhile, attacked the other soldier, driving his knife home repeatedly.

Geiger and Roesler ran up. Geiger entered the house as Ross was finishing off the Japanese soldier. He looked down at the dead man and said, "You did a good job, Bob. You looked fierce as hell."

"I don't know how I looked," he replied, gazing at his bloody knife and hand. "It hadda be done."

He wiped the knife and his hand—some of the blood was his own since he had scuffed his knuckles in the struggle—on the dead man's uniform.

"Let's move on," Lutz said.

Proceeding cautiously through the village, they searched each house, knowing there were eight more enemy soldiers around somewhere. Then Shullaw signaled a halt.

"I see smoke," he said.

"I don't see any smoke, Bob," Geiger said. "Are you sure it's not just mist?"

"It's smoke, I tell ya," he insisted. "Let's check it out."

Approaching a hedge that hid the house Ross said had emitted smoke, the team split into two groups as before. Someone in the hut heard them and shouted a warning and the Scouts opened up on the house with their carbines. Five Japanese soldiers burst from the hut, firing, only to be cut down in the fusillade of .30-caliber rounds. An officer with a pistol remained inside and the Scouts poured a rain of bullets into the house, riddling the man.

One of the Japanese was wounded and moving. His bloodlust up, Ross stood over the man and struck him on the head with his M1A1 carbine, breaking the folding wire stock. Knives finished off the rest. The enemy body count was at eight, but Junior had said there were ten, so the hunt resumed. At the last hut in the village, a small cook fire was burning, but the two Japanese who had lighted it had fled at the sound of the gunfire. After searching the enemy's abandoned personal gear, the team moved back into the village and collected the belongings of the eight men they'd killed. They took any papers they found, as well as rifles, three pistols, a flag, a sword, watches, a leather dispatch case stuffed with papers and pens, and money. One of the slain had been a medical man, possibly a physician. They saw no signs of a radio station.

By nine thirty a.m. the team returned to where they'd dropped their packs. There they sifted through the items they'd taken. Going through the wallets had its somber side.

"Look at this," Roesler said. It was a picture of a woman and children, probably the dead man's family. "Poor bastard."

"Out here it's easy to forget that they have families back home just like we do," Lutz said. "They're just average guys doing their jobs like we are, and it's by the grace of God that the boot isn't on the other foot, or they'd be going through our pockets."

★   ★   ★

The team slogged back through the mud, Junior tagging along with Ross, who was the only man he could converse with. The young Javanese came in handy, since he knew where to find drinkable water, when there was any to be found. The team reached the banks of the Arso River and settled in for the night. After washing their clothes in the muddy water, they dropped into an exhausted sleep. As happened so often on this mission, their slumber was disturbed as rain began to fall overnight. For Ross, the rain was not the only problem. As he later told his buddy Geiger, he was haunted by the man he had knifed, the first he had ever killed, and whose body lay abandoned back in the village.

By August 18, their fifth day out, the men were in sorry shape. Dirty, footsore, and unshaven, most had jungle sores and insect bites on their arms and legs and crotch itch. Leeches clung to their skin and had to be removed. Lutz had two in his mouth. Plus, Ross's damaged shoes kept falling apart, and he tried to save them with makeshift repairs.

Arriving at the Tami River, the team encountered the engineer unit that had followed them part of the way inland four days earlier. One of the Scouts mentioned they had come from Arso. The engineers were astounded.

"HQ won't let any patrols under thirty men go farther than the Tami," an engineer said.

The Lutz Team puffed up with pride, chalking everyone else off as a "bunch of softies."

Geiger recalled that, throughout the walk, Ross had a difficult time, both with his disintegrating shoes and having to lug his own rifle along with a captured Japanese weapon. At one point along the muddy trail, Junior kept tugging on a phone wire that had been strung along the path. This kept pushing Ross, beside him, farther out into the muck. Fatigued beyond measure, Ross exploded and ran screaming down the middle of the trail, until he slipped and fell in the ooze. Geiger hurried to his friend's side and helped him up.

"Let me take that Jap rifle," Geiger said, taking the now mud-clogged weapon.

"I think I'm going jungle happy, Geig," Ross fretted, sweat pouring from him.

"Come on, buddy," Geiger said. "You'll be OK."

The team walked on, finally coming across fresh water, where they stopped for the night. Ross cleaned up his muddy clothes, as well as his own and the Japanese rifles. He apologized to the team for cracking up.

"Don't worry about it," Lutz told him. "We're all on edge. We should be back by tomorrow morning."

Ross threw away his now worthless shoes and donned several pairs of socks, and the men turned in.

The trail the next day was muddy as ever and the team, sporting six days of whiskers and filthy clothes, looked and smelled like hell. Gonyea and Roesler, at point, set a brisk pace that made it difficult for Ross and Junior to keep up, especially over the rutted terrain. Utterly exhausted, the sickly Junior broke down and Gonyea hoisted the boy onto his back. The men took turns carrying him. The team finally reached the truck trail and began following it, encouraged by the knowledge that they only had about two miles yet to go. Then they heard a truck engine. While the others rested, Geiger and Ross hur-

ried toward the sound and secured a ride back for the Scouts, a blessing after five and a half days of walking.

"Thank God for those truck jockeys," Gonyea said, as the vehicle
bounced its way back along the dirt roads.

"Thank God for Ross," Geiger said and smiled. "He told them we
were desperate men and that we'd be willing to commit murder to get
our hands on a truck."

At 6th Army HQ, the ragged, dirty, smelly men drew gaping stares.
They handed Junior over to G2, only to be told they were expecting
Japanese prisoners, not Javanese laborers. "Phooey," was the Scouts'
general consensus. They had not been told anything about prisoners.
The team was also told that G2 had neglected to inform the air corps
about how far out the team had gone.

"Our planes strafe that area all the time," an officer told them.
"You're very lucky."

★   ★   ★

Finally making it back to their camp, the men shaved and hit the showers, threw away their muddy, rotting clothes, and drew new uniforms.
Then it was off to see the medics at the dispensary to treat the open
sores derisively dubbed "jungle rot" or the "New Guinea crud" on
their arms and legs and the blisters on their feet. Later, at their tent, the
men split the booty from the mission. Lutz got the sword. Anything not
wanted was turned over to the ASTC supply people to swap with the
navy. Japanese war souvenirs meant better food.

That night, the men slept on clean sheets.

★   ★   ★

At about the same time the Lutz Team was striking out for the Arso
River, Lt. Wilbur Littlefield was awaiting his first assignment. Like
Lutz, he had been a graduate of the ASTC's third class. Littlefield had
served with the 160th Regiment of the 40th Division and had gotten

himself into some trouble. A lieutenant in Easy Company on Guadal-canal, he was angered by Fox Company's commanding officer, a captain, who was griping to his mess crew about someone in Littlefield's company, and Littlefield had gotten fed up.

"You're a goddamned liar," he snarled at the officer.

Dragged in front of his own commander, Capt. Donald Moore, Littlefield was told, "Bill, you're a helluva good soldier, but you don't have enough respect for rank."

The Fox Company captain wanted Littlefield court-martialed, but in the end he was either cooled down or dissuaded, and nothing came of the incident. Still, when news arrived that the Scouts were looking for candidates, Littlefield's name was submitted.

Littlefield's team was a tough bunch, especially Samuel L. Armstrong and Allen H. Throgmorton. Prior to joining the Scouts, both had been first sergeants until jailed by military police, Armstrong for stabbing a man to death in a knife fight and Throgmorton, who, while carrying company funds he was to deposit, stopped by a bar for a drink and disappeared for two months before turning himself in.

Also part of the team was Sgt. Zeke "Chief Thundercloud" McConnell, who was half Cherokee Indian. McConnell was born in Oklahoma, where his father had abandoned his family, and his mother died when he was just five years old. His Cherokee grandmother raised Zeke until he was eight, then was unable to do so any longer, at which point the boy was packed off to the Sequoyah Orphans Training School in Sequoyah, Washington, run by the Bureau of Indian Affairs. Later, he attended Bacom Junior College, also in Washington State, and was drafted into the army in March 1942.

McConnell did his basic training at Fort Lewis, Washington, then was shipped off to Hawaii, and then New Britain as part of the 180th Regiment of the 40th Division. An athletic young man who loved football and boxing, he was employed as a jeep driver for his regimental commander, Colonel Caulkins. It was Caulkins who learned about the Alamo Scouts and nominated McConnell. Accepted for training, he became part of the third class. Littlefield liked McConnell's nature skills and selected him for his team, and by the war's end the two had forged a lifelong bond as McConnell became the brother Littlefield never had.

The rest of Littlefield's team consisted of Sgt. Alva C. Branson, from California, Pvt. Elmer E. Niemela, a nineteen-year-old Minnesotan of Scandinavian descent, and Sgt. Paul Bemish.

This would be Littlefield's team until Leyte, when several black soldiers came into a bar where Armstrong and Niemela were drinking. Armstrong, who not unlike many Americans of that era held strong racist beliefs, ordered the blacks to dance by firing his .45 automatic into the floor by their feet. He and young Niemela were immediately discharged from the Scouts and sent back to their original units, Armstrong for his actions and Niemela for not stopping him. (His army experiences would change Armstrong, who, in later life, entered the ministry.)

Littlefield's first New Guinea assignment came on August 13. He and his men were dispatched to the coastal village of Vanimo to confirm American intelligence reports that the Japanese were using the area to bypass U.S. lines at Aitape, in an attempt to strike at the 6th Army headquarters. Littlefield would be working with Alamo Scout training instructor Raymond "Moose" Watson, the burly, highly likable Australian who loved the American game of baseball and could usually be counted on to either hit a home run or strike out.

For the Vanimo mission, Watson again brought along his two native police boys. Littlefield respected the abilities of these men, recalling their remarkable skills during night exercises.

That skill aside, however, the police boys' hatred of the Japanese created problems. Littlefield needed prisoners, a concept the natives seemed not to understand. Coming across two enemy soldiers digging a machine-gun emplacement near Vanimo, he turned to the head police boy and said, "You catchum Jap fella." The natives moved forward quietly. Just before they reached the Japanese, they were spotted. One enemy soldier jumped up and yelled, "No shoot, no shoot." The police boys gunned them both down.

"Damnit," Littlefield cursed.

He had the bodies searched for documents, especially anything that might identify their unit, then moved on. Farther along the trail, the men came across an empty lean-to. In that same instant, another Japanese soldier appeared. Spotting the Scouts, he turned to run. The police boys shot him, as well.

Retreating back to Vanimo, the Scouts treated themselves and the villagers to a meal of fresh fish, which they obtained by tossing grenades into the adjacent river and having Branson wade in after the stunned catch. Littlefield, after not seeing evidence of any large Japanese troop movements, and having given up on the idea of taking live prisoners, called in the air corps crash boat they had come ashore in, and returned to Woendi Island.

Littlefield's next mission in New Guinea met with greater success. Near the end of August, the chieftain of a native village on the tiny island of Roemberpon, at the mouth of Geelvink Bay, arrived by canoe at Biak. He brought news that the Japanese had been holding a large number of Indian soldiers, captured after the fall of Singapore thirty-one months earlier, on the Vogelkop, where they were used as slave laborers. But as the war turned against the Japanese and their supply lines tightened under Allied pressure, the enemy was barely able to feed himself, let alone the prisoners. As a result, the Japanese were releasing the Indian soldiers, many already malnourished, into the jungle to fend for themselves or die.

"You and your team will accompany this man back to Roemberpon and confirm his story," Littlefield was told by the 6th Army G2 officer who briefed him. "If it is true, have the natives spread the word to the mainland to bring all the men they can find to Roemberpon, and we will arrange for their return here."

On August 29, Littlefield and his team, along with the native chieftain and Sgt. Herman S. Chanley of the Thompson Team, boarded a PT boat bound for Roemberpon. Arriving off the island and out of sight of the coastal village, with its cluster of huts built up on stilts, the Scouts put two rubber boats over the side. Littlefield called Chanley over to him.

"You ride in the boat with me and the chief," Littlefield said. "Sit behind him. If he's leading us into an ambush, kill him."

Chanley, who would later receive a battlefield commission and lead an Alamo Scout team of his own, nodded grimly.

Far from being ambushed, after the Scouts landed, buried their boats, and walked to the village, they were treated like conquering heroes. Men, women, and children mobbed them.

"I don't think they'd ever seen a white man," Littlefield still recalled sixty-three years later.

The celebration was enhanced when some natives brought out what must have been the village's most prized possession, a white linen tablecloth.

"Where in the hell did they get that from?" Littlefield said.

"Beats the shit out of me," Armstrong replied. "I haven't seen a white linen tablecloth since I joined the army."

The natives served up fresh fruit and hot coffee and the Scouts enjoyed being the toast of the town. The next day it was back to work. Littlefield had his team reconnoiter Roemberpon, which did not take long on the small island. Satisfied that there were no Japanese hiding anywhere, he arranged with the chief to bring the Indian prisoners to Roemberpon from the mainland.

"Bring em Indian fellas long place kanaka," he told the chief. "You savvy finish?"

The chief nodded.

Littlefield told the chief they would return to pick up the captives in two weeks. He then led his men back to where the boats were hidden, inflated them, and rendezvoused with the PT boat.

Word went out to the villages on the Vogelkop and soon native canoes were ferrying four or five former prisoners a day out to Roemberpon. On September 15, Littlefield and his men returned. With them they carried sacks of rice, both for the natives and to feed the hungry ex-prisoners.

Over the next two days, Littlefield watched more prisoners arrive, and what he saw was pathetic: emaciated, weak men in tattered clothes, their cheeks hollow, their eyes sunken into the thin faces. Some of the men could not climb out of the canoes without help.

The Indian soldiers were overjoyed to see the Americans and, despite their condition, greeted them with whatever enthusiasm they could muster. Littlefield recalled one practically skeletal man who had to be helped to his feet and propped up by two others. Yet he faced the lieutenant and snapped off a stiff British salute. That memory would remain with Littlefield for the rest of his life.

The Americans remained in the village for four days, during which time Littlefield decided on the best way to get the prisoners out. Scouting the adjacent beach he noticed the shore had a pronounced slope.

"We need to get the PT boats in as close as possible," he said. "Some of those men are in no condition to transfer from a rubber boat to a PT deck."

Littlefield had his team wade into the water to probe with their feet for hidden rocks or reefs. Thankfully, the bottom was clear of obstacles.

On September 19 two PT boats arrived off Roemberpon. Littlefield apprised the commanders of the condition of the ex-prisoners he would be bringing out and asked the two skippers to nudge their craft up onto the sloped beach. They agreed.

"Those skippers had balls," Littlefield said sixty-three years later.

With the PT boat prows on the sand, the Scouts, navy crewmen, and natives began hoisting the Indian soldiers aboard. When the last of the captives was loaded, the Scouts climbed onto the decks. Littlefield turned and waved to the chief as the PT commanders reversed engines and backed their boats off the soft white sand. The Scouts were carrying about forty men away from certain death in the jungle. Later, more PT boats would come back to Roemberpon and take off more sickly former prisoners. Just how many were being saved Littlefield did not know, but he and his men had accomplished their mission of mercy.

★   ★   ★

As Littlefield and his men sailed for Roemberpon for the first time on August 29, Bill Lutz informed his team they were being sent out again, this time to Salebaboe Island in the Celebes Sea, south of Mindanao, the southernmost island of the Philippines.

On September 5, as the team prepared, Lutz boarded a plane for a photo recon flight over the area. Geiger would miss this mission. Down with yellow jaundice, he would be replaced by Bob Schermerhorn, formerly of the Sumner Team.

Lutz and his men arrived at Woendi Island on September 9 and were amazed at the changes since their last visit. From a simple PT base, it had now become an area overcrowded with men and ships. Three days later the team boarded the PT tender USS *Mobjack* as part of a force sailing toward the Morotai Islands, 230 miles northwest of New Guinea and 300 miles southeast of Mindanao. Knowing they were closing on the Philippines heightened the men's eagerness.

The first stop, though, was a new PT base at Amsterdam Island just off Sansapor and not far from the site of the team's first mission less than two months ago.

The invasion at Morotai, Operation Interlude, went off as planned on September 15, but two days later the Scouts were still on the *Mobjack*. A Japanese scout plane buzzed overhead and the sky filled with antiaircraft fire, which the plane managed to elude.

The Scouts' mission, when they were finally briefed on September 20, was to travel by PT boat to Salebaboe, a three-mile-wide, fifteen-mile-long island in the Seloud Group, 150 miles south of Mindanao. It was a one-day mission with the goal of grabbing some local natives and bringing them back for intelligence-gathering reasons. Accompanying them would be a Dutch army officer, Lieutenant DeBruine. Three members of the McGowen Team would go along as the contact men.

The three PT boats departed at four thirty in the afternoon. The trip was long and over dangerous waters, and all the men—Scouts included—wore life jackets. With the night, a steady rain began falling and flashes of lightning lit the sky. One of the PT boats fell behind and the timetable for delivering the team to the island was slowed. The flotilla reached Salebaboe about three a.m. and the Scouts lowered the rubber boat into the water and paddled for shore. Reaching the island, Ross jumped out onto the beach to secure the rubber boat,

only to fall into a watery hole. The beach, which G2 told him was
made up of "black sand," was, in fact, deeply rutted coral, and Ross
had jumped into a gully. He reemerged, sputtering and cursing. The
original plan called for sending the ten-man rubber boat back to the
PT boat with two members of the contact team, who had come along
on the trip in. Now it was decided to keep it onshore and a radio message was sent to the PT boat to return in twenty-four hours. The coral
made it extremely difficult to drag the rubber boat inland and hide it,
but the men finally succeeded after much tugging and lifting. That
done, the Lutz Team cautiously worked their way inland while the
McGowen men stayed with the boat.

Salebaboe did not have thick jungle like some islands, but rather
sported dense bamboo thickets with bamboo wood lying on the
ground for a misplaced foot to crack if a man was not careful. But
bamboo wasn't the only concern. The inky blackness of the rainy night
was complete, and each man clung to the man in front of him in order
to stay together. In the dark, the team got turned around and ended
up back at the coral beach. They eventually reunited with the Mc-
Gowen Team and everyone settled in to get some sleep, which was
next to impossible in the driving tropical rain.

The team was under way by dawn with Lutz, Ross, and Roesler in
the lead. With their wet uniforms steaming as they dried under the hot
sun, the men spent much of the day reconnoitering the island. Lutz
discovered a well-used jungle trail, bordered on one side by native
gardens, leading to a village. Calling a halt, Lutz was asked by some
of the men if they could smoke. He said no. Lutz was a nonsmoker,
Roesler recalled, and his refusal pissed off the group's smokers. But
Lutz knew the smell of tobacco could carry a long way, and he was
taking no chances.

The village was within sight of the beach, so the Scouts could
watch both the shore and the trail. They allowed two native women to
walk by on the trail, passing barely ten feet from Roesler, while at sea
an occasional canoe glided past. Then a young man in a white sun
helmet, carrying both an ax and a machete, came along the footpath.

As he reached the spot where the Scouts lay concealed, DeBruine stepped out in front of him. The man stopped and turned, only to find two Alamo Scouts had emerged from the brush behind him. DeBruine told the man, obviously not a Japanese soldier, he would not be hurt, but that he was to come with them. The man willingly agreed, but as they took away his ax and machete, two teenage boys appeared on the trail. Spotting the Scouts, they turned and ran, yelling at the top of their lungs as they fled.

"They'll tip the Japs," Lutz said. "Let's go."

He led the team quickly into the underbrush and up into the nearby hills, in the direction of his next objective, the village of Moesi. Approaching to within three hundred yards of the place, the team spent four hours hiding in, what Roesler recalled, "the deepest part of the jungle we could find," watching for signs of the enemy. Seeing none, they worked their way back to the shore to retrieve their rubber boat. As the Americans reached the place the boat was hidden, Ross, at point, indicated "freeze." Ross then signaled "take cover" and the men dropped to the ground amid the underbrush as a twenty-five-man Japanese patrol approached, all armed and led by the two teenagers they had seen earlier. The Lutz Team was spread three to four feet apart, and lay in deathlike stillness as the Japanese walked directly through them, their *jikatabi* split-toe shoes within arm's reach of the Scouts, poking and probing the brush with bayoneted rifles. The Americans, sweat pouring down their faces, fingers tight on the triggers of their weapons, dared not breathe as the enemy moved on by. Maybe, Roesler thought, the Japs think the boys were exaggerating.

★　★　★

By ten p.m., the PT boat scheduled to pick them up still had not arrived.

"Inflate the boat," Lutz ordered. "It's probably safer for us floating out on the water than it is to stay here."

The men did as ordered and cast off from Salebaboe. Everyone heaved a sigh of relief when contact was finally made with the PT boat. Clambering back aboard, they were soon speeding back to Woendi Island.

During the return trip, DeBruine questioned the young man. He said he was a twenty-one-year-old islander and was glad to help the Allies.

"He says the Japs were very cruel," DeBruine told Lutz. "They forced him and others to work for them for twenty cents a day in invasion money. He claims there are about a hundred troops onshore and they have five mountain guns and several automatic weapons. They've left the villages to dig in up in the hills."

The young man informed DeBruine that the largest island in the Seloud Group, Talaud, was occupied by about one thousand troops, but that the rest of the islands were unoccupied.

When this information was relayed back to the Allied planners, it was decided to skip invading the place. Instead, the Allies' next stop would be the Philippines.

But first there were two more missions in New Guinea, involving not intelligence gathering and reconnaissance, but compassion and humanity.

CHAPTER 8

". . . By Far the Best Show I've Ever Seen."

Sumner Team: Pegun Island, August 21–23, 1944

Except for a small overnight mission to the Cape Oransbari–Cape Mambiwi area on August 12–13, Lt. Bob Sumner and his men had spent the last week or so at the navy's PT base on Woendi Island, playing beach volleyball, swimming, and just enjoying some time off. Then, on August 21, as the evening shadows were deepening, the men were relaxing and joking with each other in the comfort of their squad tent when their reverie was suddenly broken by Sumner.

"Hate to interrupt this good time," the lanky, strawberry blond Oregonian said. "Briefing on Noemfoor tomorrow morning. Consider this a mission alert. Get your gear together."

★ ★ ★

When Sumner arrived at the briefing hut the next day, he was greeted by Lt. John McGowen.

"Hi, Red," McGowen said. "We got a real doozy for you. You're gonna love this one."

The two Scouts went inside.

Waiting in the hut was Maj. Gen. Edwin D. Patrick, commander of Krueger's Cyclone Task Force, which had been formed in June 1944 for the invasion of Noemfoor. The fact that Cyclone's commanding officer was conducting the briefing suggested the unusual nature of the assignment. An army air force officer was also present.

The general cut right to the chase.

"This is not a recon mission, Lieutenant," he told Sumner. "This is a rescue mission. Three days ago, a picket boat carrying several air force enlisted personnel sailed here"—he pointed to a map—"to the Mapia Group. The Mapias consist of several small islands and three large ones, Bras, Pegun, and Fanildo. They are, as you can see, separated by narrow stretches of water. The men were sent to locate a British Beaufighter that had been forced to land on one of the small islands near Pegun and recover the two-man crew or, if possible, repair the plane so the crew could fly it home. The air corps guys in the picket boat included some mechanics."

He paused, then continued.

"As they passed near Pegun, three of the air force men asked to be dropped off to search for souvenirs and the boat skipper, for whatever the hell reason, agreed and let them go ashore."

"I take it that Pegun is occupied?" McGowen asked.

"The little yellow bastards are like ants at a picnic basket," Patrick replied. "Our G2 estimates between three hundred and four hundred are stationed throughout the Mapias.

"Anyway, the others found the plane and got it back into the air. On the return, the picket boat stopped at Pegun to pick up the air corps guys. As they approached the shore, one of the men ran out onto the beach, waving and yelling at them to get the hell out, that the Japs were on to them. Then he was hit by fire from the tree line and fell right there at the water's edge. The Japs also fired at the picket boat. Naturally, they hightailed it back to operational HQ to report and Woendi Ops passed it on to us."

"I gather our job is to go ashore and see if we can find the three airmen, or two now, probably," Sumner said.

"Yes," Patrick replied. "I have discussed this with General Krueger and he agrees. Go in, look around, see if you can find them, and get the hell out in one piece. Personally, I think the men are dead, but air force HQ has asked for our help." He cast a glance at the air corps officer. Then he added, "Besides, General Krueger and I both have an aversion to leaving any of our men behind if there's any chance of getting them out."

"Do we have any intelligence on the island?" Sumner asked.

"It's fairly flat, with a narrow beach and jungle vegetation," Patrick said. "Before the war it was an American and Dutch agricultural experimentation station, whatever the hell that is. What's left of that station is a cluster of huts not too far inland. We don't know the specific number of Japs on Pegun, but they use the place as an OP. Being four hundred miles south of Morotai and a hundred twenty-five miles east of Biak, it's a good place for the Nips to monitor any air or sea movements we make in the direction of Morotai or the Philippines."

Sumner looked at the map, nodding slowly in contemplation.

"The decision is yours, Lieutenant, on whether or not you want to undertake this assignment," Patrick told Sumner. "As I said, I believe these men are dead and I'm hesitant to risk more lives to prove it."

Sumner looked at Patrick, then to the air corps liaison officer.

The air corps man said, "Will you see if you can find our people?"

"Yeah," Sumner said. "We'll do what we can."

"Figured you'd say that, Red," McGowen said. "I and some of my guys will be the contact team. We'll get you ashore, bring the rubber boat back, and then stand by offshore to come get you. We will remain in radio contact. We don't expect you to be onshore for more time than it takes to see if they are dead, or bring them back if alive."

"And if they're POWs?"

"Don't take any extreme risks, but if you can free them, do it," Patrick said. "Then get back to the beach. You'll have plenty of fire support. In addition to the PT boat you'll be on, we're sending along two more plus a destroyer escort. The PT boats will take up station off Bras and Fanildo to prevent any Japs from crossing over to reinforce in case you get into a fight, and the frigate will remain beyond the horizon, out of sight unless needed."

"One more thing," McGowen said. "You're aware that our usual standing orders are to avoid enemy contact as much as possible. In this case, enemy contact is almost guaranteed. Arm yourself and your men accordingly."

"Weiland will be glad to hear that," Sumner said. "He's been aching for a chance to drag that damned BAR into the field."

"Use extreme caution, Lieutenant," Patrick said. "And remember, no matter how much we'd like to bring them back, General Krueger simply will not permit the loss of a valuable Scout team on an operation of this type. If those arrangements are understood, then you may make the attempt as soon as possible."

"We'll leave tonight at midnight," Sumner said.

He saluted and left.

★ ★ ★

Sumner and his team boarded the PT boat just before midnight and soon were skimming across the black water. With Cpl. Bob Schermerhorn down with malaria, the team consisted of Sumner, Blaise, Coleman, Weiland, Renhols, and Jones.

For the contact team, McGowen had brought along Pfc. Raymond Aguilar, a Mexican Indian who would serve as boat handler, as well as Staff Sgts. Ray W. Wangrud and Harold N. Sparks, and Pfcs. Jack C. Bunt and Charley D. Hill. They would help Sumner's men prepare for the mission.

The firepower of the three PT boats, along with the frigate, with its three five-inch gun turrets and 40- and 20mm dual-purpose guns, was comforting to Sumner.

"Let's get some sack time," he told the team as the PTs raced out to sea. "We'll need to be sharp in the morning."

Sleep was difficult on a PT boat bouncing across the waves at thirty miles per hour, but the team managed to snatch enough to rejuvenate their minds and senses.

At about two a.m. McGowen woke Sumner.

"We're about an hour out," he said.

Sumner nodded and began rousing his team. He told them to check their equipment and weapons.

"Souvenir hunting?" Coleman said. "Do you believe those guys?"

"Why not?" Blaise replied as he tested the radio. "You know how it is. We bring in souvenirs and trade them to the air corps and navy in exchange for better chow. Maybe these air corps guys decided our prices were too high and wanted to cut out the middleman."

Sumner had already decided this would be a quick, in-and-out, "pistol-type operation." Aside from a few tropical chocolate bars and their canteens, there would be no rations and the only equipment, other than their weapons, would be extra medical packs.

For the weapons, each Scout had at least seventy-five rounds, although Coleman, with his "grease gun," had two hundred. The imposing six-foot-two, 180-pound Weiland, who seemed to enjoy shooting down Japanese, was toting the heavy Browning Automatic Rifle, and also carried two hundred rounds. Since these two weapons would provide the team with a base of fire if needed, each Scout carried one extra clip for both Coleman and Weiland.

Every team member had hooked two fragmentation grenades on his web gear, and Sumner and three others also carried one smoke grenade apiece.

By three a.m. the PT boat was nearing the island. The tide was high and the sea calm, allowing the PT skipper to take his fifty-one-ton vessel, with its shallow five-foot-three-inch draft, through the island's surrounding reefs with little difficulty.

Sumner and McGowen had been studying the radar screen, trying to get a feel for the island's western topography, since there were no aerial photos available. The two Scout team leaders determined that if the surviving airmen were anywhere, it would be as prisoners around the old agricultural experimentation station. Sumner's plan was to land his men five hundred yards farther up the coast, away from the station, then make their way to the buildings and observe.

At three twenty a.m., the PT boat, its muffled engines gurgling through the underwater vents, slowed to a halt. The two other PT boats continued on, headed for their assigned spots off Bras and Fanildo, a short distance to the north. The frigate was already on station fifteen miles out to sea.

"This is it," the skipper whispered.

The inflated rubber boat was lowered into the water on the sea-ward side of the PT, and the men loaded in. Sumner and Aguilar stayed to the rear of the craft. Aguilar brought with him a towrope, the other end of which was attached to the PT boat. As the Scouts rowed the rubber boat toward the dark shoreline, Aguilar played out the rope.

Just before four a.m., the rubber boat reached the shore and Sumner and his men jumped into the shallow surf. Aguilar turned the rubber boat and began rowing back, aided by crewmen aboard the PT boat reeling in the towrope.

The tree line began just twenty feet from the narrow beach. As drilled, the men moved into the natural cover, then fanned out into a semicircle, backs to the sea, and waited while Renhols and Weiland, the beach security team, brushed away their footprints in the white sand.

The island's vegetation was mostly coconut trees mingled with sparse shrubs and low grass less than a foot tall. With daylight still some two hours away, Sumner let the men nap, rotating between sleepers and guards every thirty minutes. The only "enemy action" the team encountered during the rest time occurred around five fifteen a.m., when a palm frond fell, landing on Weiland, who had been sitting against the tree trunk. Luckily, he had been hit by the leafy end of the thick branch, and was unhurt, although the men stifled a laugh as Weiland, jolted suddenly awake, assumed he had been jumped by a Japanese soldier and briefly wrestled with his attacker.

In the faint glow before the six a.m. dawn, during what is called the morning nautical twilight, Sumner was preparing to move his men out when he heard Jones give two sharp warning raps on his rifle butt. A nine-man Japanese patrol was moving toward them from the south. Signaling the team to silence, Sumner and his men lay hugging the ground, quiet as death itself.

The patrol was on a path, unseen by Sumner until now, that would take them just fifty feet from the Scouts' position. From their manner, Sumner knew they were not expecting trouble. They walked along almost casually. Their weapons, all bolt-action Arisaka rifles, were slung over their shoulders, and some were munching on fruit. The soldiers were all in good physical condition, wearing, for some reason, blue shorts with regulation short-sleeve shirts, socks, and the typical split-toe *jikatabi* rubber-soled shoes. The Scouts hugged the ground, not daring to breathe, as the patrol walked by, continuing off to the north.

Once the enemy was out of sight, Sumner told Blaise to conceal the radio as the team prepared to start their search.

As the sun continued its climb above the eastern horizon, its rays illuminated the buildings of the experimentation station, a few hundred yards to the south. Sumner could see six of them in various stages of disrepair, thanks to air corps bombs. From this distance, no signs of movement were evident, but a small plume of smoke rising from one indicated a cooking fire. Also now visible was a large, single-story house, just seventy yards to the team's right. The home's screened veranda faced the shore, giving its inhabitants a postcard-perfect view of the South Pacific.

Somewhere near the house, a rooster crowed.

"Maybe instead of the flyboys, we ought to rescue ourselves a chicken dinner," Jones muttered.

"We have to check it out," Sumner told Coleman. "If it's occupied, any Japs inside could block our return."

Using hand signals, Sumner directed the team toward the house, crawling forward two at a time. Twenty yards from the house, they came upon a depression, three feet deep and twenty feet wide and running north to south. They crawled into it. For the next fifteen minutes they lay there, watching for movement, but the only sign of life was the clucking of chickens.

Suddenly the door opened and a Japanese officer decked out in boots, light khaki breeches, a white shirt, open at the collar, and an olive drab jacket with red collar tabs, each with two or three stars, emerged. Stepping off the screened veranda, he calmly opened the front of his pants, and began to urinate.

Finishing his chore, he turned and strode off in the direction of the experimentation station, unaware of the Americans watching him barely fifteen yards away. Assigning Weiland and Jones to keep a watch to the rear for any sign of the return of the nine-man patrol, Sumner and the rest left the depression and approached the house. Entering, weapons at the ready, they found it empty, as Sumner had expected. As in any army, Japanese officers and enlisted men do not intermingle.

The team returned to the depression and, following Sumner, headed toward the experimentation station, moving forward, hunched over, in short rushes from cover to cover, until they got to within one hundred feet of the cluster of buildings.

The Scouts could hear voices, but could not be certain where the speakers were or what was being said. One thing was obvious, though. The men talking were not the Americans they were seeking, a point confirmed by laundry, including Japanese military garments flapping from a wash line in the light breeze.

Sumner, at the edge of the depression, took much of this in with his binoculars. Through the glasses, he watched a mess cook busily at work over a fire. Since the air corps had worked over the station, Sumner could see inside some of the buildings, where supplies were neatly stacked under what remained of the roofs.

To his left, Sumner saw a sailboat on stocks, near the water and hidden from aerial view.

After some few minutes of observation, he shifted the team a short distance to the west to afford a different perspective. From this vantage point, Sumner saw only one other man in one of the buildings, and no sign of the officer. He did, however, spot a smaller structure with several lead-in wires stretching from an extensive array of radio antennae. Personal equipment was also visible and the breeze carried to the Scouts the smell of whatever the cook was preparing.

Sumner handed the glasses to Coleman and indicated where he was to look.

"With that radio setup, this could be the headquarters that controls all the barge traffic along this part of the New Guinea coast," Sumner whispered. "The one thing I don't see that I had hoped to find is a guard shack where those flyboys might be kept prisoner. I don't see one. Nor does it seem like anyone's looking for them."

"That patrol earlier?" Coleman asked quietly.

"Routine," Sumner answered. "They were too casual to be a combat patrol."

"You think those air corps guys are dead?"

"And buried here on the island somewhere," Sumner said. "This place is just too damned small and too damned flat for them to hide out long." He looked at his watch. It was nearly nine a.m. They'd been onshore four hours. "Maybe we'll keep looking, but the longer we stay on this island, the better our chances of ending up in that Jap's cook pot."

Just then, Jones, on the right flank, spotted two Japanese heading in the Scouts' direction. As he passed the warning to the others, he saw two more enemy soldiers to the rear of the first pair. Sumner focused on them with his binoculars, estimating them to be about 150 yards away. Then, just as quickly as they were there, they were gone.

"That cuts it," Sumner said. "We've been seen."

A shrill whistle pierced the quiet air, grating on the Scouts' already taut nerves, followed by the flat crack of an Arisaka rifle. More firing broke out and the air became alive with the whizzing and buzzing of passing rounds.

"Make 'em duck," Sumner told Coleman, who cut loose with his grease gun, emptying a thirty-round magazine in the direction of the gunfire. The shooting stopped.

"Weiland, Blaise," Sumner said. "Keep a lookout for that patrol. Jones, you're the eagle-eye here. Have you seen any sign of those airmen?"

"No, sir," he replied.

The firing resumed from a stand of vegetation in front of the team, kicking up dirt plumes around them. Coleman sent another long burst of submachine-gun fire that way. Leaves and pieces of twigs flew in all directions, and the Japanese return fire, when it came, was greatly reduced.

Sumner was certain the airmen were dead, otherwise one of them would have tried to make their presence known at the first sound of the skirmish, particularly the distinctive ripping sound of the 450-rounds-per-minute submachine gun. No voices were heard, nothing to indicate they heard the battle.

"Back to the beach," Sumner said. "Weiland! Suppressing fire."

Weiland, a big grin creasing his face, aimed along the sights and, with the nineteen-pound BAR resting on its bipod, emptied a twenty-round clip at the Japanese, replaced it, and emptied another. All firing stopped and the team scurried along the depression, heads bent low.

★　★　★

Cruising just to the north of Pegun, McGowen and the men on the PT boat heard the gunfire echoing from the island.

"Shit," McGowen said. He turned to the PT commander. "Call for the cavalry."

"Already on it," the navy lieutenant said, his ship-to-ship radio mic in hand.

"Aguilar!" McGowen said. "Get that rubber boat ready."

★　★　★

It took just fifteen minutes for Sumner and his team to reach their pickup point. Thrashing noises from behind let Sumner know that Japanese were in pursuit. Sumner directed Weiland to provide a base of fire while he and the others dashed from the depression into the underbrush. They, in turn, covered his withdrawal.

At the beach, Blaise and Renhols recovered the radio, switched it on and, as soon as it warmed up, contacted McGowen. Out from the beach, they could see the PT boat swiftly approaching, then glide to a halt three hundred yards from shore.

"We've got company, sir," Blaise said into the handset.

"We know," McGowen replied. "Did you find the airmen? Over."

"Negative," Blaise said. "We are coming out."

"Roger," McGowen said.

With a nervous eye to the north, Sumner watched for the nine-man patrol he knew had to be hightailing it in his direction. He deployed his men in a defensive semicircle.

"Tell Red we need a point of reference," McGowen said into the radio. "We can't spot you in the underbrush."

Blaise relayed the message.

Sumner nodded. Hoping the Japanese had not yet discovered their exact position, he stood up and stepped out from the vegetation onto the sand, facing the sea. Renhols joined him, facing inland.

Blaise said, "Roger." Then to Sumner he said, "They see you, sir." The two remained standing, back-to-back, a human landmark.

*　　*　　*

At about this time, McGowen's radio crackled with a different voice. The pilot of an Australian Beaufighter, Flight Sgt. Mostyn "Mos" Morgan, who, along with his navigator, Flight Sgt. Fred Cassidy, was scanning radio frequencies, had picked up the conversation between the PT boat and the island.

After identifying himself as a member of the Royal Australian Air Force's 30 Squadron, Morgan said, "I don't mean to eavesdrop, mate, but could you use a hand? Over."

"In fact, yes," McGowen said, looking up at the approaching drone of the aircraft. "I have a six-man patrol with Japs to their front and the sea to their backs. We need to get them off. We could use some air support. Over."

"What an amazing coincidence, old man," Morgan quipped. "It just so happens I have an airplane. I'll stand by until I see your lads are clear. Over and out."

* * *

A burst of gunfire from Sumner's right alerted him to the fact that the much-anticipated arrival of the nine-man patrol had taken place. The firing also alerted the other enemy soldiers, who now began to close on the team's position. With the firepower he had, Sumner knew he could stave off the estimated thirty or so Japanese to his front. This new threat on his flank, however, made his situation more precarious. Blaise alerted McGowen to the new development.

"We can't provide covering fire because we can't see the positions of the rest of your team," McGowen said. "Stand by. We are sending the boat."

He turned to Aguilar.

"Ray! Get going."

Aguilar nervously hesitated. McGowen shot him a hard glare.

"I said go! Now, damnit."

Aguilar put the rubber boat over and he and a PT crewman climbed in and shoved off.

Sumner watched the PT eagerly. Farther out to sea, the frigate was in view, racing toward them at flank speed. In the distance, Sumner could hear heavy weapons fire. The other two PT boats were working over Fanildo and Bras, keeping the enemy's heads low and preventing them from sending reinforcements across the narrow channels to help their comrades on Pegun.

The sea was calm and the PT boat bobbed about three hundred yards offshore. Then the rubber boat emerged from the seaward side, turned, and, powered by Aguilar and the sailor, headed toward shore. Seeing the rubber boat, Sumner and Renhols dropped to a knee.

"They're dead meat on that thing," Coleman said, watching the rowers.

Sumner agreed.

"Unless we give the Japs something else to shoot at."

Coleman stared at him.

"Us?"

Sumner nodded, then said to all, "We're going to wade out backward to meet Aguilar. We don't have a choice. Jonesy, you're first. At my signal, fire to your left and head for the water. Go!"

Jones fired his carbine as ordered and scampered across the sand and into the surf. Turning to face inland, he began wading backward toward the approaching rubber boat. Japanese bullets splashed around him like jumping fish.

"Weiland, Coleman, suppressing fire. Renhols, firing to your right. Go."

As the automatic weapons sprayed the brush, Renhols dashed into the water, firing his carbine to the right. He followed the retreating Jones.

"Suppressing fire! Blaise, go."

Weiland, Coleman, and Sumner laid down covering fire as Blaise, lugging the thirty-five-pound radio with the handset still to his ear, took off across the sand and into the water after his two comrades.

The Japanese were doing everything they could to prevent the escape. Waterspouts from bullets kicked up all around the men.

"Weiland, you're next," Sumner said. "Reverse marching fire! Go."

As Coleman and Sumner laid down covering fire, Weiland stepped out of the vegetation and walked backward, sending three-round bursts from the BAR at the concealed enemy. Sumner marveled as Weiland, emptying one clip, expertly removed it, jammed it into his fatigue jacket, took a new one from his ammo pouch, rammed it home, and continued firing.

As Weiland entered the water, spraying lead to the left and front, the .30-caliber rounds buzzed by his team leader's head. Sumner called to Coleman, "Pull back on me, diversion fire to the front and right."

The two broke cover together and ran for the water, with Coleman laying down suppressing fire in all directions with short bursts from his submachine gun. Sumner thanked God for the hard, sandy ocean floor, which afforded good footing. In addition, the water got deeper the farther out they went, but not so deep that the men could not wade. In fact, the depth was perfect, since it left the men with only their heads and shoulders exposed, giving the Japanese small, hard-to-hit targets. Still the Japanese tried, and hot lead whirred and hissed into the water all around them. The fire seemed especially hot from the nine-man patrol on the right. Sumner ordered Weiland to direct his BAR in that direction.

As he waded backward, Sumner glanced over his shoulder. Jones and Renhols were just reaching the rubber boat, which was about a hundred yards offshore, and were being hauled into it by Aguilar and the sailor.

"We might make it after all," he thought.

★　★　★

Watching the watery escape from the PT boat, McGowen grinned.

"Outstanding," he said to himself.

The radio crackled. It was the Aussie pilot.

"I see six men in the water. Is that everyone? Over."

"It is," McGowen radioed back. "Give 'em hell, my friend. Over and out."

The Beaufighter winged over to the left and Morgan gunned his engines as he made his run toward the beach.

★　★　★

Waist-deep in the water, still facing the shore, Sumner was unaware of the air cover until he heard the whine of the two Bristol Hercules engines. Raising his eyes skyward, he saw the plane screaming down, lining up on the tree line. Then the Beaufighter's six heavy .50-caliber machine guns and four nose-mounted 20mm cannons opened fire, tearing up the vegetation just twenty-five yards in front of Sumner. To cut the margin of safety that close, Sumner knew, this guy had to be good.

A hundred feet off the ground, the Beaufighter, its engines roaring, raked the shore, sending clouds of dust and debris high into the air and diminishing the Japanese fire by half. The plane then climbed into the sky.

The PT boat held its fire until Sumner reached the rubber boat, then the eager gunners squeezed their triggers. Brightly burning tracer rounds streaked overhead and disappeared into the jungle. Between each tracer, Sumner knew, were five unseen rounds.

In the sky, the Beaufighter had completed his turn and came scream-ing down for a second pass. Again his guns hammered the Japanese positions, their heavy slugs shredding the vegetation as the men in the rubber boat cheered.

"God bless that Aussie," Coleman said, voicing the team's praise. "He saved our sorry asses."

Arms reached out and pulled Sumner into the rubber boat. Bullets from shore now had ceased, but not before a few struck home. Por-tions of the rubber boat had been hit and deflated, but the craft's internal compartmentalization kept it afloat. Manning every available oar, the men rowed the wounded, sluggish craft toward the PT boat, coming around the seaward side and out of the Japanese line of fire. Scouts threw their gear on board before climbing up themselves with the help of the contact team.

As Sumner reached the PT deck, he heard McGowen's radio crackle to life.

"Are all aboard? Over," Morgan asked.

"Recovery complete, no casualties. Over."

"Good show, Yanks. Tell your swagmen to keep their peaches up! Any sign of your other ranks? Over."

McGowen turned to Sumner, who shook his head.

"Apparently not," McGowen relayed. "Thanks much for your help, we are in your debt. If you get to Sixth Army HQ, look us up. The name is Lieutenant McGowen, and the beer's on us. Over."

"Right-o. Glad to help out. Cheerio," he said, and the plane faded away.

Once all were aboard and the damaged rubber boat recovered, the PT skipper opened his exhausts.

"Guess they know we're here now," he said.

He headed the eighty-foot Elco out beyond the reefs. The other two PT boats had by now returned, and the three opened fire on the island again. The skipper of the frigate, cruising about five miles out, came over the radio and asked for instructions.

"Near the southern end of the island are a cluster of shacks," Sumner said. "It's a supply base. You should be able to see the roofs."

Scanning with his binoculars, the frigate commander said, "Yeah. Got 'em."

Almost instantly, 40mm fire from the ship was directed at the experimentation station, followed by the loud boom of the five-inch guns. The shells tore through the air and burst among the buildings. Sumner watched in grim satisfaction as the huts seemed to dissolve under the heavy fire. The hidden sailboat, too, was blown into kindling. Then, at Sumner's direction, the frigate turned her guns on the officer's house, which was soon smothered by high-explosive rounds.

"I pity them poor, damned chickens," Jones said.

Despite the pounding they were taking, the Japanese sent small-arms and mortar rounds at the PT boats.

"Plucky bastards, aren't they?" Weiland said.

As the PTs lessened their fire, McGowen and Sumner descended below to the wardroom.

"That was by far the best show I've ever seen," McGowen said. "And your withdrawal from the island was brilliant. It took guts."

"There was no other way," Sumner said.

"True," McGowen agreed. "I know it made Aguilar unhappy. He was crappin' his pants at the prospect of rowing that rubber bull's-eye to shore."

"But he still came," Sumner observed.

McGowen said, "The PT boats are going off in another direction, so we will be transferring to the frigate at twelve hundred—that's about an hour from now. Meanwhile, tell me what you found onshore."

Sumner proceeded to brief McGowen on their movements after reaching the island, up to and including the moment they were spotted by the Japanese.

"I'm convinced General Patrick was right," he concluded. "Those men are dead. Had they been alive, they'd have tried to contact us, especially after we began mixing it up with the Nips."

An hour later, the team scrambled up cargo nets onto the frigate and, they felt, into the lap of luxury. Billeted in the sick bay for the eighteen-hour cruise back to Noemfoor, they had clean sheets, air-conditioning, showers, and the best food they had tasted in weeks.

After dining and cleaning up, the men turned in and slept soundly.

Not long afterward, the Australian fliers, Morgan and Cassidy, dropped by the Alamo Hotel, where they and the Scouts got happily sloshed.

★ ★ ★

Several nights after the Pegun Island mission, the propagandist Tokyo Rose broadcast that, "Imperial Marines have repulsed an Allied attack on the Mapia Islands with losses."

Jones guffawed at the report.

"Hey, baby," he said to the sultry voice on the radio. "We had no casualties, so it musta been your side who had the losses."

Three months later, on November 15, elements of the 2nd Battalion, 167th Infantry Regiment, Sumner's old unit, landed on Pegun Island with no enemy resistance. The Japanese were gone.

The commander, Lt. Col. Leon L. Matthews, reported that his troops had discovered the bodies of three enlisted men in a common grave. Two of them had their hands tied behind their backs with telephone wire and had been shot in the back of the head. Although none of them had dog tags, their uniforms bore markings of the army air corps.

★   ★   ★

On New Year's Day 1945, in a ceremony on Leyte, Sumner's men were each awarded the Bronze Star for their rescue attempt on Pegun Island.

CHAPTER 9

The Rescue at Cape Oransbari

The Nellist and Rounsaville Teams: October 4–5, 1944

On September 9, the ASTC graduated its fourth class, two teams under Lt. William E. Nellist of Eureka, California, and Lt. Thomas J. Rounsaville of Atoka, Oklahoma. Nellist, who had served with the 511th Parachute Infantry Regiment of the 11th Airborne during the fight at Buna, was an easygoing man. An avid duck hunter and fisherman since he was seven years old, he was at home in nature and had earned the nickname "the White Indian." A California National Guard rifle champion, he was the best marksman among all of the Alamo Scouts.

"Stud" Rounsaville, twenty-five, was also a rugged soldier, coming to the Scouts from the 187th Glider Infantry Regiment of the 11th Airborne. Tall and gangly, with a contagious sense of humor, the all-arms-and-legs Oklahoman was an exceptionally fine leader and tactician, as he was about to prove.

Rounsaville was justly proud of the tough and diverse team he had assembled. There was the Hawaiian-born Tech Sgt. Alfred "Opu" Alfonso and Sgt. Harold N. Hard, a schoolteacher from Coldwater, Michigan, and Pfc. Franklin Fox of Dayton, Ohio. Pfc. Francis H. Laquier was a Chippewa Indian from the White Earth Reservation in Early, Minnesota, who, like Rounsaville, had been a paratrooper. Laquier had served with the 503rd Parachute Infantry Regiment and, to Rounsaville's delight, had a keen eye for detail and could draw a map as well as any engineer. And last was Pfc. Rufo V. Vaquilar. Bearing the nickname "Pontiac," the outbreak of the war had found Vaquilar in a Pontiac, Illinois, jail. He won a pardon when he volunteered for the military and served, for a while, with the 1st Filipino Regiment until, at the ripe old age of thirty-four, he joined the Alamo Scouts.

Late September found the Rounsaville and Nellist teams attached to the Netherlands East Indies Administration on Roemberpon Island, three miles off the eastern coast of the Vogelkop. The Scouts had been keeping an eye on Japanese barge traffic and supply bases operating near the Maori River south of Manokwari. The duty had been relatively uneventful. They had spent the few weeks since their graduation "conducting small patrols on the mainland and with the navy riding around in PT boats," Nellist recalled. Then, on September 28, Rounsaville was approached by a Dutch lieutenant decked out in jungle fatigues topped by an Australian bush hat with the brim characteristically turned up.

Following up on Alamo Scout Bill Littlefield's mission from August, Lt. Louie Rapmund of the Netherlands-Indies Civil Administration was using Roemberpon as an evacuation point for Indian prisoners and natives who had been released by the Japanese on the Vogelkop. Rapmund had been told by one of the native men that the former Dutch governor of the area, along with his family and a number of native servants, was being held by the Japanese in a small village at Cape Oransbari, near the Maori River. Rapmund, accompanied by the ex-prisoner, passed the information to Rounsaville, who was in daily contact with 6th Army G2.

Although operations in New Guinea were nearing an end, so far as MacArthur and the top brass were concerned, there were still some 200,000 Japanese stranded on the big island and on smaller isles offshore in bypassed pockets of resistance. In several of these pockets the enemy held hostages, mostly Dutch, Melanesian, and Australian, usually serving as laborers for the emperor.

Some two thousand of these stranded Japanese were holed up around Cape Oransbari, and about thirty of those were in a small village-turned-prison-camp near the Maori River, two and a half miles inland from the coast.

Shortly after relaying the information to his headquarters, Rounsaville and his team, along with Rapmund and the former hostage, were paddling ashore at Cape Oransbari, landing at the mouth of the Wassoenger River, about six miles north of the village. The jungle terrain was difficult and it took several hours to pick their way through the tangled growth. Having finally arrived at the edge of the village, the Americans lay concealed as they observed and took notes. With his sharp eye and training, Rounsaville noted the approximate number of the enemy, the location of the huts, covered approaches leading to the village, and other details. Moving toward the coast, he mapped out an evacuation point, but found it guarded by a Japanese machine-gun emplacement. When Rounsaville felt he had all the information he needed, the men withdrew.

This would be a two-team job.

★ ★ ★

Like Rounsaville, Bill Nellist was an excellent soldier and tactician. One of the few married Scouts, he and his wife, Jane, had wedded shortly before shipping out. He was "rough and tough," she recalled in 2007.

Nellist originally planned to become a sniper because of his excellent marksmanship. He could hit rocks thrown into the air, as well as targets, by shooting backward over his shoulder with the aid of a mirror. Instead, he volunteered for the Alamo Scouts, and he and Rounsaville had been the only two officers retained from the fourth training class. They knew each other very well—how the other man thought, his abilities and talents—and they had formed a close bond.

Like Rounsaville, Nellist also felt he had assembled the best possible team. Twenty-four-year-old Sgt. Andy Smith was beyond tough. Voted the 6th Army's top athlete, he was a superb basketball player and a deadly accurate knife thrower. Pvt. Galen C. "Kit" Kittleson, formerly of the 503rd Parachute Infantry Regiment, was a top-notch soldier who had won the Silver Star for knocking out a Japanese machine-gun nest on Noemfoor. The team included two Filipinos in Pfc. Sabas A. Asis and Staff Sgt. Thomas A. Siason. Rounding out the group was Pfc. Gilbert Cox, a large man, built like a defensive football player, and Tech Sgt. Wilbert C. Wismer.

When informed by Rounsaville about the mission, Nellist eagerly joined in, and they decided to ask Lt. Jack Dove to serve as the contact. Dove assembled a scratch team of Tech Sgt. William Watson, Pvt. Charley Hill, and Naval Machinist Mate 1st Class K. W. Sanders. In addition, the escaped prisoner would accompany Rapmund, and, once ashore, the group would be met by three native guides secured by Rapmund.

On October 2, the teams arrived on Biak and held a briefing with 6th Army G2, laying out plans for the twelve-hour mission.

"The boats will drop us here," Rounsaville told the others as they bent over a map lying on a table in the briefing hut, "at the Wassoenger River. We will then have to walk about six miles to the village. Expect about thirty Japs there, but there are two thousand more some twenty miles away, so we get in, hit them, free the hostages, and get out as fast as possible. By the way, the guys holding the Dutch governor are Kempeitai, Jap secret police."

Using four PT boats, the flotilla slipped out of the base at Biak that evening, but were turned back by a heavy storm. The second attempt the next night was foiled when one of the PT boats hit a submerged log and bent a screw. On October 4, just after the tropical nightfall at five p.m., they tried again. Cruising across the black ocean on a moonless night, the PT boats slid to a halt off the dark coastline around midnight.

"Get the boats over the side," Rounsaville ordered.

While loading into the dinghies, Rapmund lost his balance and would have tumbled overboard had Kittleson not grabbed his web belt. Within a few minutes, three rubber boats were silently gliding toward shore, their occupants somewhat disconcerted by the newly risen bloodred moon that rode low in the eastern sky.

"Don't worry too much about being spotted," Rounsaville had told Nellist before departing. "Rapmund took the liberty of having all the native canoes in the area temporarily confiscated, so no night fishermen will see us and get a message to the Japs."

The beach was narrow—only about a yard wide—and as the Scouts came ashore forty-five minutes after leaving the PT boats, three dark-skinned natives, dressed in khaki shorts, materialized from the jungle.

"Kit," Rounsaville whispered to Kittleson. "You and one of the guides take the point. Everyone, stay together. It's blacker than a witch's heart in that jungle. Let's go."

As the teams disappeared into the dark woods, Dove and Charley Hill lashed the three rubber boats together and rowed back to the PT boats.

The dense canopy of foliage overhead blotted out what little moonlight there was, casting everything into pitch-darkness. The only natural light was the twinkling foxfire created by decaying vegetation. Despite the blackness, the natives quickly found the path that led away from the Wassoenger River toward their objective. The footpath was narrow and muddy, and Kittleson made his way forward by the red glow of a flashlight taped to the muzzle of his Tommy gun, its beam invisible fifty feet or more away. Others used red-hooded flashlights as well.

"Hell, the last thing the Japs will be expecting is for an enemy patrol to be snooping around the jungle at night carrying flashlights," Rounsaville said, when he OK'd their use.

Flashlights aside, even though the guides assured the Scouts that Japanese security was lax, the GIs were taking nothing for granted, and Kittleson tested each step before putting his weight down. After picking their way through the jungle in this fashion for more than two hours, Rounsaville ordered all flashlights doused, after which, Kittleson later recalled, the trip grew "hairy."

The trail took the men south, across Cape Oransbari, to the Maori River. As they neared the dark waterway, the distant but distinct *crack crack* of two rifle shots rang out in the dark. The Scouts froze and dropped to a knee. One of the guides said something to Rapmund, who told Nellist and Rounsaville, "The Japs hunt wild pigs at night." Rounsaville nodded, but the men waited unmoving in the brush for fifteen minutes. Then Nellist crept forward to tell Kittleson to move out. After reaching the bank of the Maori River, the Scouts held their weapons up and cautiously waded through the knee-deep water, just upstream of the village.

The low moon was below the tree line when the Scouts arrived at the village at about three a.m. In the darkness, they dropped to their knees within reach of each other to observe and listen. The scent of smoke was in the air—hopefully, Rounsaville thought, from last night's cook fires. The attack depended upon surprise.

Rounsaville turned to Rapmund.

"Think you could send one of the natives in to check things out?" he whispered, barely audible. "I need to confirm the number of Japs and where they are."

Rapmund nodded and then spoke softly to the former prisoner, who had served as an orderly for the Japanese garrison before he took flight. The man slipped away as quietly as a passing cloud. As they waited for the native's return, the men sat silently in the night, watching the village. A dog barked somewhere off in the darkness and a rooster crowed, both sounds eerie in the stillness of the jungle. About an hour later, the native returned, carrying three Japanese rifles he had stolen. He spoke to Rapmund, who whispered to Rounsaville. Rounsaville then gathered the men around him and spoke in a low voice.

"There are twenty-three Japs in the village and five manning the outpost," Rounsaville began. "Eighteen of them are asleep in the long nipa hut, which is set up on stilts. There's another hut about twenty yards beyond it with five more. That's the Kempeitai HQ. I'm told they have the governor there. By the shoreline are shallow machine-gun emplacements—a heavy Dutch MG and a light Jap gun. There are four men there. But there are no sentries anywhere so they must feel pretty damned safe."

"The hostages are confined to various huts in the village, with orders to stay inside or be shot."

Rounsaville nodded.

"We go at oh four hundred," he said. "That will give us all time to get in position. My first shot will be the signal."

The assault had been laid out beforehand, based on Rounsaville's earlier reconnaissance. It would be a three-prong attack with Rounsaville, his team, and Rapmund hitting the main barracks. Asis, Wismer, Smith, and one of the guides were to enter the Kempeitai hut, kill the soldiers, and take the commander prisoner if possible. Nellist, the rest of his team, and a guide were to trek to the coastline and knock out the gun emplacements. That was to be their exfiltration point, and Rounsaville needed the beach secured in order to call in Dove.

"Let's go," Rounsaville said.

The men split up and went about their assignments.

★ ★ ★

Rounsaville and his men slowly worked their way around the village through the underbrush and got into position near the long nipa hut. Palms and other vegetation grew around the outside of the makeshift barracks, so the space under the elevated hut was in total darkness. Signaling the others to follow, Rounsaville cautiously led his men up to the building, and then ducked under it, bending low so as not to bump their heads on the floor above. All was quiet from the room overhead except for the soft snoring of sleeping men.

Splitting the team in two, Rounsaville led some of the men to the ladder at one end of the hut, while the rest of the team moved toward the ladder at the opposite end. There they waited, sweat pouring from their bodies, nerves taut. Rounsaville kept an eye on his watch for what seemed like an eternity. When four a.m. finally arrived, he crept out from under the hut and slowly climbed the ladder. At the other end of the building, his men did the same thing. The doorways to the hut, as well as all of the windows, were covered in mosquito netting. Rounsaville slid the netting back and peeked inside. An oil lamp glowed dimly, casting deep shadows around the interior. A soldier wearing only a loincloth was putting a teapot on a woodstove. Rounsaville looked at Opu Alfonso, who was next to him, brandishing a Remington twelve-gauge pump-action shotgun with a flashlight, now minus its red hood, taped to the barrel, and nodded.

Rounsaville looked at his watch again. It was four ten a.m.

Taking a deep breath, he threw back the netting and stepped inside, flicking on his flashlight. He fired a lone round—the signal shot—into the man making the tea, then emptied his magazine at the sleeping forms. Scouts burst in from both doorways. The Japanese scrambled to get up as their peaceful slumber had suddenly been converted into a madhouse of gunfire, muzzle flashes, screams, and the blinding glare of flashlights. A few managed to reach for their weapons, but most died in their beds, cut down by the savage fire. A few dove through the windows, hit the ground, and scampered into the jungle. The Scouts fired after them as they ran. Two were hit and tried to seek shelter in a ditch, but the Scouts finished them off with quick, short bursts. Alfonso and Fox started chasing the other fugitives into the jungle.

"Let them go," Rounsaville called. "Let's gather up the hostages and get the hell out of here before they bring back help."

★   ★   ★

When Smith saw Rounsaville climb the ladder of the barracks twenty-five yards away, he, Asis, and Wismer gathered at the doorway to the Kempeitai hut. Inside, four Japanese were asleep, two in cots to the right of the door and two to the left. Another man, doubtless the Kempeitai officer, slept in a bed at the rear. Smith and Asis slipped inside, bumping into a bookcase in the dark. The thump did not wake the sleeping men. At the sound of Rounsaville's signal shot, Smith leveled his carbine at the two on the left and fired. Emptying the fifteen-round clip, he dropped it, reloaded, and resumed firing until there was no more movement.

"Sayonara, assholes. Pleasant dreams," he snarled after the second magazine was empty.

Meanwhile, Asis riddled the men to the right.

The officer was still in his bed, eyes open wide in surprise, watching the Americans. Smith approached him, leveling his carbine at the man. It had been decided earlier that he was to capture this officer, so Smith had memorized the phrase demanding his surrender. Now Smith told the man to give up and he would not be harmed.

The officer glared at him as Smith dropped his empty clip and loaded in a fresh one. The Japanese officer did not move.

"Surrender, you crazy sonofabitch," Smith yelled in English, having suddenly forgotten the phrase in the heat of the moment.

Without warning the officer threw back his mosquito netting and sprang at Smith, a bayonet materializing in his hand. Smith took a swipe at the officer's head with his weapon, but missed. Asis shot the man, who fell back on his bunk, dead. The Scouts found and freed the governor, then quickly searched the hut for documents. Finished, they stepped outside. Wismer slipped a phosphorous grenade from his belt, yanked the pin, and tossed it into the hut. The Willie Peter exploded and the hut began to burn.

★   ★   ★

The attack had taken less than three minutes. After the cease-fire order, the Scouts fanned out to search the rest of the village. The hostages huddled in their huts, uncertain of what was happening, until Rapmund began calling them out. As they were being collected, Rounsaville sent a runner to Nellist to have him radio Dove to send in the rubber boats.

In one hut, a Japanese radio was found. A few well-placed .30-caliber rounds converted it into junk. In another hut, Smith discovered a table holding a gramophone and several 78-rpm records, all American, including several by Bing Crosby. Smith put his weapon aside and removed Crosby's recording of "My Melancholy Baby" from its sleeve and placed it on the turntable. As Crosby began to croon,

Smith sat down on a crate, closed his eyes, and propped his muddy boots on the table to enjoy the music and think of home back in St. Louis.

As Smith was reveling in the moment, Vaquilar, the ex-con, strode in and, without a word, leveled his Tommy gun and sent a burst of lead buzzing by Smith's head. The startled Smith jumped to his feet.

"Goddamn it, Pontiac, what the hell are you shooting at!" Smith screamed at Vaquilar, who stood there, smoke curling from the muzzle of the Thompson. "The fucking fight is over!"

Vaquilar, who spoke little, simply nodded and left the hut. A shuffling noise behind Smith caused him to turn. A Japanese soldier, blood pumping from holes in his tunic, a gleaming bayonet fixed firmly on his rifle, was leaning against the bullet-scarred rear wall. Smith watched as the soldier began to sink slowly to the floor and fall dead just behind where he had been relaxing.

Smith stared at the dead man, then at the record player from which Crosby's voice still crooned unconcernedly, and sighed, "Jesus Christ."

It would be the last time Smith would let down his guard on a mission.

Rounsaville and the others, meanwhile, had assembled all of the hostages. The Dutch governor, who spoke English, was dazed but otherwise in good shape. With him was his wife and twelve children, ages seven through teenage. The Scouts also freed his native staff, mostly women and children, the men having either been executed by the Japanese or fled into the jungle. However, instead of the thirty-two prisoners Rounsaville had planned on, he found he now had sixty-six captives to bring out.

After all the hostages were freed and the village scoured for documents, the Scouts went about tossing phosphorous grenades into the huts until all were burning briskly, the bamboo walls and thatched roofs crackling. Smoke and flaming embers drifted into the night sky as the Scouts led the captives toward the pickup point. It had been just four minutes since the first shot had been fired.

★   ★   ★

Because of the dense jungle, Nellist had not heard Rounsaville's signal shot, nor the gunfire that followed.

Reconnoitering the Japanese defensive position, he had discovered a bamboo hut with a palm-thatched roof, mounted on stilts. A ladder led up to a small porch. Nearby were three foxholes, two of which held machine guns. None of the guns were attended.

Nellist waited anxiously for Rounsaville's signal. At one point he and his men had been forced to lie low as two Japanese soldiers emerged from the hut. One man carried his tunic and stepped into the bushes nearby to relieve himself. The other spoke to him as he stoked the fire and put a pot of water on to boil. One of the men, possibly having heard some slight noise, rose, picked up his rifle, and walked to within a few yards of where Kittleson and Siason lay hiding. He spoke to his comrade, who said something back, and the man returned to the fire. Two other soldiers now emerged and strolled into the bushes to attend to nature.

After waiting close to an hour for the signal, Nellist decided he needed to attack. He and Cox, who carried a twelve-gauge Remington automatic shotgun, crept to within ten yards of the fire. Then Nellist, one of the few Scouts who used a Garand, took aim and fired. The impact of the round tossed his man over onto his back. Cox leveled his shotgun and blasted the second man, who was thrown as if hit by a brick.

Kittleson and Siason leaped to their feet, ran forward, and cut down the other two. Siason saw an unexpected fifth man dive into the bushes, and, investigating, found an officer, pistol in hand but too terrified to fire. Siason leveled his carbine and squeezed off three rounds.

"Bastard," the Filipino hissed at the dead man.

"Search them to make sure they're dead," Nellist said. "Check the hut for documents, then burn it. And grab those two machine guns."

While this was being done, Rounsaville's runner arrived and Nellist got on the radio to Dove.

"Nellist One," he said. "Recover."

"Roger," Dove replied.

Dawn sunlight was starting to stream in through the trees when the caravan of Scouts and freed hostages arrived. As preparations were made to depart, Alfonso thought he heard a noise in the jungle, and pumping a round into his shotgun, he went to investigate. A skinny white man jumped up from the undergrowth, shouting in broken English, "Me no Jap. Me Frenchman. Me got wife and ten children. Go with you."

"What the hell?" Alfonso muttered to himself, then said to the frightened man, "Well, come on if you're goin.'"

Thus, the Scouts' troupe of refugees was increased by twelve, bringing the total number of escapees waiting to board the PT boats to seventy-eight. By seven a.m. the boats were idling offshore and the loading had begun. It was a slow, tedious process, as Dove's scratch team helped the civilians get from the beach to the boats while the Scouts set up a defensive perimeter around the pickup point. When all was done, the eighty-foot Elcos were jammed with bodies fore and aft.

As the PT skippers pointed their bows toward Biak and sped for home lest they be caught in the open by enemy aircraft, the refugees, happy their ordeal was over, broke out in song. Regaling the Americans with the Dutch national anthem, they gleefully pounded the Scouts and sailors on the back.

News of what Rounsaville later called a "flawless mission" and a "textbook operation" brought instant recognition to the previously unknown Alamo Scouts. Although the mission was officially classified until February 1945, word leaked out and on October 13, 1944, less than ten days after the completion of the mission, Bradshaw's hometown newspaper back in Mississippi, the *Jackson Daily News*, ran a headline proclaiming, BRADSHAW WINS MEDAL FOR TRAINING PACIFIC SCOUTS and told of his being awarded the Legion of Merit by General MacArthur for the Oransbari raid. Two days later an Associated Press war correspondent, Murlin Spencer, arrived to pen a three-part story recounting the exploits of the Scouts.

As for Nellist and Rounsaville, their adeptness in delivering the prisoners unscathed from Japanese hands would not be forgotten by Krueger. In January 1945, they would be called upon to repeat this performance as part of another rescue mission, this time in the Philippines at a POW camp near the city of Cabanatuan.

* * *

The rescue at Cape Oransbari marked the last mission by the Alamo Scouts in the New Guinea area during World War II. Between February and October 1944, the Scouts conducted thirty-six missions, from Los Negros in the Bismarcks to Sansapor on the Vogelkop. They had been awarded nineteen Silver Stars, eighteen Bronze Stars, and four Soldier's Medals. They had rescued five hundred civilians, killed eighty-four Japanese soldiers, and captured twenty-four more without loss to themselves other than men hospitalized by jungle ailments.

Their next stop would be the Philippines.

CHAPTER 10

"Maybe We Can Save the World."

Leyte and Samar Missions: October–December 1944

In the early morning hours of Friday, October 20, 1944, Gen. Douglas MacArthur stood on the bridge of the cruiser USS *Nashville* and watched with satisfaction as ships of Adm. Thomas Kincaid's 7th Fleet and Adm. William F. Halsey's 3rd Fleet pounded the coastline of the island of Leyte with their big guns. Through binoculars, he followed LSTs and Higgins boats loaded with men and tanks of General Krueger's 6th Army as they circled the troopships like gnats, then turned and headed for land. Seeing the smoke and the flame, and hearing the rumble of battle from the distant shore, MacArthur smiled grimly. This was the day of fulfillment of the promise he had made thirty-one months earlier after his harrowing escape from Corregidor on Lt. John Bulkeley's seventy-seven-foot plywood boat. This was the first day of his retribution against those who had caused his defeat and humiliation.

This was his return to the Philippines.

Code-named Excelsior, the Philippines stretch for 1,150 miles, which, if laid over a map of the United States, translates to the distance from the Great Lakes to Florida. The archipelago's 7,083 islands, of which just 466 are larger than one square mile in size, cover 114,400 square miles. In 1944, only 2,773 of the islands, or about a third, bore names, and only between 600 and 700 were inhabited by any people, many of whom spoke a language called Tagalog.

Called Hito or Firippin by the Japanese, the Philippines were vital to Nippon as a natural barrier between the advancing Allied tide, the Japanese homeland, and their Dutch East Indies conquests, with their wealth of much-needed natural resources, particularly oil and rubber. Or at least what resources could safely slip through the American submarine network, which was taking an ever-higher toll on merchant shipping.

Volcanic in origin, the Philippines largely consist of rocky terraced ridges and deep valleys, mostly running north to south. Hardwood forests of teak, ebony, and cypress cover 70 percent of the land, while the lowland plains are extremely fertile.

Leyte, the island chosen for the Americans' initial assault, is the perfect example. Located 340 air miles south of Manila, Leyte is 115 miles long and 45 miles wide. The eighth largest island in the chain, most of its 2,799 square miles is rugged, mountainous terrain, with a narrow coastal plain to the south, which widens to 5 to 10 miles in the central area, facing Leyte Gulf, where Krueger's men were now coming ashore. To the north, the island's coastal plain becomes the 25-mile-wide Leyte Valley, running out to the Samar Sea. Climate-wise, there is on average only ten degrees difference between Leyte's hottest and coldest months, and rainfall, as the Americans were about to find out, averages seventy inches a year, with some spots getting two hundred inches, especially during the monsoon season of October to April.

About one million people called Leyte home in 1944, mostly in the more hospitable northern region, especially in the Leyte and Ormoc valleys and near the city of Tacloban, which had a population of thirty-one thousand and sits at the mouth of the San Juanico Strait, which divides Leyte from Samar. Tacloban was especially poignant for MacArthur, for it was here that he had first come, fresh from West Point, to the Philippines as a second lieutenant exactly forty-one years and one day earlier, on October 19, 1903.

The island's biggest asset, however, was its magnificent anchorage in Leyte Gulf.

★   ★   ★

The invasion MacArthur was now observing from the bridge of the *Nashville* almost did not come to pass. Adm. Chester W. Nimitz, MacArthur's coequal in the Pacific, did not share the general's passion for retaking the Philippines. Unlike MacArthur, his pride was not tied up in the islands, and he proposed a strike directly at Formosa. This, he argued, would seal off the Dutch East Indies from Japan and place U.S. forces in a position to land in China at Hong Kong, or maybe Formosa, and establish airfields from which to bomb Japan into oblivion.

MacArthur countered that the Philippines were American soil, and that national pride demanded they be freed from Japanese control. Besides, he said, it would be easier to take and the Filipinos were loyal and could be counted on to give the utmost help.

To sort out the difference, FDR ordered Nimitz and MacArthur to meet with him in Honolulu in July. MacArthur bristled at the order from "Mr. Big," as the secret order referred to the president, complaining about "the humiliation of forcing me to leave my command and fly to Honolulu for a political picture-taking junket."

But the "junket" proved successful. FDR supported the Philippine operation.

Planning for the return to the Philippines began on September 21, 1944, and called for U.S. forces to hit the southernmost island, Mindanao, the second largest in the chain. However, aerial reconnaissance reported meeting so little resistance that the high command decided to bypass Mindanao and go straight to Leyte, just to the north across Surigao Strait. In addition, Halsey was encouraged by reports from a downed pilot who had been rescued by a submarine, and by reports from other fliers, that Leyte was more lightly defended than first thought. Indeed, U.S. planners began to believe the entire central Philippines were a hollow shell.

The date for Operation Cyclone, as the invasion of Leyte was code-named, was set for December 20, but was advanced two months in light of Halsey's reports.

The attack was to be led by the 6th Army under General Krueger, and would be launched along an eighteen-mile front north to south from San Jose to Dulag. This would secure the Tacloban area, as well as sealing off the San Juanico Strait and isolating Samar island to the north. As a prelude, the 6th Army Rangers would strike the offshore islands of Dinagat, Suluan, and Homohon on October 18, knocking out any observation posts and radar stations that might forewarn the Japanese of American intentions. On the night of October 19, the Rangers would set up beacon lights to guide the fleet into the gulf toward the invasion beaches.

The Japanese garrison on Leyte consisted of twenty-three thousand men of Lt. Gen. Shiro Makino's 16th Division, reputed to be the toughest unit in the 35th Army. Except for four companies detached to Samar, most of Makino's men were concentrated to the north, in the Ormoc area, where they would defend Leyte in depth. There would be little resistance on the beaches. Makino's job was to fight the Americans for as long as he could, buying time for General Yamashita and the 14th Army to bolster defenses on the main island of Luzon.

For the Alamo Scouts, the Philippine campaign would mark a change in their operations. Now, instead of reconnaissance missions to scout possible beach landing zones and enemy numbers and defenses, they would conduct intelligence-gathering missions ranging from three to seventeen days, during which, for the most part, they would work closely with Filipino guerrilla groups. They would arrange for the resupply of arms, ammunition, medical supplies, and other materials to the guerrillas, as well as coordinate guerrilla movements with American troops advances, and establish radio networks to report on Japanese activity.

★   ★   ★

At one p.m. on Friday, October 13, four Alamo Scout teams under Bill Nellist, Tom Rounsaville, Jack Dove, and Wilbur Littlefield boarded the PT tender *Wachapreague* at the Woendi Island PT base, their destination being Leyte. After a refueling stop at Palau on October 16, and slogging through rough seas on October 19, the ship dropped anchor in Leyte Gulf on October 21; the invasion onshore was twenty-four hours old. There, in Leyte Gulf, they were surrounded by the powerful 3rd Fleet, which included sixteen aircraft carriers, six sleek new battleships, and eighty-one cruisers and destroyers. Closer to shore was Kincaid's 7th Fleet, with several smaller escort, or jeep, carriers, and a few of the navy's older battleships. While the 3rd Fleet was to protect against an attack by Japanese naval units, the 7th Fleet, also known as MacArthur's Fleet, provided support for the men on Leyte. The Scouts watched from the ship's rail as the battleship USS *West Virginia*, which had been sunk at Pearl Harbor almost four years before, lobbed shells at unseen targets on the island.

On October 23, the fleet was subjected to a Japanese air raid. The sky filled with antiaircraft fire and, as the Scouts watched, a Japanese plane, trailing smoke and flame, arced downward into the sea a few hundred yards from their tender. Anxious to get off the vulnerable ship, the men were relieved when they were able to go ashore on October 25, even though they had yet to be given a mission.

★   ★   ★

The Lutz Team was sent to Leyte ahead of the other Scouts. Arriving with the invasion force aboard the PT tender *Oyster Bay*, the team—minus Cpl. Cliff Gonyea, who had been recalled to the 31st Division and replaced by Staff Sgt. Glendale Watson—had come ashore on Red Beach with the landing force on October 20. The fighting front had moved inland, but enemy snipers still abounded, either tied to their posts in some of the tall trees or hidden in camouflaged foxholes called *takotsubo*, or octopus traps. There, they kept GIs ducking until rooted out and killed.

Despite the fact that the war was just half a mile inland, the beach, Jack Geiger recalled, looked as if "Hollywood had set it up." There were microphones, recording equipment, and photographers milling about, watching as a landing craft made its way toward a pier that jutted out over the water. The craft ran aground fifty yards from shore. After a few minutes' hesitation, the ramp was lowered and several men walked down it, stepping into the surf. The lead man, in pressed khakis, sunglasses, and gold-braided cap, clenching a long-stemmed pipe in his mouth, was unmistakable. MacArthur strode through the knee-deep water—he had hoped to come ashore dry at the pier—with determined steps, covering the distance in forty paces. He was followed by Sergio Osmena, the Philippine president since the death in July of Manuel Quezon. Newspaper photographers snapped away.

Stepping to a microphone, MacArthur said, "People of the Philippines, I have returned." After a few remarks by Osmena, everyone climbed into jeeps and sped off.

Geiger shook his head in wonder and said, "Boy. That was a great opportunity for a sniper. I wonder where they were."

★ ★ ★

While Mindanao had been bypassed in favor of a landing on Leyte, Allied planners still considered putting troops ashore. To pave the way for a possible invasion, Bill Nellist was called into a briefing on October 20.

"So long as the Japs control northern Mindanao, they could threaten our operations in southern Leyte and maybe even seal off the Surigao Strait," Nellist was told by a 6th Army G2 officer. "We're going to put you ashore. We want you to check into Jap troop strength and defenses, as well as look for possible landing beaches, water sources, road networks, and so forth."

On the night of October 23, Nellist and his team boarded PT-132, the *Sea Bat*, under Ens. Paul H. Jones, the same boat and skipper that had taken Sumner's team on its Geelvink Bay excursion back in July.

Traveling at night to avoid roaming Japanese Zeros, a PT boat's worst enemy in daylight, Jones and his boat arrived off Mindanao near the small coastal village of Ipal, around six a.m. The Scouts rowed ashore, where they were met by their contact, a short, dark native man in dirty khaki shorts carrying an old American-made '03 Springfield rifle. The man was overjoyed to see them, and in Tagalog told them of a 75mm gun at an eight-man outpost near Bilaa, overlooking the beach where the Scouts had landed. The Japanese had seen them, he said, but had held their fire. Nellist asked the man to send a runner to the headquarters of the 114th Guerrilla Regiment to inform them that they were coming, and to supply a guide to lead the team up into the hills.

En route to the camp, the team met a group of guerrillas advancing toward them carrying American and Philippine flags. They led the Scouts to the guerrilla camp, where Nellist was introduced to the group's leader, Philippine army lieutenant Jones B. Castillo. The guerrilla band consisted of forty to fifty men, who were gathered in a bamboo hut when Nellist arrived. Nellist noted that their arms consisted of old Springfields, assorted Japanese rifles, a Japanese mortar, and an aging American Gatling gun.

The Scouts spent the next several days patrolling the valley with the guerrillas, reporting back any findings to Siason, who had set up a radio station in the camp. The guerrillas reported that a twenty-seven-man Japanese patrol, aware of the Americans' presence, had kidnapped four native men, including the chief of the village of Ipal, bound them, and were taking them to the nearby Kempeitai unit.

"We can cut them off and hit the bastards and free the hostages," Kittleson suggested.

Nellist thought for a moment, then said, "No. Our mission is to pinpoint the Jap garrison, defenses, and gun emplacements. We have our orders."

He then directed Asis and Smith to check out a Japanese observation point reportedly manned by forty men with a heavy machine gun, and told Kittleson and Cox to see if they could spot any more barges hidden in a nearby cove. As the men prepared to go about their assignments, Nellist took Kittleson aside.

"Kit," he said. "I'd like to have acted on your suggestion, but I have to think of our mission first. We can't save everybody, but maybe we can save the world."

★ ★ ★

The team's pickup from Mindanao did not go well. On the night of October 26, huddled by the water's edge, Nellist flashed three blinks of his flashlight seaward. He waited, then flashed the signal again. No response.

"Something's wrong," he said, then told Siason to turn on the radio. Nellist finally made contact with Lt. Jack Dove, who was coordinating their pickup. After talking briefly to Dove, Nellist hung up the receiver and turned to his men.

"The boats aren't coming," he said. "The Jap navy is coming through Surigao Strait. We'll move to the alternate location and try again tomorrow night."

The new rendezvous point was three hundred yards south of the village of Ipal. During the night, as they hiked up and down the mountain ridges toward their new pickup point, far out in Surigao Strait they watched the sky light up from searchlights and muzzle flashes and heard the faint roll of distant naval gunfire.

"Somebody's catchin' hell out there," Andy Smith muttered.

The next morning, the Scouts saw smoke billowing from burning ships. Overhead, Japanese floatplanes hovered like carrion birds.

"Wonder who won last night," Cox said.

"We'll find out if no one is there to pick us up tonight," Nellist replied.

As they resumed their hike, the team continued their reconnaissance. A native runner found Nellist and informed him of a small Japanese force that had landed in barges at Bilaa Point. Nellist led his team in that direction, arriving around seven p.m. There he discovered that two barges had put ashore a thirty-eight-man observation team, who had established an outpost equipped with a heavy machine gun. The barges were still moored to a jetty. Pinpointing the site, the team withdrew and headed for their pickup site.

Two PT boats, Jones's *Sea Bat* and PT-326, the *Green Harlot*, commanded by Ens. Howard L. Terry, arrived the next night with Jack

Dove on board. "Thank God," Nellist thought as he received Dove's signal that the boats were standing by.

Rubber boats were dispatched to pick the team up, manned by members of Tom Rounsaville's team, which had been aboard the *Green Harlot* coming back from a mission of their own. Their arrival back on the *Sea Bat* left a lasting impression on the sailors. One crewman, Motor Machinist Mate 1st Class Sherb Bowers, who operated the forward twin .50-caliber gun tub, later wrote that he had never "seen a more qualified bunch of mean, vicious, murderous-looking sons of bitches than them Alamo Scouts.

"I mean those bastards would kill you, and give you change," he wrote. "Everything about them said *kill.*"

As soon as the Scout team had been recovered, Nellist reported the Japanese observation post to Jones.

"Let's go leave our calling card," Jones said.

With their engine exhausts muffled in the water, the two boats skimmed silently through a Japanese minefield—the five-and-a-half-foot draft of the PT boats being too shallow to set off the explosives—and approached the position Nellist had indicated. Just offshore, the two boats opened fire with everything they had. Machine-gun tracers and 20mm and 40mm shells arced through the darkness, raking the coastline. The barges were "blown to smithereens," Jones later recalled. Fuel drums exploded in huge balls of fire, setting the water aflame. Another barge was spotted pulled up on the beach by a small shack. The boats came about and poured deadly fire on the position, shredding the barge and hut, as more gas and ammo exploded onshore.

Some meager Japanese fire came back at them, and in the melee the 326 boat ran aground. Jones steered the *Sea Bat* around, a rope was thrown, and, as the crews continued firing at the enemy, the *Green Harlot* was pulled free. The reprieve was short-lived, for soon the *Sea Bat* was wedged on some underwater coral. Instantly, Jones, along with crewmen Quartermaster 2nd Class Herb Betz, the chief engineer, and Boatswain's Mate 2nd Class Donald Koepke, leaped into the water.

Col. Frederick Bradshaw, the original commanding officer of the new all-volunteer reconnaissance unit named the Alamo Scouts.

Sgt. Bill Blaise earned two Silver Stars and a Bronze Star while serving with the Sumner Team.

The Alamo Scouts receive training in hand-to-hand combat, Fergusson Island, January 1944.

Instructor Preston Roland fires a tommy gun at Alamo Scout trainees in the water as Scout commander Frederick Bradshaw (*center, with hands on hips*) and Gen. Innis Swift (*right, in helmet*) look on. Fergusson Island, January 1944.

Sumner Team members Harry Weiland (*left*) and Bill Blaise at weapons training.

Scouts on a twenty-six-mile training hike through the jungle on Fergusson Island, February 1944.

Class 3 graduates from the Alamo Scout Training Camp stand at attention. Finschafen, June 22, 1944.

Team leader Lt. John McGowen.

Team leader Lt. Robert Sumner.

Sgt. Terry Santos in the Philippines, circa 1944.

Santos speaks at the Alamo Scouts reunion
in October 2007.

Sgt. John "Jack" Geiger.

2nd Lt. Irvin Ray.

Lt. Bill Littlefield, circa 1944.

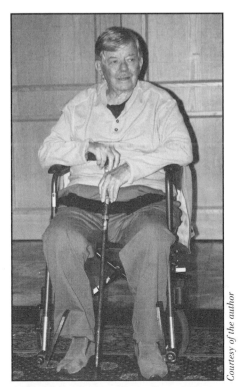

Bill Littlefield at the Alamo Scout reunion
in 2007.

Lutz and McGowen teams on a PT tender after the mission to Salebaboe Island.

Courtesy of the U.S. Navy

PT 132, the *Sea Bat*, which took Scout teams on several missions.

Courtesy of the Alamo Scout Association

Alamo Scouts in a rubber boat rowing ashore from PT 379.

Nellist and Rounsaville teams after the legendary Cabanatuan Raid: (*rear, from left*) Gil Cox, Wilbert Wismer, Harold Hard, Andy Smith, Francis Laquier; (*front, from left*) Galen Kittleson, Rufo Vaquilar, Bill Nellist, Tom Rounsaville, and Frank Fox.

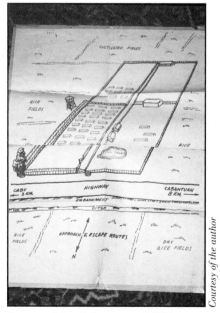

A map of the Cabanatuan POW camp, now in the possession of Alamo Scout Harold Hard.

Courtesy of the U.S. Army

(*From left*) Alamo Scout leaders Tom Rounsaville, Bill Nellist, Robert Sumner, and John Dove, after the four received Bronze Star medals on January 1, 1945. Rounsaville, Nellist, and Dove received medals for their participation in the Cabanatuan raid, Sumner for the Pegun Island rescue mission.

The Sumner Team after receiving the Bronze Star for the Pegun Island mission, January 1, 1945: (*rear, from left*) Harry Wieland, Paul Jones, and Ed Renhols; (*front, from left*) Bob Sumner, Lawrence Coleman, and Bill Blaise.

The Nellist Team after the Cabanatuan Raid: (*rear, from left*) Gil Cox, Wilmer Wismer, and Andy Smith; (*front, from left*) Galen Kittleson and Bill Nellist.

Alamo Scout team leader Bill Littlefield (*left*) speaks to Scout Lee Hall (*right*) at the 2007 Scout reunion in Denver. Sitting between them is Les McConnell, son of Scout Zeke McConnell.

Lee Hall, who graduated among the first class of Scouts in 1944, with his wife, Maude, at the 2007 reunion.

Scouts and family at the 2007 reunion dinner: (*from left*) Terry Santos, Bob Buschur, Rita Buschur, Maude Hall, and Lee Hall.

Several Scouts joined them and, with the *Sea Bat*'s XO, Bob Muller, throwing the boat into reverse, rocked the 132 loose.

When the men in the water reboarded, they found Jones was missing. A strong current had swept him away. Struggling desperately, he freed himself and made it to shore.

"Get a boat over the side," Nellist ordered, after Jones was spotted. "Then get us a little closer and give us covering fire."

The PT laid down a "murderous stream of fire," Bowers wrote, and in a strange reversal of fortune, it was Alamo Scouts picking up a PT skipper instead of the other way around. They delivered the wet, and somewhat chagrined, Jones back to his vessel.

"I thought I was a goner," he said, safely back on board.

But the bad news wasn't over. The coral had badly damaged one of the *Sea Bat*'s propellers. Worse, two of her three engines had quit, cutting her speed to about ten to twelve knots. It was about two a.m. and they had 120 miles to go to reach safety, hopefully before the sun came up.

"That's not good," Dove told Nellist. "We have to run up Surigao Strait and across Leyte Gulf to Tacloban, and that's four hours with a healthy boat. We need to put as much water as possible between here and there before daylight because this whole area is crawling with Jap ships and planes."

He told Nellist of the big naval fight on October 25, a three-prong Japanese attack that history would dub the Battle of Leyte Gulf.

"That's why we couldn't get you last night," Dove said. "Every available ship in this area was engaged. The navy sank two Nip destroyers and two battleships, but up north, at Leyte Gulf, another Jap force got in among our jeep carriers and raised hell."

★   ★   ★

The trip back was as miserable and slow as expected as the *Sea Bat* limped her way through Surigao Strait, her bent screw rattling horribly. The *Green Harlot* kept pace protectively. The PT crewmen offered the Scouts food on the trip, but the GIs' appetites were diminished in part, thanks to the six-foot ocean swells that tilted the 132 boat up and down in a sickening motion.

At four a.m. the boats were illuminated by a harsh spotlight. The light came from the Royal Australian Navy ship HMAS *Hobart*, and a booming voice through a loudspeaker ordered them to halt and give the password. Jones did, but was told it was no longer valid. A new word had made the rounds in the PT boats' absence. In response, he began shouting "Babe Ruth" and "Betty Grable" and other things over the radio, trying to convince the Australians he was an American. But the Australian officer was taking no chances.

"You will heave-to until dawn to be recognized," Jones was told.

The boats sat about a thousand yards from the ship for another two hours, then tried again to move. Darkness was running out. But the Australians prevented their leaving, threatening to blow the PTs out of the water if he tried.

Jones snapped.

"Goddamn you," he bellowed into the mic. "I have a crippled boat, and waiting here until daylight makes us a target for every fucking Nip plane in the Philippines."

There was a pause from the *Hobart*.

"Stand by to be boarded," the voice said.

"Aye, aye," Jones said. Then to Nellist and Dove he snarled, "Do you fuckin' believe this?"

A boarding party soon arrived in a whaleboat, and once the Australians were satisfied that the PT boat was not loaded with Japanese infiltrators, Jones was given the OK to proceed.

"This is bullshit," Jones cursed to the Australian in charge. He pointed to the east, where the first streaks of dawn were painting the horizon. "This crap is going to get me and my passengers killed."

"I'm sorry," the Australian lieutenant said. "I have my orders. You may proceed."

They left and Jones fired up the remaining Packard and wended his way through what he could now, in the early dawn, see was a screen of destroyers and light cruisers. Once beyond the ships, he pushed the throttles open as far as he dared. The *Sea Bat* rattled as if she was going to shake herself apart. The *Green Harlot* dutifully kept pace to starboard.

★ ★ ★

At around eight a.m., the Japanese found them.

Cruising a mile south of the island of Dulag, still twenty-five miles from their base, the 132's young radar man, Ray Vining, called out, "Five bogies, coming in from the east."

The crewmen at general quarters scanned the sky but saw nothing. Jones, in the cockpit, removed his shirt and hung it over the cockpit door and said to Muller, who was steering the boat, "Well, it looks like—"

Then came the cry, "Japs!"

It came from Scout Gil Cox, who was standing on the starboard side with Kittleson.

The first plane came in low, using the backdrop of Dulag to help hide its approach. It came in so low, Kittleson recalled, that he could see the pilot's white *Hachimaki* headband with its brightly painted rising sun in the center.

The Zero's nose-mounted machine guns opened up, raking the *Sea Bat*, and two hundred-pound bombs dropped from the plane.

"Incoming! Hit the deck!" Kittleson yelled.

He and Cox dropped behind a torpedo tube just as the bombs hit the water close by the *Sea Bat*'s port side. Geysers of water lifted from the sea and descended onto the men and boat as shrapnel tore through the already injured craft.

In the forward gun tub, Bowers swung his gun around, but not in time. Shrapnel from the bombs ripped through his position, tearing off his kapok flack jacket and leaving him slashed and bloodied.

"I figured I'd been cut in half," he wrote. Later, at the hospital, surgeons would dig kapok out of Bowers's insides.

Kittleson heard Bowers scream in pain when hit. He jumped up and ran to the gun tub. Stepping over the injured sailor, he swung the weapon up at the plane, but his sudden movement, plus the wind-driven spray from the fighter's propeller as it zoomed by overhead, nearly blasted Kittleson overboard.

Shrapnel from the same bombs that wounded Bowers also riddled the cockpit. Jones received a slight head injury and a more serious wound in his side, and the *Sea Bat*'s XO, Muller, had the back of his neck and both shoulders gashed. A wound to his left arm left that hand paralyzed for eight months.

Vining, the young radar man, was mortally wounded.

Shrapnel from another bomb that landed just astern of the *Sea Bat* struck Torpedoman 2nd Class William J. Speer, a twenty-year-old North Hollywood boy who had transferred from submarines to PT boats and served as the *Sea Bat*'s 40mm loader. Hit in the back and abdomen, he was dead within fifteen minutes.

Motor Machinist Mate 2nd Class (MoMM2c) Bill Fox, who had been in the engine room but had just come topside and was talking to Speer, was hit in the leg and thrown into the cable near the engine room hatch. MoMM2c Bob "Parry" Parazinski, at the 20mm mount with MoMM3c Dewey Hiner, was struck in the foot. Fox, who at twenty-seven was the "old man," took over Parazinski's position, but could no longer see the Japanese plane.

Radioman 3rd Class (RM3C) Owen Beach, a twenty-year-old New Englander at the number-two twin .50, saw a bomb drop, recalling, "It had a large detonator, like a stinger, about eighteen inches long." He ducked down as it exploded and got a small nick on his leg, but he never got off a shot from his machine guns.

With both Jones and Muller down, RM3c Thomas Gibson, after sending out a distress signal, took over the boat. He thought of his assistant, young Vining, who just a day earlier had confided to chief engineer Bowers the fear that he was going to die.

"Don't worry about it," Bowers had told him, trying to calm the boy's nerves. "We're gonna make it fine. I got two years in here, and we're gonna be all right."

Now Vining's fears had come true. In fact, within minutes, half the

Sea Bat's crew were casualties, including two, Vining and Speer, who were dead or dying.

The Alamo Scouts fared a bit better.

About an hour before the attack, Jack Dove had gone below to get some sleep. He planned to use Jones's stateroom, but Muller said, "Use mine. I have a fan at the head end. You'll be more comfortable."

"I'll buy that," Dove replied.

The decision saved Dove's life, for Jones's room was shredded by bomb shrapnel. Dove was also saved by his not using a pillow. A chunk of steel ripped through the PT boat's wooden hull, leaving a hole so big, Dove recalled, that he could stick his head through it. The shrapnel grazed Dove's nose. Had his head been raised on a pillow, he might have been blinded or, more likely, killed outright. He also caught a bullet in the leg from a strafing plane.

Nellist treated Dove's wounds after sticking him with a morphine syrette.

Andy Smith had been talking to crewman Betz just before the attack. Betz had shown him photos of his two young daughters. Smith then lay down on the deck to get some sleep, propping his head up on some spare kapok jackets. But the sun was in his eyes, so he reversed his position, lying flat and propping his legs up on the jackets. When the Japanese attacked, he was jolted awake. Smith saw his legs were bloodied, but it wasn't all his blood. Most of it was from Betz. The young father lay seriously wounded near the base of his 20mm gun mount. Smith, with just minor injuries, jumped up and began helping to care for the bloodied man, and thought that Betz might survive. However, the young Missourian died three days later on the hospital ship USS *Comfort.*

Scout Bob Asis took a shrapnel wound to the arm while using the forward gun tub as cover.

American fighters, responding to Gibson's distress signal, arrived and chased the Zeros back over Dulag.

The 346 boat had miraculously sustained little damage, and now her skipper, Ensign Terry, brought her close to her stricken sister craft.

His XO, Ens. Pete Rardin, had been a medical student before the war, and now came aboard the 132 boat with his medical kit and ministered to the wounded, for which he would receive a Silver Star.

The two PT boats then continued to limp their way home.

They arrived at Tacloban on October 27, where Nellist filed a report that there were between six hundred and eight hundred Japanese on Mindanao, although many seemed to be unarmed, and they were short on food. He provided 6th Army G2 with a detailed map of troop positions, ammunition dumps, supply depots, and travel routes, as well as sources of fresh water and whether or not the beaches could sustain an invasion. But even in Tacloban, now in American hands, the men were not safe from the enemy. The day after Nellist got back from the Mindanao mission, a Japanese fighter strafed the beach where he and several other Americans were sunning themselves. The men scattered but Nellist was grazed by bullets in the leg and neck.

★   ★   ★

Since the invasion at Leyte, the 24th Division had been engaged in heavy fighting near the city of Palo on the coast of San Pedro Bay. The division's goal was to move south and link up with the 96th Division, and the 24th's commander now requested a reconnaissance mission between Palo and Tanauan. Sixth Army HQ selected Bill Littlefield for the job, and he arrived for a briefing on October 22. Sleeping near the HQ tent that night, the Scouts, jolted awake by gunfire, grabbed their weapons and dashed outside. Japanese soldiers were attacking the camp and a wild melee broke out. When it was over, Littlefield found dead enemy soldiers within thirty yards of his tent.

The team moved out at ten a.m. the next day, passing through American lines. Cherokee Indian Zeke McConnell recalled, "The Japs were on both sides of us all the way. Between the Japs, the American bombing, strafing, and navy shelling, we were all plenty scared."

The Americans lucked out. Tanauan was unoccupied. Littlefield radioed the information back to army HQ and the next day, the American 381st Regiment arrived and the advance continued. Returning to the PT tender *Wachapreague*, Littlefield and his team were dispatched to Samar by PT boat to spot enemy activity, but there was none to be seen.

★   ★   ★

On November 9, the Lutz Team was alerted for its first Philippines mission since they had watched MacArthur slosh ashore, although by now they were no longer the Lutz Team. Bill Lutz had come down with a jungle rash that required his being sent back to the States for treatment. In addition, Glendale Watson was gone and Bob Shullaw had been transferred to George Thompson's team. Thus only Jack Geiger, Bob Ross, and Oliver Roesler remained, and they were now led by John McGowen. This was a happy move, Geiger recalled. Mc-Gowen was not just the most experienced of all Scout team leaders but he had won a Soldier's Medal and two Silver Stars. He was an easygoing man and not a stickler for military protocol.

The three-day mission involved contacting Filipino guerrillas in the mountainous region of Burauren and obtaining information on Japanese supply routes between Burauren and Dagami. Infiltrating through Japanese lines was easy. Getting cooperation from the Filipinos was more difficult. When the Scouts reached Burauren, the town's mayor told them that the guerrillas had moved farther up into the hills.

"Can we hire a guide to take us there?" McGowen asked.

"No, no," the mayor said. "There are many Japs and you are just four men."

"Then we'll find them on our own," McGowen resolved. "We won't turn back."

The next day a guide agreed to take them as far as Malaihaw, the next town to the west. They saw no Japanese, but the cratered landscape, splintered trees, and shattered huts gave proof that American artillery had been at work.

The team moved to the San Joaquin River, which skirted the densely forested mountain range that runs the length of Leyte. There they crossed the river and moved inland, where they discovered several abandoned Japanese pillboxes. They saw no Japanese but the soft earth was heavily scarred with footprints and hoof prints.

"The Japs are using pack animals," McGowen muttered.

Approaching the town of Camire the next day—it was October 24— the Americans froze at the sound of small-arms fire off in the distance and to their rear. After waiting silently in place for about fifteen minutes, the team pressed on into the town. Finding it empty, they passed on through. The source of the gunfire remained a mystery.

Moving into the mountains, the team's trek became steep and difficult. Reaching the lip of a precipitous gorge that offered no way across, they backtracked, soon coming upon an elderly Filipino man with a water buffalo, or caraboa, harvesting rice. Unable to understand the heavily armed men with the fiercely painted faces, he led them to the nipa hut he shared with his granddaughter and her husband. Luckily, the girl spoke English.

"You fooled my grandfather with your uniforms," she said. "He thought you were Japanese."

McGowen explained his mission and his need to contact the guerrillas. She told McGowen the guerrillas were camped just a few miles away, and invited them into the hut to eat. As they downed a meal of black beans and rice, the door to the hut burst open and in barged a guerrilla brandishing a Tommy gun in both hands and wildly shouting orders. The woman spoke rapidly to the man and calmed him down. She explained who the strangers were, then she turned to McGowen.

"This man thought you were Germans," she explained.

"Germans?" McGowen said. "Why in the hell would he think that?"

"He heard that Germans had landed by submarine to help the Japs," she replied.

Once the confusion was straightened out, the guerrilla agreed to lead McGowen and his men to his headquarters. Picking their way into a jungle ravine, they passed through several checkpoints, and, as darkness descended, reached a small bamboo hut lit by a single candle. By the flickering light, McGowen outlined his mission to the guerrilla commander, who refused to cooperate, saying it was impossible. He then left the hut carrying the candle so the Scouts could get some sleep.

He awoke them at daybreak, and while he still would not lead the Scouts into the mountains, he agreed to have men escort them east to the mouth of the Kabugnan River, where the Scouts could obtain two native canoes. From there, their reconnaissance would be by water.

Escorted by a few guerrillas, they reached the river by mid-afternoon and found the dugout canoes waiting. As they skimmed over the water, they passed makeshift shelters occupied by refugees who had fled inland from the Leyte invasion beaches in response to American leaflets warning them of the upcoming landings.

Stopping to talk to the refugees, McGowen learned that the Japanese were short on food and that they had abandoned their prepared positions along the highway running between Tanauan and San Joaquin, to take up new ones inland.

With this information in hand, McGowen decided to return to base even though his main goal of locating Japanese supply routes in the mountains had not been accomplished. The reluctance of the guerrillas to help him left McGowen with a bitter taste in his mouth for their fighting ability.

McGowen's bad luck as leader of the former Lutz Team would continue.

On November 19, seven days after their unhappy experience in the hills above Burauren, McGowen, Geiger, Ross, and Roesler were headed on a new assignment. They were to load up supplies, including stretchers and medical gear, on a PT boat and rendezvous with George Thompson and his team on Ponson Island, where Ormoc Bay meets the Camotes Sea, off Leyte's western coast. Thompson and his men had been there since November 6, watching Japanese shipping activity in the bay, and had picked up two wounded airmen.

The team would hop a ride with three PT boats from Squadron 33, which were scheduled to conduct a patrol of the bay. During the course of this patrol, their boat, PT-495, the *Gentleman Jim*, would stop at Ponson so McGowen's men could unload the supplies and evacuate the wounded fliers.

The boats cruised along the western coast of Leyte. Onshore the Scouts could see lights, possibly fires lit by GIs. At about twelve fifteen a.m., the boats intercepted several wooden Japanese barges, eighty to ninety feet in length and armed with machine guns. The PTs circled, then swarmed in for the attack and a wild firefight ensued. Japanese 7.7mm machine guns and American .50 calibers blazed and flaming tracers cast their reflections on the black water as they streamed to and fro. American 20- and 40mm guns joined the melee.

A Japanese barge, burning and badly holed, nudged into the *Gentleman Jim*, and the PT boat's starboard .50-caliber machine gunner riddled it. A man screamed in the darkness, and Roesler recalled the barge dissolving under the heavy fire "like a sugar cube in a hot cup of coffee." The barge disappeared into the sea. Three more barges were burning and sinking.

Then, in the confusion, the skipper of the second PT boat in the formation, a new officer with little night patrol experience, cut his wheel to port and took his boat out of position. The 20mm gunner on board the PT, his adrenaline flowing and unaware that his boat was out of line, spotted a large shadow two hundred yards to starboard. He swung his gun around and opened fire.

The shadow was the PT-495.

Rounds from the errant PT boat peppered the 40mm gun position on the *Gentleman Jim*'s fantail, and men screamed in pain and shock. The executive officer of the wayward boat saw the mistake and immediately ordered the gunner to cease fire, but the damage was done. At least five sailors were hit, and one would shortly die. Of the wounded, one sailor suffered a bad leg wound and another had an arm blown off, while a third seaman was down with a head wound. A young sailor, his arm badly mangled, staggered forward from the carnage and told his skipper, "Get the hell out. We're all hit back here."

He did not have to tell the skipper of the *Gentleman Jim* that news. He was one of the seven men who received minor wounds, having been nicked in the shin by shrapnel. Another of the wounded was

Alamo Scout Oliver Roesler, who had a piece of an exploded 20mm shell lodged in his neck.

No one on board knew the fire came from another PT boat, and initially no one cared. Help for the wounded was now the job that needed to be done and everyone pitched in. Geiger, who said he would never forget the sight of the bloodied men, helped the XO navigate the boat, while everyone else, including the Scouts, assisted in first aid. Even Roesler, his neck and uniform bloodied from his own wound, helped Ross, who was tending the boy with the mangled arm. As they dumped sulfa powder on his wounds and hit him with morphine before applying a tourniquet, they spoke to him to get his attention off his injury.

"What's your name, son," Ross asked as he worked on the boy.

"Wilbur," the sailor muttered.

"Wilbur, huh?" Ross said. "We got a couple of Wilburs in the Scouts. Nice name. Been with this boat long?"

"No," he replied, groggily. "This is my first cruise."

"Well, you're gonna spend some time in a nice clean hospital, with good food and pretty nurses," Ross said. "Maybe you might even get to go home and see your family. Would you like that?"

The youth smiled through his pain and the two Scouts looked at each other, certain he would lose the arm. Whether it was the sight of the crippled boy, or the effects of his wound, or both, Roesler was soon sickened and had to go below. Geiger relieved Ross.

"Take a break, Bob," he told his friend. "Grab a smoke."

"Thanks, Geig," Ross replied. "This has me fuckin' unnerved."

Of the twenty-two men on board the 495 boat, twelve had been hit. Still, things could have been a lot worse. Two of the 20mm shells had struck near the *Gentleman Jim*'s fuel tanks. Had they been a bit closer to the mark, they would have touched off the boat's high-octane aviation gasoline and the boat would have been blown into matchsticks.

Then the rain began to fall. Blankets were brought up from below to cover the wounded and make them comfortable. It was about three thirty a.m. by now, and PT-495 had lost contact with the other two boats. Suddenly one of the PTs, probably the same one that had shot them up, piloted by the same disoriented skipper, materialized out of the darkness, heading for the 495 boat. The *Gentleman Jim*'s injured commander tried to wheel his boat out of the way, but the oncoming craft struck the 495's stern. Smoke billowed from the rear of the 495 and someone yelled, "Fire!" However, it was quickly discovered that the smoke was coming from the smokescreen generator on the fantail, which was damaged in the collision.

The third PT boat soon pulled up. The badly injured men were carefully transferred and the boat sent on its way toward its base at Linoan. The PT-495 and the boat that rammed it limped home together, so badly damaged that the men wore life vests just in case.

Safely back at Linoan, McGowen, Ross, and Geiger helped the PT-495 crew clean the bloodied deck. Roesler was sent to the army hospital at Hollandia, New Guinea, and would be out of action for three months, returning on November 21.

The mission to resupply the Thompson Team was scrubbed. It was also the last mission for the Lutz Team. With its leader gone, the team was dispersed. Ross was sent to the Dove Team. Geiger and Roesler would be recalled by their original units.

★   ★   ★

Keeping tabs on Japanese troop movements within Leyte's mountainous interior was a priority for American planners.

On November 12, the Dove Team, under the command of Lt. Woodrow Hobbs since Jack Dove's wounding, along with Bob Sumner's team, were sent to watch Highway 2, the main road from Ormoc north through the Ormoc Valley to Carigara Bay. Sumner's team was to watch the southern stretch of road from Ormoc City to Valencia, while Hobbs and his men kept an eye on the northern leg of the highway from Valencia to Cananga, as well as the road rolling eastward to Carigara, thus putting the entire highway under surveillance.

Hobbs, along with Staff Sgt. John G. Fisher, Sgts. John E. Philips, John E. Hidalgo, Denny Chapman, Irv Ray, William R. Watson, and

Ray W. Wangrud—these last two formerly with the Reynolds Team—left the PT tender *Oyster Bay* that afternoon, arriving at San Isidro at three a.m. Met by natives, they were rowed ashore by canoe and spent the night in a nearby house.

On November 15, the team was ferried seventeen miles to the south to the village of Abijao, where they linked up with Maj. Jose Nazareno and his 96th Philippine Regiment, who led them on a mountainous trek eastward to the village of Maulayan, which overlooked the Ormoc-Carigara road. There they set up a radio station and spent the next two weeks reporting enemy activity. Arriving at Maulayan, Hobbs got word through a civilian scouting unit called the Volunteer Guards that three thousand Japanese were massing at Cananga, with another thousand congregated some five miles to the east.

Hobbs radioed that there was a strong possibility that the Japanese were preparing to evacuate across the Camotes Sea to Cebu, adding a report he had received that the enemy already on Cebu were slaughtering entire villages in retaliation for their own losses on Leyte. The lightly armed guerrillas on Cebu were unable to prevent it.

Even before Hobbs radioed his disturbing news, on November 14, Lt. George S. Thompson's Team, which consisted of Thompson, Sgts. Leonard Scott and Charley Hill, Cpl. Gordon Butler, Pfcs. Joseph Moon and Joseph Johnson, and Pvt. Robert Shullaw, formerly of the Lutz Team, along with Vincent Nuivedo, a Filipino radio operator, were dispatched to Poro Island in the Camotes Island group, to watch for enemy barge traffic between Leyte and Cebu.

Landing in rubber boats on the island's northeast coast, they were met by guerrillas, who told them as many as one thousand Japanese were in the vicinity. The Scouts set up a radio station and interviewed civilians. Thompson established a civilian information network as a means of conveying news to the scattered villages. Results weren't long in coming, as the Scouts were informed about enemy barges ferrying troops from Talang Point on Pacijan Island to Ormoc. Japanese forces also reinforced Ponson Island, just northeast of Poro, where they ruthlessly raped, tortured, and bayoneted civilians.

Enemy presence among the Camotes Islands was intense, causing the Scouts to keep on the move, and it was amid this busy time that the Japanese found the Thompson Team.

On the night of December 7, Thompson and his men had settled among a small seaside collection of shanties on Poro Island. Selecting a two-story house right at the water's edge, the men bedded down.

"Indoor accommodations," Charley Hill said as he stretched out beside Thompson. "That is a rare luxury indeed for us Scouts."

"Yeah," Thompson said. "When word gets out to the other teams, we'll be regular celebrities. They'll be wanting autographs and asking to touch us."

Hill chuckled, then said, "Tommy, can I see your fancy pistol?"

Thompson reached into a shoulder holster and slid out his .38-caliber revolver. He handed it to Hill, who held it lovingly. He especially admired the wooden pistol grips, with Thompson's name carved on one side and "Alamo Scouts" on the other.

"Who carved the grips for you?" Hill asked.

"Bob Ross," Thompson replied. "He's handy as hell. It's native wood—ash, I think."

"No shit? Big Bob Ross of the Lutz Team?" Hill asked, then handed the gun back. "But how come you use a thirty-eight? Where's your forty-five?"

"I could never hit shit with a forty-five," Thompson replied, slipping the revolver back into his holster. He then rolled over to get some sleep.

In the dark of the night, the team was awakened by engine noises. Six barges loaded with Japanese soldiers were landing just outside. At Thompson's signal, the men slipped quietly up to the second floor and kept silent vigil. They watched in growing concern as some of the enemy troops approached the two-story hiding place and a few men went inside.

As the enemy tromped around the ground floor, Thompson said quietly, "Hold your fire."

Then the sound of boots on the steps was heard as two Japanese climbed the stairway.

"Let's get the fuck outta here," Thompson said, then he and three of the team leaped from the window and splashed into the sea. Sergeant Scott and the remaining three rushed down the back stairs, pushed past the startled Japanese on the steps, ran out of the house and into the surrounding jungle, gunshots and shouts of surprise and outrage following them.

Reaching dense underbrush, the men dove for cover. Before long, Japanese soldiers approached, and with bayonets mounted on their Arisaka rifles began probing the bushes. The tip of a bayonet nicked Scott in the stomach, drawing blood, but he did not flinch. Soon satisfied that the Americans had escaped, the enemy withdrew back to the village.

Miraculously, the entire team escaped unscathed except for Scott's slight wound, and the men reassembled. However, they had lost their radio and most of their supplies. They eventually linked up with Company I of the 88th Infantry Cebu Command, the only native military group in the Camotes. The Filipinos in this unit were armed with eight carbines, ten Japanese Arisaka rifles, and twelve sidearms. Thompson, using the guerrillas' radio, arranged to supply them with seventy-five M1 rifles, two .30-caliber machine guns, and plenty of ammunition.

★ ★ ★

By late November, the only experienced Scout team not deployed was Lt. Thomas Rounsaville's, but he wouldn't be idle for long. On November 21, he and his men, along with Sgt. Lleandro Reposar, a Filipino radio operator, and a guerrilla officer named Captain Avela, who would serve as guide, boarded a PT boat for a trip across a narrow strip of the Visayan Sea to the north, this time to Masbate Island, just off the southeast tail of the main Philippine island of Luzon. Their mission was to help local guerrillas set up a radio and observation network to assist with the upcoming invasion.

The team went ashore from the PT boat at the village of Tenke on the southern tip of Masbate, traveled overland to Esperanza, then by native sailboat, where, sitting on the boat's outriggers, they watched for attacking planes, both American and Japanese. American navy planes soon arrived, diving out of the sky. Everyone went over the side as bullets churned up the sea around them.

"Everyone stay in the water," Rounsaville ordered, then turned to Sergeant Hard. "Harold, follow me."

Rounsaville climbed back into the boat, followed by Hard. Both men stripped off their shirts, exposing their white skin. The fighters came swooping down again, noticed the shirtless white men, and peeled off, dipping their wings in apology.

Arriving at Masbate on November 23, Rounsaville was informed that the guerrilla radio operators in the area were unable to help him communicate because they did not know how to decode the incoming messages, so he left Sergeant Reposar behind to create a reliable radio station, and headed along the coast to establish observation posts, both on Masbate and the smaller island of Ticao, just to the north. Observing Ticao across the short strip of water that separates it from Masbate, Rounsaville noticed heavy Japanese air traffic. Through Captain Avela, Rounsaville was informed by natives that the air activity was covering a Japanese attempt to reinforce Leyte with troops from Luzon, sending them on transports through the Masbate Passage and down the slot between Masbate and Samar.

Rounsaville passed the intelligence on, with the result that he and his men had ringside seats as torpedo planes of the 5th Air Force delivered a series of vicious attacks on enemy shipping.

A few days after learning of the reinforcement attempt, the team spotted a Japanese troop convoy steaming through the passage. Rounsaville radioed the coordinates to the 5th Air Force, and before long, American planes were swarming over the ships. The Scouts were mesmerized as they watched water geysers erupt around the enemy convoy. Smoke and flame shot up from some of the vessels, which began to burn and sink. Survivors leaped from the ships to the point where, Rounsaville recalled, the "water was black with Japs." Fighter planes strafed the men thrashing in the ocean.

In all, six enemy transports were sunk.

Rounsaville's team also called in bomb strikes on Masbate itself, where the Japanese had a major airfield on the outskirts of Masbate City. The raids forced the Japanese to relocate several times.

★   ★   ★

By early December, twenty-three thousand Japanese troops were trapped in north Leyte's Ormoc Valley. The American advance combined with Allied airpower had established a firm stranglehold on the enemy by all but eliminating any chance of resupply or reinforcements.

To eliminate this pocket of resistance, the Americans were planning to land troops near Ormoc City on December 7, and drive to the north and cut the enemy force in two. However, 6th Army HQ needed last-minute information on Camp Downes, one of the proposed invasion areas, west of Ormoc. Reports were that the enemy had been reinforcing the area. Attempts to send in PT boats to reconnoiter had failed. A Scout team was needed.

Bill Littlefield and his men had been idle since their reconnaissance of Samar in late October, and had spent much of the past several weeks escorting General Krueger. The men and their officer were itching to go. Part of the reason for their inactivity had been because Littlefield had suffered an attack of appendicitis, and though it did not require surgery, Krueger feared Littlefield might have a flare-up in the field and that he might lose a team, since the men would never abandon their leader.

It was Doc Canfield who intervened and put Krueger's fears to rest.

"Hell, he may never get another attack," Canfield replied when asked his opinion. "He's fine to go."

On December 2, Littlefield was in a jeep, bouncing along a road toward the village of Baybay to check out the reports on enemy presence, and also to get some depth soundings and look for mines. With him rode team members Zeke McConnell and Alva Branson. The jouncing trip took ten hours, but the three men soon arrived at Baybay on the west coast of Leyte, where Littlefield recruited local fishermen to deliver him and his men behind enemy lines, some thirty miles to the north, by canoe.

Gliding along the water, the canoes stayed well offshore—the natives did not want to risk getting too close—while Littlefield took notes. As the natives paddled, they pointed out to Littlefield the locations of mines and obstacles, and described the slope of the beach, all of which Littlefield relayed back to his headquarters. The information he gathered aided greatly in the invasion five days later, and by December 11 Ormoc fell to the Americans.

★ ★ ★

Lt. Rafael M. Ileto, a native Filipino, was happy to be back home. A member of the ASTC's fifth class, which had graduated on October 28 at Cape Kassoe, at Hollandia, New Guinea, he was about to lead his team, Sgts. Fredirico Balambao, Paul E. Draper, James Farrow Jr., and Peter Vischansky, and Cpl. Estanislao S. Bacat, into their first mission.

Accompanied by Lt. Marion Myers of the ASTC staff, the team boarded a navy J-boat on December 8 from the newly established ASTC camp at Abuyog, near the mouth of the Cadacan River on central west Leyte.

Sixth Army HQ wanted to know what the enemy was up to near Balangiga on the southern coast of Samar. Ileto and his team landed at Guiuan, just west of Balangiga, where they were met by guerrillas and led to their camp near the town of Salcedo. Natives rowed the Scouts by sea to Balangiga, where they reconnoitered the shoreline. Ileto also interviewed locals, from whom he discovered that some 250 Japanese were concentrating in the hills five miles north of the city. Enemy patrols frequently raided the towns, terrorizing the inhabitants.

By December 14, six days after setting out, Ileto had assessed Japanese strength, as well as the strength and capabilities of the guerrillas, and returned to base.

Two days before Ileto returned, newly commissioned 2nd Lt. Herman S. Chanley and his team left on their first mission. Chanley, formerly of the Hobbs Team until his promotion, departed on December

12, landing near the town of Pawikan. There he established a radio station and OP and sent back reports on enemy movements in Carigara Bay and Biliran Strait.

Chanley's return on December 20 marked the end of Alamo Scout operations on Leyte.

CHAPTER 11

Samar/Ormoc Bay

Sumner Team: October–December 1944

Lt. Robert Sumner and his men had the honor of performing both the shortest and one of the longest missions ever done by an Alamo Scout team, both within two months.

On October 22, 1944, an L-5 Piper Cub flying from an offshore aircraft carrier to American lines on Leyte was in serious trouble. Coming in low over Samar, the westernmost island of the Visayan chain, just northeast across the half-mile-wide San Juanico Strait, the plane's sixty-five-horsepower engine struggled to keep the 640-pound aircraft aloft. Outside, the moonless night made it black as the devil's soul. Straining, the pilot saw the dim form of a landmass on the water below. According to his charts, this had to be Samar.

Lowering the scout plane, the pilot, a sergeant who flew for an ad hoc messenger unit called the Guinea Short Line, brought the nose up gently and set the wheels down. Moments later, the *Grasshopper*, as the small plane was nicknamed, rolled to a halt. The pilot radioed his position, thanked God when he got a "Roger," and cut the laboring engine.

Now the army courier had a bigger problem. In a satchel on the seat beside him was a six-inch-thick notebook filled with the complete field orders for the 14th Corps, including the tactical and logistical plans for each division: times, dates, troop movements, locations, and unit strengths—in short, the works. The idea had been to deliver the document to 6th Army headquarters, and not to the Japanese on Samar. Capture of the plan could jeopardize the entire Leyte operation.

The sergeant had arranged to be picked up by a PT boat on the coast. However, there was a very high risk of meeting Japanese, both while on his way to the coast and while awaiting the arrival of the rescue boat. Not willing to risk that the plan would fall into enemy hands if he himself did, the pilot stepped off some distance, made a mental note, and buried the satchel in the earth.

Then he struck off for the coast.

★   ★   ★

Seven days after the L-5 went down, Colonel Bradshaw summoned Red Sumner to his tent.

"Red, you and your team draw up a plan quickly," Bradshaw said. "I'm sending you over to Samar. Seven days ago, a Piper Cub headed for corps headquarters was forced to land due to engine trouble. The sergeant flying it brought the plane down in a coconut grove somewhere near the village of Balangiga."

Bradshaw pointed to a location on the island, just across the Gulf of Samar from where they now were.

Sumner asked the nature of the documents. Bradshaw told him.

"Jesus," Sumner moaned.

"Exactly," Bradshaw said. "The pilot buried the documents in a B4 bag, in case he got captured, and made his way to Legaspi, then by PT boat to Tacloban and Sixth Army HQ. This is high-priority. You'll go as soon as you assemble your team. I've commandeered a picket boat from one of the engineer regiments to take you across the gulf. Sorry it's in broad daylight, but it can't be helped."

"How will we find the plane and the bag?"

"The pilot will be going with you," Bradshaw said. "This should be quick in and quick out. The skipper of the picket boat figures he can get you across the gulf in thirty minutes."

Sumner studied the map and aerial photos spread out on Bradshaw's table.

"It might be wise, so we don't draw attention to the village, that the boat approach the island here, about two miles to the west. Then we can cruise along the shore to here," he said and pointed. "That will put us just half a mile from Balangiga."

Bradshaw and Sumner agreed that while the team would take a radio with them, they would break radio silence with headquarters only to confirm landing and to announce their departure.

Sumner hurried back to get his men ready. Sticking his head in the squad tent, he said, "Saddle up. We've got a quick in-and-out job." He looked around and saw one man missing. "Where's Renhols?"

"He took some clothes to the dry cleaner," Blaise replied.

"You guys didn't throw his shit out in the street again, did you?" Sumner asked, a smile creasing his lips.

The team joke was how the ex–drill instructor and ever-neat Blaise, who somehow managed to look well-pressed even after coming in from the jungle, got fed up with Renhols's slovenliness and, along with Paul Jones and Harry Weiland, had gathered up all of Renhols's clothes one day and threw them out into the company street. When Renhols returned, Blaise told him, "You can live in the street until you get your stuff in order."

Renhols apologized to the team and kept his things neat from then on.

"No, sir," Blaise told Sumner.

"Well, get him back here at the double quick. We need to shove off."

★   ★   ★

The trip to Samar was unopposed. Rowing in from two hundred yards offshore, the team's noontime landing went smoothly. As directed,

Sumner had Bill Blaise fire up the radio to announce their arrival, "Red One," which was acknowledged by Bradshaw's laconic "Roger."

Sumner left one man to guard the boat, then headed inland with the flier and the Scout team. The terrain was generally open and cultivated, with no evidence of any people, friend or foe. After a walk of about half a mile, the Scouts saw the L-5 sitting near a clapboard schoolhouse built among a number of coconut palms. He had managed to land among the trees without striking any.

"Jesus Christ," the pilot sighed. "It was pitch-dark when I landed. I didn't even see the damned trees or the school."

"You're one lucky bastard, Sergeant," Sumner said.

The Scouts spent the next fifteen minutes observing the plane for any signs of an ambush, but the only sound was the buzzing of insects and the lazy offshore breeze rustling the palm leaves. Keeping the pilot by his side, Sumner and the team advanced. As they reached the plane, Sumner stationed the men around it. Then he, the pilot, and one team member headed for where the bag was buried a few hundred feet from the aircraft. After some initial difficulty getting his bearings, the courier led the Scouts to the hiding place.

"I didn't realize I was this close to the beach," he said, spotting the ocean a few hundred feet away.

The bag was recovered intact. They returned to the plane, where the pilot removed several key engine parts, rendering it useless to the enemy. Sumner, meanwhile, ordered the school and some nearby houses searched. The men discovered a stash of Japanese military documents, including papers that showed the area to be a staging point for barge and light naval traffic along the coast of Samar en route to Leyte and Mindanao.

The Scouts also found some personal gear, mostly uniforms and equipment. They took possession of several thin blankets, a mixture of wool and silk, which the men found very warm, yet light, and practically indestructible. They used these until the end of the war.

When Sumner was satisfied that the Scouts had thoroughly searched the buildings, he directed Blaise to notify the picket boat skipper to recover the rubber boat and man he had left there, and then put in at a rickety pier built out from the shore near where the bag had been buried. The men were back on the boat by three p.m.

The mission had lasted just three hours.

★   ★   ★

During late October the American effort on Leyte was hampered by severe weather, including a major typhoon, that created serious problems for the navy in its efforts to support the invasion with reinforcements and supplies. These problems were multiplied onshore by bad roads and worse terrain. To resist the Americans, the Japanese began reinforcing the Leyte garrison from other islands with the intent of launching a major counteroffensive. Sixth Army headquarters was aware of the enemy plan, thanks to the guerrillas, and knew it had to eliminate the Japanese threat on Leyte. The key to this was Ormoc Bay, located on Leyte's west coast, where the Japanese had established a main supply base. To guarantee success, coordinating activities with the local guerrillas was a necessity, as was supplying them with sufficient arms and ammo to disrupt the enemy. It was decided that an Alamo Scout team would work with the guerrillas, and for that, Bob Sumner got the call.

Back just eight days after retrieving the satchel of secret documents on Samar, Sumner and his men found themselves on a PT boat on the evening of November 5, heading for a landing that night at Palompan. Shortly after setting out, however, the PT boat was recalled to Tanauan to await further instructions.

"The reason we scrubbed the mission," Sumner was informed by Lt. Col. Frank Rowalle of 6th Army G2, who boarded the PT boat the next morning to meet with Sumner, "is that the Nips landed a sizable force in Palompan the night before, and the entire town is completely in enemy hands. The guerrillas in that area have fallen back into the bush rather than fight the Japs and put the twenty thousand civvies living there in even more danger."

Rowalle rolled a map out on the PT's superstructure.

"What we're gonna do instead, Red, is you're gonna leave tomorrow night in the company of two other PTs to provide extra cover, go north, around Leyte, and land at Abijao, about thirty miles from your objective. The guerrillas under Major Nazareno will meet you there. Your recognition signal at Abijao, as usual, will be your nickname, 'Red,' which they will flash to you by Morse code. You make no reply. We don't want the Japs spotting your light flashing out on the water. Instead, you will approach shore. If you fail to make contact, expect to return at the same time for the next two nights. You'll take in some arms and ammo—the guerrillas are short of both. If you need more supplies, we can arrange for airdrops as needed. You will, of course, monitor all Jap land and sea movements. Plan to stay in the bush until we order you out, a few weeks at least, so equip yourself and your men accordingly."

Loaded down with two tons of weapons and ammo, plus a three-man Filipino radio team and their equipment from the Philippine Message Center, the PT boat left Tacloban Bay, cruising across the San Juanico Strait between Leyte and Samar after dark to avoid Japanese aircraft. As he guided his boat across the black water, the PT skipper was contacted by radio and told that the two other boats assigned to provide him support for the mission were being detached and sent elsewhere.

"Damn," he said as he signed off. He turned to Sumner. "I don't like this, but I'm willing to go on. It's your call, Lieutenant."

"We have a lot of shit to unload and we're gonna have our asses hanging out while we do it," Sumner replied. "But it can't be helped. We keep going."

Gliding across the dark strait, the PT's radar picked up what appeared to be a Japanese destroyer sitting dead in the water just ahead of them. Tensions were high and battle stations manned, gunners and torpedomen alike, until the skipper located a 1925 chart that revealed the "destroyer" to be a large rock projecting up from the water.

"All hands, stand down," the skipper ordered, and a sigh of relief was heard all around the boat.

Rounding the north tip of Leyte and entering Carigara Bay, the boat skipper located Abijao. Muffling the PT's Packards, he steered the boat toward the dark coastline. Everyone's nerves were on edge. Then a light was spotted. It flashed "Red" in Morse code.

Continuing to glide slowly toward shore, everyone was wary of a trap and all weapons were trained on the jungle. Suddenly lights began to appear, and as the boat drew closer, buildings and people came into view. As the PT closed on the coast, Sumner ordered Ed Renhols to flash "Scouts ashore." Renhols did, and a cheer came up from the island. Squads of guerrillas deployed along the beach, forming a protective cordon. Sumner asked the boat skipper to come about and present his beam to the shore to ease in unloading the supplies. As he did, the rubber boat was inflated. As it was prepared for launching, the craft swung abruptly. It struck Sgt. Lawrence Coleman, pitching him off the boat's fantail and into the water. His teammates quickly fished him out, but not before his right hand was severely cut by one of the PT's razor-sharp propellers. One look at the wound and Sumner knew Coleman's mission was over.

"I've got to send him back to the base hospital," Sumner told the skipper, who nodded in agreement. "If we don't, he might lose that thumb. He might anyway."

The guerrillas were so overjoyed to see the Scouts that, as the rubber boat approached the beach, a group of them hoisted Sumner from the craft and carried him ashore. In that less-than-graceful manner, he was presented to Maj. Jose Nazareno, commander of the 2nd Battalion, 96th Infantry Regiment, of the Leyte Area Command.

"We are so glad you have come," said Nazareno, who, at five feet nine inches, was unusually tall for a Filipino. "You have brought us guns, yes?"

"I have brought you guns, yes," Sumner replied. "Let's get some help to unload them."

Nazareno ordered two large canoes, or baratos, to proceed to the PT boat. Sumner boarded one. As the supplies were being unloaded, the guerrillas turned over two Japanese prisoners, who were ordered to sit on the PT boat's fantail. Contrary to their warrior code of Bushido, they remained there with no apparent interest in trying to escape.

"A pair of realists," Sumner said to Blaise.

Unloading the PT boat took forty-five minutes, during most of which the young skipper fidgeted. He wanted to get back to Leyte before daylight. Shortly after one a.m., all gear was ashore. Sumner checked once more on Coleman, who, cradling his bandaged hand, appeared to be in a state of mild shock. He did not want to leave the team and the mission.

"We can't treat you properly," Sumner told the distraught man. "You're no good to me with one hand. Besides, if you don't get medical help, you might lose that thumb, and then I lose you permanently. I need you healthy. You're going back."

Coleman nodded meekly.

★　★　★

Once in the village of Abijao, the team was not prepared for what they saw. More than two hundred festive partyers jammed the street in a noisy victory celebration. Wine and local cuisine was featured, and dance music—Visayan tunes, Filipino melodies, and American big band—was provided by musicians playing an accordion, a violin, and a motley assortment of horns. Speeches were given by anyone wishing to be heard, although few were over the revelry.

To guard against a sudden Japanese attack, two companies of guerrillas manned picket posts on every road leading into Abijao.

On November 7 the team moved on to San Isidro, where Sumner established a radio station in the village and detailed Schermerhorn and Jones to remain behind and run the communications operation and coordinate supply drops. A second radio would stay with the team. The next day Sumner's group, less Schermerhorn and Jones, along with a company of guerrillas headed inland toward the central mountain range, whose jagged, mist-enshrouded peaks jutted four thousand feet into the sky before sloping down into the fertile Ormoc Valley.

Assisted by the guerrillas and members of local militia groups called the Volunteer Guards, Sumner's first destination was the barrio of Matag. Upon reaching a small village along the trail, the team was billeted on the second floor of the largest bodega, or house, in town. They would sleep on low-framed beds with woven rattan mattresses, Sumner's first experience, he later wrote, with "this peculiar form of punishment."

As his Filipino hosts prepared to leave to allow the Scouts to get some rest, a young man of about twenty told Sumner, "Sir, we are so happy to have the whites back. You will never know what the Japs did to us. Thank you for coming back."

The comment left Sumner deeply touched.

The team had been asleep about three hours when a bugle call blasted them awake.

"Latrine dis away," a Filipino guerrilla announced.

Breakfast consisted of chicken and duck eggs fried in coconut oil, fried plantains, pork chops, steamed rice, and locally grown coffee. It was sumptuous, but proved hard on the digestive systems of men not used to island cuisine.

After eating, the Scouts opened the weapons crates and issued carbines and M1s, along with ammunition, to two companies of guerrillas who had little in the way of armament. Sumner noted that they were in desperate need of clothing, too. The guerrillas wore a mixture of civilian attire, mainly captured Japanese gear, U.S. web equipment, and maybe shoes. Socks were a luxury. Headgear included straw buris, U.S.-issue tropical helmets, and a few U.S. campaign hats, these last mostly worn by the professionally trained Filipino Scouts. No Japanese helmets were worn for fear of being shot by friendly fire.

Striking out for Matag, a barrio in the lower foothills of Leyte's mountainous spine, the column of men moved without incident. In each village, new Volunteer Guards relieved other VG men, taking over the duty of carrying supplies. Also at each stop, Sumner was introduced to the barrio chieftain, or *tente*. This man, who was either elected or appointed, or had succeeded to the post by heredity, controlled every aspect of life in the barrio. His word was law.

In each village the natives foisted fresh water, fruit, flowers, chickens, and eggs on the grateful Scouts until they could carry no more.

They were also regaled with comments, more inquisitive than derogatory, about their height, skin, and hair color, especially the strawberry blond Sumner.

The team reached Matag around four p.m., and the command post (CP) was set up in the largest house. That night, the Americans were again treated to a festival with food and music, safe from Japanese discovery thanks to the guerrillas' effective alert system, which would spot enemy forces miles before they reached Matag.

During the party, Sumner sat with Nazareno.

"You have a finely disciplined group of men here, Major," Sumner said.

"*Sí*," Nazareno replied. "But we need more weapons and equipment to kill more Japs."

"Make me a list of your needs, and I'll arrange an airdrop," Sumner said. "Is there a place where we can establish a drop zone that won't jeopardize our operations?"

Nazareno thought, then said, "I think the barrio of Mas-in would be good. It is on our way."

Sumner agreed. Besides, he thought an airdrop behind Japanese lines would have an unsettling effect on enemy morale.

That night he sent an "eyes only" message to Colonel Rowalle with the request for arms, ammo, web gear, and clothing for two hundred men. The drop would be in forty-eight hours.

The guerrillas' need for ammo and automatic weapons was highlighted the next day, when they got into a hot skirmish with a Japanese patrol near the village of Picoy. Besides being outgunned, the Filipinos, undisciplined in combat skills, fired off twice as much ammunition as was necessary.

Their journey was delayed by a fierce tropical storm that forced the men to find whatever meager cover they could to protect themselves from the heavy rainfall. The storm passed as suddenly as it had appeared, and the column resumed its march. At a bridge near the barrio of Sabang-Boa, the guerrillas at the point ran into a Japanese patrol. A hot skirmish ensued, with weapons blazing and men shouting excitedly. The fight ended as quickly as the earlier storm, with no casualties suffered by either side. However, the enemy was now aware of the Americans' presence. Worse, the radio had broken down and time was lost having to repair it.

After arriving at Mas-in, the guerrillas began hacking out a drop zone, bordered by mounds of underbrush to be set alight as needed. The C-47s, three of them, arrived on time at two p.m. Sumner guided them to the target area by having the piles of debris set ablaze. The Skytrains made two passes over the smoky triangle, dropping thirty-six large bundles, which floated to earth under red and white canopies. As the men hastily unwrapped the bundles, their eyes lit up as they found Garands, carbines, BARs, ammo, clothing, gasoline, coffee, cigarettes, and bundles of *Stars and Stripes* and *Life* magazines. Clearing the DZ quickly, the column soon struck out along the valley bound for Puerto Bello, which would afford them a vantage point to keep tabs on the Japanese at Ormoc.

Sumner spent the next several days in the Mas-in area, setting up a radio station and organizing a twenty-one-man intelligence unit consisting of guerrillas and local constabulary.

Ordering Blaise to remain with the radio and keep in communication with Schermerhorn, Sumner led the rest on to Puerto Bello. They spent two days there before Sumner sent a runner back to Blaise with instructions to bring the radio forward.

Inexplicably, the Japanese did not send patrols to try to find Sumner and his men, even though, he felt, the enemy had to know of his whereabouts, the airdrop was so blatant. Sumner could only assume that the Japanese commander at Ormoc did not choose to risk his men with little hope of finding the Scouts.

Still, there was always the risk of betrayal.

"There are people in Puerto Bello we suspect of being *makapili*, Jap collaborators," Nazareno's intelligence officer told Sumner. "We keep them under watch."

"I have complete confidence in your people," Sumner told him.

★   ★   ★

Following the several sea battles off the Leyte and Samar coasts, Japanese prisoners—both soldiers and sailors from sunken ships—began arriving at Sumner's CP, under Filipino guard. From these Sumner was able to ascertain that elements of the Japanese 1st and 6th divisions had been transferred from China to Leyte, coming ashore at Palompan.

While at Puerto Bello, Sumner's HQ was a twelve-foot-by-twenty-foot bamboo house with a palm-thatch roof and a small porch, built on a hillside. The whole thing was set up on stilts about four feet off the ground. The team spent several weeks there, scouting throughout the Ormoc area, "showing the flag, as it were," Sumner later recalled.

After about two weeks, the Japanese could no longer tolerate the Americans' presence and troops were landed just six miles from Puerto Bello. Now there were ever more frequent clashes with the guerrillas. Falling back to Mas-in to avoid contact, guerrilla scouts alerted Sumner that Japanese troops were on both sides of him, at distances of less than a mile.

"The Japs are trying to squeeze us," Sumner told his men. "Plus, for all I know, our radio broadcasts are being monitored and maybe even deciphered."

"I think we relocate, and fast," Blaise said.

"I agree," Sumner responded, unfolding a map. "We'll displace north and west to the slopes of Mount Naguang." He pointed to a place on the map. "From here we can better protect our radio setup and we have several escape routes in case the Nips come at us in force."

Sumner turned to the Filipino radio officer, Lieutenant Cabrido.

"Send a signal to Sixth Army headquarters that we will be out of commo [communication] for a couple of days, and that once we've relocated, I will be requesting another airdrop. We're running low on ammo, medical supplies, and rations. We've been living off the generosity of our hosts too long. It's time we give something back."

By the latter, Sumner was not just referring to food, but sewing machine needles. There were many sewing machines on the island, but since 1943 the civilians had been out of the needles necessary to make new clothes. This odd request sent Alamo Scout procurement officer Mayo Stuntz scrambling. Locating several army and navy supply units, he managed to secure needles in all sizes. As a bonus, he also sent along parachute silk for garments. Most of the natives had been wearing outfits of coarse abacca, made from a thread derived from banana plants.

The drop was made on November 18, and not a moment too soon. By Sumner's reckoning, the guerrillas had only twenty minutes' worth of ammo remaining, enough for one good fight.

As Sumner's column moved toward its new position on Mount Naguang, they passed through a series of small villages, and in each they were again treated as liberators. Sumner felt the people "were starved for the American presence and an end to the Japanese." Up until this point, the natives' morale had been bucked up by broadcasts from Radio San Francisco, and they risked death by listening to *The Voice of Liberty*, a news program aired daily through the U.S. Office of War Information. They were also bolstered by underground newspapers that were typewritten and mimeographed, when possible, for circulation. Now, at last, the Americans were back.

One stop on the trail to Mount Naguang was near the village of Valencia, five miles west of a Japanese airfield. There, the irascible radio broke down again and seemed beyond repair. Unbelievably, a day or two later, a Japanese airplane droning overhead, the pilot obviously disoriented, released a wicker supply basket attached to a parachute, which drifted down on the Americans' position. The guerrillas retrieved it. Opening it, Sumner's jaw dropped. Inside was a Japanese radio with spare tubes.

"What the hell?" he muttered. He turned to Blaise. "A gift from Tojo, Bill. Can you cannibalize this stuff and get our goddamned piece of junk working again?"

"I think so," Blaise replied.

He and the three Filipino radiomen, Lt. Inoconcio F. Cabrido, Pvt. Trinidad Sison, and Pvt. Agapito Amano, went to work and soon had Sumner back in radio communications.

The radio would break down again about a week later, and would incredibly be repaired thanks to yet another misdropped Japanese radio.

★   ★   ★

Sumner's new CP on Mount Naguang was in the village of Cagdaat. His base of operations was a large house tucked into the trees with a spring-fed pool some thirty feet beyond. The radio shack was about a hundred feet away, sited for direct communication with 6th Army headquarters across the island. The Filipinos created a drop zone about a thousand yards to the east and north. With the help of Nazareno, a native intelligence network was established to report on Japanese movements, troop strength, and locations. Often, the guerrillas attacked Japanese outposts and patrols.

During the trek, Sumner had also picked up five downed American pilots, some of whom were enjoying a life of leisure among the grateful natives. These men he sent back to San Isidro in the company of guerrillas.

"Time to get you boys back to work," he said as he packed the fliers off.

★   ★   ★

In early December, about a month into the lengthy mission, Sumner received a radio report about well-camouflaged Japanese warehouses on the outskirts of Ormoc City that reportedly contained stores of food and ammunition. The 6th Army had called in air strikes, but the planes had been unable to spot the buildings beneath their camouflage netting. The task of knocking out the warehouses was thus passed on to Sumner and his men. He sat down with Nazareno and drew up plans to form a special contact company.

After laying out the mission, he said, "In your command you have a number of Philippine Scouts. I need enough men to make up three platoons of three squads each. I want veterans, men with good, solid combat experience."

Nazareno agreed and word went out. Within days, highly trained Philippine Scouts, some with as many as twenty years in the army, began trickling in to Sumner's CP. He quickly divided them into squads with nine riflemen and one automatic weapon, either a BAR or a submachine gun. Sumner would also take with him a captured Japanese 82mm mortar, and parachute flares to light up the area if needed. Should they be discovered and attacked and have to get out in a hurry, the mortar was considered expendable.

Before departing, Sumner requested another airdrop, this time to supply him with not just small-arms ammo but incendiary grenades and quarter-pound blocks of TNT.

After taking a day or two to rehearse his ad hoc company on how to function as a unit, the column struck off toward Ormoc City, arriving at their objective in the early evening hours. There they settled down in the underbrush to wait for darkness. Sumner knew the layout. While the Scouts had been assembling, he had made several personal reconnaissance trips to the area and discovered three expertly hidden warehouses. He had also dispatched his most reliable guerrilla agents to creep to within just a few yards of the buildings. There they took detailed notes of the number of guards, the size of the structures, the distances to the doors from the nearest cover, and the distances between buildings, including the guard shack.

As he waited for nightfall, Sumner called in his team, Renhols, Weiland, Blaise, and Jones (who had since rejoined the team from Abijao), and his three platoon leaders for a final briefing.

"Third platoon will provide our base of fire," he told the group.

Addressing the third platoon leader, Sumner continued.

"You will set up your line about two hundred yards from the main gate. Deploy in two-man positions, but do not dig in. As for the rest of us, first and second platoons will go with me into the warehouse area. There's about a squad of Japs stationed there, but only about three or four are on duty at a time. We will take them out quickly and silently. Under no circumstances is anyone to fire his weapon. Stress that to your men. If any shot is fired, we will abort the mission and fall back on third platoon. Clear?" Everyone nodded. "OK. We go at twenty-two hundred."

★   ★   ★

Slipping into the warehouse at ten p.m. as planned, the Filipinos went about, knives in hand, dispatching the Japanese guards. The enemy soldiers in the guard shack were not disturbed; however, one squad of Philippine scouts was posted outside with orders to cut them down should they suddenly emerge.

With the sentries dead, the platoons split up and entered their assigned warehouse. Entering one building, which measured thirty by sixty feet, Sumner—by the eerie glow of a red-hooded flashlight—found the place stacked with fifty-kilo bags of rice and crates of canned goods piled eight feet high. Working rapidly, the men began placing TNT charges with five-minute fuses, pushing them back into the stacks of supplies. Sumner knew that in the other warehouses his men were doing the same thing. With the TNT in place, the fuses were ignited.

"Let's go," Sumner said in a loud whisper.

As they fled, Sumner sent a runner to alert the guardhouse squad to withdraw. It was ten fifteen; the entire operation had taken just fifteen minutes. They now had four minutes to get away. Confirming all present, Sumner assigned one squad as rear guard and they all headed back up into the hills. By the time the charges were to blow, the group was about five hundred yards from the warehouses. Sumner called a halt so the men could watch their handiwork. Moments later, a series of blasts rocked the night, sending shock waves through the air as the warehouses were blown apart. Flames ignited the camouflage netting, adding to the inferno. Then another, bigger explosion erupted as fuel drums in one of the warehouses began detonating, sending balls of fire hundreds of feet into the air. Burning embers descended around Sumner's force, starting small fires.

The rolling explosions continued as more fuel drums and ammo ignited, and in the glow of the fires, Sumner felt he and his men were naked and exposed to "every Jap on western Leyte."

"Let's get the hell out of here," he yelled, and the group fled quickly for the concealing safety of the jungles and mountains.

Pursuit was not long in coming. From behind them came angry shouts and the sound of weapons being fired into the underbrush. Sumner knew the Japanese had not spotted them, and that the shooting was random, but that made it even more dangerous. Yet despite the hot pursuit, the raiders slipped away and returned to the safety of their CP around four a.m.

The foray came with a price, however. The Japanese called on the local civilians, as well as guerrilla bands and even bandits, to turn over to them the raiders of the supply dump or face retaliation. In surrounding villages, natives were tortured to death by the enemy bent on finding the Americans. Many were bound and used for bayonet practice and one man was skinned alive. Yet Sumner and his men were never betrayed by the loyal Filipinos.

★   ★   ★

At six a.m. on December 7, 1944, Sumner received a radio message from 6th Army HQ that the 77th Infantry Division would be landing at Ormoc at seven a.m. He quickly moved his team to a vantage point overlooking the beach. It was like having the best seats in the house for a spectacular show.

That same morning, a Japanese convoy arrived bearing five thousand infantry replacements from Yamashita on Luzon. The simultaneous arrival of the two forces at the same spot led to a spectacular collision. Aircraft from both sides tangled in the air overhead as fifty-six P-47 Thunderbolt fighters from Tacloban bombed and strafed the Japanese surface fleet. Planes began falling from the sky and enemy ships erupted in flames, many either capsizing or rearing up in the water and sliding below the waves. American ships were hit as well, and two destroyers went down, their spines broken by kamikazes. The

Japanese finally withdrew, but not before losing most of their ships and what proved to be two-thirds of their remaining bombers.

On the beaches below the Scouts' position, large naval guns pummeled the landing zone, tearing up jungle and the Japanese defenses. The prelanding bombardment was brief, then the Higgins boats and amtracs, swarming like water bugs, moved in, beached themselves, and disgorged their human contents: battle-toughened veterans of the 77th Division who had gotten their baptism of fire on Guam and Tinian.

With American troops overrunning their only local supply base, the Japanese were quickly driven back, although once they recovered from the shock, they managed to launch several violent counterattacks over the next few days. On December 10, after a fierce fight, Ormoc City fell into American hands. A huge pall of smoke hung over the city and the air was gray with concrete dust from buildings pulverized by artillery fire.

Sumner and his men were ordered to assist the incoming troops by furnishing them with guerrillas to serve as scouts and for guarding supply dumps.

The invasion presented Sumner with a new problem. With the 77th Division pushing the Japanese from the south and the 1st Cavalry, which had driven across Leyte from the October invasion beaches and were now pressing down from the north, the enemy was being driven back on Sumner's position. Skirmishes between the guerrillas and enemy units became more frequent, sometimes as many as three or four times a day, but the guerrillas and Scouts had enough firepower to keep the Japanese at bay.

About ten days after the 77th Division came ashore, Sumner received a radio message from its commander, Maj. Gen. Andrew D. Bruce. He wanted to meet with Sumner as soon as possible. Taking his team and a platoon of guerrillas, Sumner headed for one of the division's regimental CPs as instructed, arriving the next day.

The Scouts, with their camouflage gear, soft hats, airborne M1A1 carbines, and painted faces, were a source of curiosity, not just to the soldiers of the 77th but to their commander as well, and he interrogated Sumner at length.

"What are you men doing out here?" General Bruce asked.

"Monitoring Japanese troop and barge movements in conjunction with the local guerrillas," Sumner replied, giving a simplified answer.

"How long have you been out here?"

"About six weeks, sir."

"Are you men survivors of Bataan and Corregidor?"

"No, sir. We're Alamo Scouts attached to General Krueger," Sumner said, and went on to explain the Scouts' function. Bruce listened with intense interest. The 77th had served mostly in the central Pacific, so Bruce had never heard of the Scouts.

Bruce then began asking detailed questions about the beach area and terrain at Palompan. Sumner turned the questions over to his guerrilla intelligence officer, who used maps and aerial photos Bruce's staff provided to answer the general's questions. The discussion lasted about half an hour, after which Bruce told Sumner that he was planning an amphibious landing, an end run, at Palompan on Christmas Day.

Bruce thanked Sumner, and he and his men returned to their mountain lair.

As the American advance continued, Sumner's area of operations was increasingly constricted, and the guerrillas were constantly engaging Japanese stragglers in fierce firefights that resulted in casualties on both sides. It was plain to see the time had come to leave. After bringing Renhols back to the CP from Abijao, Sumner radioed 6th Army HQ with his decision.

"Leave the radio and the Filipino crew, and enough guerrillas to serve as a guard detachment with the 77th Division," Sumner was instructed.

Once back inside U.S. lines, Sumner was directed to contact Gen. John R. Hodge's 14th Corps for transport back to 6th Army HQ.

With a guerrilla escort, the team reached the village of Morgen, a short distance from the 307th Infantry Regiment's lines. The team cautiously approached the line on December 20, but were fired on by a nervous sentry. Sumner quickly pulled his men back. After all they had been through, the last thing he wanted was for one of them to get shot by a jumpy GI.

Retreating back to the village for the night, Sumner thought that perhaps the reason they were fired on was that they were unrecognizable. The Scouts were dirty, their clothes were grungy, and they did not look at all like American troops. Even the normally neat Bill Blaise, a stickler on appearance, looked terrible.

"Let's clean up," he told the men. "I want everyone to bathe, wash his uniform, clean his boots and equipment and get a haircut. I want us to look as if we're coming off the parade field, and go in with pride, heads high, looking as if this little jaunt we've been on has been a piece of cake."

The Sumner Team passed through lines of the 393rd Infantry Regiment the morning of December 21, forty-seven days after setting out, the Scout record to date. By six p.m., Sumner was reporting to General Hodges, nicknamed "the Mayor of Ormoc," who insisted Sumner and his men join him for dinner in the officers' mess tent. Sumner accepted the invitation, and that evening, as they ate, he was amused to find that Hodge dined on standard, no-frills army rations. He did not tell the general that he and his men ate better food during their lengthy mission, thanks to the grateful Philippine people.

Sumner was put on an L-5 scout plane and flown back to the ASTC ahead of his men to report to 6th Army G2, arriving back on December 23. His men followed a day later, where Coleman, stitches mending his injured hand, rejoined them.

Christmas 1944 marked a rare moment in Alamo Scout history. For the first time since August, all of the Scout teams were together. On Christmas Day, this elite unit of men gathered in the mess hall for a lavish holiday dinner, and gave thanks that, after forty-nine missions, many fraught with high levels of danger, all of them were there, safe and sound.

Now it was on to Luzon.

CHAPTER 12

"Only an Act of God Is Going to Get You Out."

Luzon, January–February 1945

At ten forty-five a.m. on January 4, 1945, 850 ships of MacArthur's Luzon invasion force, including two PT tenders carrying several Alamo Scout teams, sailed out of San Pedro Bay between Leyte and Samar, then steamed south across Leyte Gulf. The next day found them cruising through the Surigao Strait under a sunny, clear sky, then gliding across the Mindanao Sea, bound for the broad expanse of the South China Sea.

Actually, the invasion of the main Philippine island of Luzon had begun on December 15, 1944, with a surprise landing by the Americans on Mindoro, separated from Luzon by the seven-and-a-half-mile-wide Veroe Island Passage. Defended by one thousand Japanese soldiers and some two hundred sailors marooned from sunken ships, the enemy garrison was quickly driven back into isolated pockets of resistance, where they would hold out until being annihilated in late January.

Now the main show was to begin, and the invasion force bound for Lingayen Gulf hoisted anchor and steamed away.

Luckily for the men on the troop transports, they were three days' sailing behind the bulk of Adm. Jesse B. Oldendorf's warships. These heavily armed vessels, nine aircraft carriers and several battleships, including two battle-scarred veterans of Pearl Harbor, the *West Virginia* and the *California*, ran a gauntlet of Japanese air strikes, including kamikaze attacks. On January 4, a kamikaze slammed into the escort carrier *Ommaney Bay*, killing ninety-seven men and creating so much damage the small carrier had to be scuttled. The next day sixteen kamikazes hit nine U.S. and Australian ships, and on January 6, in desperation, daylong suicide raids roared out of the clouds. One plane hit the bridge of the battleship USS *New Mexico*, killing twenty-nine men, including the ship's captain and Lt. Gen. Herbert Lumsden, British prime minister Winston Churchill's personal liaison to MacArthur. In fact, that day proved to be one of the worst in U.S. naval history, with eleven ships damaged, a minesweeper sunk, and hundreds of men killed.

On January 8, a kamikaze nosed into the escort carrier *Kitkun Bay*, and burning aviation fuel and exploding ammo made the ship glow like a red-hot coal. Yet somehow, the ship was saved.

As the Japanese launched strikes, so did the Americans, and planes from the invasion fleet, along with B-25 Mitchell bombers from 5th Air Force airfields on Leyte and, now, Mindoro, plastered the former U.S. base at Clark Field.

Miles behind all of this carnage, the GIs in the troopships sailed unmolested.

MacArthur's landing on Mindoro surprised Yamashita, who had assumed the Americans would rely on air cover from the bases he knew they were building on Leyte. Yamashita had no way of knowing that heavy rains had delayed the completion of those airfields, forcing MacArthur to turn his attention to Mindoro. In response, Yamashita ordered more air strikes, including by kamikazes, this time at the forty-mile-long American convoy of troop and supply ships. While many of these planes, generally flown by inexperienced pilots, did not get through the wall of antiaircraft fire, some did with devastating results. The ammunition ship *John Burke* vanished in a spectacular explosion and another, the *Lewis L. Dyche*, blew up so violently it picked up two

PT boats a quarter mile away and dumped them back into the water with heavy damage, while a hail of falling debris, including unexploded shells, rained down on adjacent ships, causing more damage and casualties.

Yamashita was a pragmatist. With the fall of Leyte, he knew he had no hope of stopping an American landing on Luzon and little chance of defeating them once they were ashore. He had lost half of his shipping and thousands of men trying to reinforce Leyte. His naval force now consisted of two submarine chasers, nineteen patrol boats, ten midget subs, and 180 one-man suicide boats, mostly in the Manila Bay area. Perhaps worse, all but about two hundred planes of his air force had been shot down or destroyed on the ground, and by the time the Americans actually came ashore, that number would be reduced to a few dozen.

Luzon is 340 miles long and 130 miles across at its widest. To defend it, Yamashita had six infantry and one armored division, or about 275,000 men, to draw on, but this number was deceptive. Many of his men were not frontline caliber, including convalescing sick and wounded, and most were poorly armed and equipped. There were also about 16,000 naval personnel around Manila, mostly sailors whose ships had been sunk in Leyte Gulf in October, under the command of Adm. Sanji Iwabuchi. But interservice rivalry meant Yamashita had little authority over them.

Unable to prevent a landing, Yamashita ordered that the beaches would not be defended. Instead, he would fight a battle in-depth, making the Americans pay in blood for every yard and to deny for as long as possible the Americans' use of Luzon as an air base to strike at the Japanese homeland. To accomplish this, he broke his defending force into three main elements. His main force of about 152,000 men, called the Shobu Group, were sent into the mountainous regions to the north with orders to tie down the Americans for as long as possible. This would also allow the Japanese to control one of the island's main food-producing areas in the Cagayan Valley. Yamashita remained in command of this unit, setting up his CP in the village of Baguio, a summer mountain resort five thousand feet above sea level.

Another eighty thousand men, called the Shimbu Group, under the command of Lt. Gen. Shizuo Yokoyama, were sent to the south to hold the high ground east of Manila and thus control the city's water supply. The remaining thirty thousand troops, the Kembu Group, under Maj. Gen. Rikichi Tsukada, were to hold the Caraballo Mountains and the west side of the Agno-Pampanga Valley, where the former U.S. bases of Clark Field and Fort Stotsenburg were located, and stretch south to Bataan. They were to hold as long as possible, then retreat to the Zambales mountain range and fight a delaying action.

Manila was indefensible, Yamashita decided, so he ordered his men out except for a small detachment to protect supply routes and blow the highway bridges leading from the city. Iwabuchi decided otherwise and commanded his sixteen thousand sailors to hold the city, which would soon be turned into a charnel house of death and destruction.

★ ★ ★

The landings, Operation Mike I, started the morning of January 9. Even though guerrillas onshore had radioed that there would be no Japanese resistance on the beaches, Oldendorf ordered his big naval guns to fire, which they did, needlessly destroying homes and public buildings. At nine thirty a.m., the first of sixty-eight thousand men of the 6th Army came ashore to find, as the guerrillas had said, the Japanese gone. The Scouts landed the next day, setting up their camp near a captured airfield.

As on Leyte, the Scouts were told that their mission on Luzon would mainly be to establish and maintain communications between the various independent guerrilla groups. Information coming from the guerrillas was often exaggerated and sometimes self-serving, meant to boost the prestige of the guerrilla band's leader, and thus was of questionable reliability. The Scouts would also set up observation posts to watch the roads and radio stations, and teach the guerrillas how to gather accurate information, and what to look for, especially numbers of enemy, their armaments, and types of equipment.

The Scouts in the field relied on the natives and often paid them. The teams were issued American dollars or Philippine pesos. When the paper money was gone, they wrote IOUs, which the 6th Army honored. On occasion the Scouts would barter information in return for clothes, food, and ammunition.

Bill Littlefield and his team drew the first Alamo Scout mission on Luzon, a twenty-four-day excursion that began near the town of Tarlac on January 14 and would end February 7 near Manila. Their mission was to reconnoiter southeast of Tarlac, where Highways 3 and 13 intersected. Passing through the American lines and moving well ahead of the advancing army, Littlefield and his men were the first Americans the Filipinos in this region had seen in three years who were not prisoners of war. They responded by giving the Americans flowers and singing songs, including "The Star-Spangled Banner," that left the Scouts moved. The people wrote a letter of tribute about the Scouts' arrival, with all men signing it on the front and the women on the back.

The villagers also heaped food items on the GIs, especially eggs. Initially, the Scouts appreciated this gesture, but as it was repeated in village after village, they soon had more eggs than they could carry. Littlefield tried to dispose of some by gulping them down raw, but upon cracking open one egg and finding a partially developed chick inside, that culinary experiment quickly ended.

Part of Littlefield's mission at Tarlac was to contact the three-thousand-man Marking Guerrilla unit under Col. Marcos V. Agustin, and to assess their value as a fighting unit and if they could be relied upon to work with the 6th Army. Littlefield met and talked extensively with Agustin and was convinced by the training and discipline of his men of Agustin's reliability as a leader. He radioed back a recommendation to the 6th Army that the Marking group be used in conjunction with U.S. units, and soon the guerrillas would be fighting alongside men of the 43rd Division.

Littlefield continued his mission south toward Manila.

Since the Scouts were out in front of the main body of troops by several miles, many of the Japanese garrisons in the area were as yet unmolested. On several occasions, Littlefield and his team had to creep around enemy garrisons. One night, as he lay silently in the underbrush, Littlefield fought the urge to jump or flinch as a Japanese soldier strolled up to the bushes where the Scout leader lay hidden, opened his fly, and urinated. Littlefield remained immobile as he felt the warm liquid splatter on his leg.

About four days into the mission, Littlefield and his men were offered transportation by a friendly Filipino via several skinny horses that, Littlefield later said, "hadn't had a square meal since December 7, 1941." The horses had blankets but no saddles, and within just one day the Scouts were all rubbed raw between their legs.

"It damned near killed us," Littlefield recalled sixty-two years later.

They unanimously decided walking was better.

Littlefield soon discovered that the horses were the least of his problems. As the mission neared its end, Zeke McConnell was stricken with appendicitis and could not keep up with the team. McConnell insisted that the team go on ahead, and that he would follow at his own pace. With great reluctance, Littlefield agreed, but assigned a guerrilla to escort his Cherokee friend and carry his rifle. However, McConnell snatched the weapon from the man, saying, "No, you won't." The guerrilla carried McConnell's pack and web gear instead.

The team proceeded on ahead, finally reaching American lines, where, to his relief, Littlefield spotted an ambulance loading up injured men. He hurried up to the driver.

"Hold this vehicle here," he said. "I have a very sick man coming in."

The driver, nervous at being so close to the flying lead, said, "I can't wait, sir."

"Yes, you can, son," Littlefield replied.

"I have no room, sir," the man insisted. "The ambulance is full. And the Japs might attack us here."

"You are not going anywhere until my man gets here," Littlefield commanded, and the nervous driver waited. Finally, Littlefield spotted McConnell and the guerrilla approaching and ran out to meet them. He helped his friend into the ambulance and the vehicle sped off.

McConnell had surgery, but even the hospital wasn't safe. As Mc-Connell lay recuperating, Japanese attacked the base and the patients in their beds were told to lie still while outside the battle raged as marines held off the enemy assault. McConnell ached to get up and get into the fight, but could not.

While hospitalized, however, McConnell met two POWs released from Cabanatuan prison camp just days earlier, both from his own home state of Oklahoma. He and the skinny, sickly men had a "nice reunion," he later recalled.

★   ★   ★

As Littlefield continued moving south, Bill Nellist was summoned to a briefing. In the mountains east of Lingayen Gulf and the town of Santo Thomas, the Japanese had built an intricate cave and tunnel network stockpiled with supplies, food, and weapons. Protecting the installation were an undetermined number of 240mm howitzers, mounted on tracks so that after being fired they could be rolled, via an elaborate pulley system, back through camouflaged doors into a mountainside cave and hidden from the prying eyes of American spotter aircraft. The tracks also allowed the Japanese the mobility to shift the guns' firing positions.

Seven men gathered in the CP for the briefing that, to Nellist's surprise, was delivered by General Krueger himself.

"Our troops can't get across the Rosario Road because of those goddamned Jap big guns," Krueger said. "You've got to locate and pinpoint those bastards, Bill. But I have to tell you, the area is crawling with Japs. They have a defensive perimeter running from San Jose south to Urdaneta. You've got a fifty-fifty chance of getting in. And if you do get in, only an act of God is going to get you out."

Nellist knew this would be a tough nut to crack and that, as a Scout, he could refuse any mission. But that ran against his grain. The Jap guns had to be taken out.

The next day Nellist climbed into a small L-5 scout plane for a look-see. Gazing down at the rugged landscape, with its steep ridges and deep valleys, he saw no signs of the guns. That evening at five thirty the team boarded a Higgins boat at White Beach One, which carried them down the coastline, nearer to their target. The boat stopped three hundred feet offshore when its keel scraped the sandy bottom. The ramp went down and the men waded to shore in chest-deep water, weapons held high, with Gil Cox out in front. The landing boat backed off the sandbar and turned out to sea.

All was quiet along the dark shoreline ahead as the men waded in, except for the distant barking of a dog. Then, while the Scouts were still a hundred yards or so from the beach, the sky lit up as a flare fired from a navy ship, probably at the request of American troops onshore, burst overhead, bathing everything with a bright light. Wismer thought he had pissed his pants, but was unsure because of being in the water.

The men froze, lowering themselves so that the water was lapping against their chins. Nellist hoped the flare was not a signal for a bombardment, or he and his team would be "left with our asses hanging out." After the flare had burned itself out, the team cautiously waded to shore.

The guns were tucked away in the mountains three or four miles inland, so once the team reached the sand, Nellist began pushing forward immediately. He wanted to close as much distance to his target before dawn as possible in order to find a suitable place to set up an OP. They were barely on dry land when they stumbled upon a footpath. Wanting to make time, Nellist decided to take it.

"What about Jap patrols?" Tom Siason asked.

"I doubt they use this trail much," Nellist replied. "Look how overgrown it is."

Nellist put Kittleson at point, and they began the trek. The starless night was as black as six feet down a cow's throat and Kittleson didn't even see the native village until he almost walked into it. Huts of nipa palm suddenly loomed in the darkness, and Kittleson raised one arm and dropped to a knee. The others dropped also. For the next thirty minutes the seven men remained silent as ghosts. No sound came from the collection of huts. Satisfied the place was empty, the team crept through the village like shadows in the night.

Beyond the village, the path widened into a weed-choked road. With a red-hooded flashlight, Nellist checked his map.

"The road joins Highway Three at the village of Rawis," Nellist said. "Let's go. Kit, take the point again."

As the team followed the empty road, the thinning vegetation on both sides told Nellist they were gaining altitude.

Daylight dawned cloudy, with a threat of rain. A gray mist clung to the mountaintops. Nearing Rawis, Nellist split the team in two, with Kittleson, Cox, and himself advancing along one side of the road, and Smith, Siason, Asis, and Wismer on the other. Smith took point. They had not gone far when Smith dropped to a knee, as did the others. Smith turned toward Nellist and drew the flat of his hand across his throat. The signal was clear: there were Japanese ahead. Nellist indicated for the team to hold, then tapped Kittleson and pointed toward the village. Kittleson nodded and moved forward. As he drew closer to Rawis, he dropped to all fours, testing each move before committing his entire weight.

Kittleson came to a tangled patch of rhododendron. Crawling through it, he reached a small rise. Ahead was a short concrete bridge spanning a trickle of water that passed for a stream. Beyond the stream, in the village, sat a Japanese truck. A small breakfast fire burned by the stream bank. By its meager flame squatted three Japanese soldiers, brewing tea, smoking and chatting, then laughing over some joke one of the men told. A soldier poured himself some tea into a tin cup and, slinging his weapon onto his shoulder, stood up. As if this were some signal, the other two also rose and walked up the slight embankment and onto the bridge. There they continued chatting, leaning their weapons against the railing of the bridge.

Kittleson went back to report.

"You just saw the three Nips?" Nellist asked. Kit nodded. "Then that's probably all there are. The Japs don't have the manpower to post large garrisons at every town." He thought for a moment, then turned to Smith. "Andy, you, Asis, Siason, and Wismer take out the two jokers on the bridge. The rest of us will go for the third Nip. I'd like a prisoner if possible."

The men moved silently into position. When they were all ready, they charged forward. Nellist yelled, *"Jishu,"* ordering the Japanese to surrender. The two enemy on the bridge grabbed for their weapons and the Scouts opened fire. One bridge guard crumpled to the ground as the other toppled over the railing and into the streambed below. The tea drinker flipped up his rifle and aimed at the Americans. Nellist squeezed off several quick rounds with his Garand. The .30-caliber slugs knocked the man three steps backward before he sat down heavily. Coughing blood, he slumped over onto the ground and died.

"Shit," Nellist said. "Let's get these bodies out of sight. Kit, check out the village."

As they went about their tasks, Kittleson, entering Rawis, suddenly dropped into a ditch. Ahead an old man on a rusty bicycle was peddling toward him, followed by a lumbering caraboa and a mob of waving villagers, shouting, "Americans come." The villagers swamped the GIs and happily took over the task of dragging off the dead Japanese. The cheering went on for several minutes as Nellist, for security reasons, tried to calm them down. He had at last succeeded, when one native asked, "MacArthur come?"

"Yes," Nellist replied, setting off another wild round of celebration.

In the midst of the hubbub, Nellist was introduced to a native named Philip, who had been forced to work for the Japanese manning the guns. He pinpointed for Nellist the location of the tunnels. All the while the revelry continued and the Scouts, growing more concerned about the Japanese hearing the ruckus, finally fled the town, pursued for some distance by their not-easily-dissuaded well-wishers.

★ ★ ★

By midday, the team was sitting on a wooded ridge. Far below them, in the valley to their rear, they could see the village of Rawis.

"Wonder if they're still partying?" Smith mused.

Ahead of them, and below, was Highway 3, along which enemy trucks and tanks could be seen rumbling. The Scouts watched for any signs of the big guns, knowing there was nothing much they could do until dark, when, should the guns fire, they could spot the muzzle flashes, and then triangulate a position.

Shortly after nightfall, near the crest of the ridge, about three-quarters of a mile away, a big gun roared, its muzzle flash lighting the night. The Scouts instinctively ducked down as the 240mm shell roared overhead like a freight train, its passage rustling the grass and leaves around them.

"Jesus Christ," Wismer said in a low tone that reflected his awe.

The men compared notes, but were unable to come to an agreement on the gun's location. The gun fired again an hour later, and continued to fire every hour. After a few firings, the team worked up a grid location, which Nellist made each man memorize; however, Nellist fretted that there seemed to be just a single artillery piece.

"I hope to hell it isn't just one fucking Jap gun holding up the entire U.S. Army," he cursed. "Let's go back."

Nellist's destination was the town of Cabaroan, located on the coast. There he hoped to hire a boat to take them back to U.S. lines. The team reached the town, all right, but the only vessel available was a rickety banca, or outrigger canoe. Deciding it was better than nothing, the men boarded the boat and began to sail southward. The banca was not up to the task and began taking on water. The Scouts had no choice but to abandon the sinking craft. They swam to shore and went the rest of the way on foot.

The 158th Regimental Combat Team (RCT) was holding the line at the town of Damortis, and as Nellist and his men drew near, it occurred to them that, without a radio—it had been deemed too heavy to carry on this mission—they were out of touch and did not know the current password.

"We could just shout out that we're Americans," Asis said.

"No," Nellist replied. "The Japs know that trick, too." He looked at Cox. "Gil, take off your shirt." Cox complied, baring his pasty white chest and upper arms. "Great. You walk out in front like that yelling that you're an American."

Cox balked.

"Go on, Gil," Nellist urged. "You're the tallest guy on the team, certainly taller than any Nip. And with that white skin and blond hair, even if their outpost is manned by a total idiot, he'll never take you for a Jap."

So it was that the Nellist Team arrived back behind U.S. lines, led by a bare-chested Gil Cox waving his shirt and calling out, "We're Americans."

The position of the Japanese guns—there turned out to be two of them, made in Germany by the Krupp ironworks—was handed on by the 158th RCT's headquarters to the 43rd Division artillery, which blanketed the area in 105- and 155mm fire. Both guns were knocked out, and the way was cleared for the continued drive on Manila.

Learning that Nellist had not only been successful but had come back unscathed thrilled Krueger and swelled him with pride.

"My Alamo Scouts always come back," he boasted. "I can send them anywhere—*any damned where*—and know they'll accomplish their missions."

★ ★ ★

For Nellist, the success of this mission, coupled with his participation in the hostage rescue at Cape Oransbari in New Guinea back in October, made him the first choice to lead what would become the Alamo Scouts' most famous raid.

CHAPTER 13

First In, Last Out

Cabanatuan, January 27–February 1, 1945

Galen Kittleson and Wilbert Wismer were lounging in the afternoon sun in front of their tent at 6th Army headquarters near Calasio, south of Lingayen. In was January 26, and they had been back just eight days from their last mission to spot some large Japanese guns holding up the American advance on Manila. As Wismer lit a cigarette and blew the smoke lazily into the air, he noticed a strange apparition. A reed-thin American major in a well-worn uniform and mounted on a bay horse was riding into camp and making straight for them. He poked Kittleson and the two enlisted men rose to attention as the officer drew rein. They saluted him.

"Can you fellas tell me where the HQ tent is?" the major asked, returning the salute with a very informal flip of his hand.

"Straight down this street, sir," Wismer said, pointing. "You can't miss it."

The officer nodded, turned his horse's head in the direction indicated, and moved on. The two Scouts watched him go.

"Who in the hell was that?" Kittleson asked.

"You don't know?" Wismer said. "That was Major Lapham. The guerrilla leader."

★　★　★

Robert Lapham had been twenty-four when the Japanese invaded Luzon in 1941. In April 1942, Lapham, then a lieutenant, and thirty-five other men volunteered to infiltrate fifty miles behind Japanese lines and blow up enemy planes parked at Clark Field. They had made forty of those miles when they received the news that Bataan had fallen. With that, the men opted to split up and filter into the hills to avoid capture. Lapham made his way to Nueva Ecija Province, near Cabanatuan City, and began to recruit guerrilla fighters. When the number of recruits hit two thousand the army promoted Lapham to major.

Shortly after the fall of the Philippines, the Japanese established a large prisoner-of-war camp just a few miles east of Cabanatuan City. Made up of men who had survived the infamous Bataan Death March, the camp encompassed about twenty-five acres in the midst of an open plain. Inside, at its peak, it housed about seven thousand prisoners, a number that began to slowly dwindle as men forced into slave labor died either of disease or at enemy hands, or were shipped to Japan to work in servitude.

Throughout this whole time, Lapham had kept close watch on the camp, and burned with a desire to set his suffering comrades free. He had made friends inside the wire, and managed to smuggle in food and even a few weapons that were stockpiled for eventual escape.

In June 1944, he made MacArthur's headquarters aware of the prisoners and their plight, and requested that several submarines stand to offshore while he and his guerrillas attempted to free the approximately three thousand prisoners left in the camp. He even relayed his plan of attack. MacArthur refused, saying the men in the camp would be too ill and weak to make the trek over the Sierra Madre mountains to get to Debut Bay. They would be recaptured and, quite likely, executed by the Japanese. Lapham's reply was that if a rescue was delayed too long, all of the surviving prisoners could be carried out in one caraboa cart.

It would be the first of several such pleas he would make, and all were rejected.

Then came the grim news from Puerto Princesa prisoner camp on Palawan, an elongated island that marks the western border of the Sulu Sea. There, on December 14, more than 150 prisoners had been herded into crude air-raid shelters on the pretext of an incoming American air strike. Once the prisoners were in the shelters, Japanese guards doused them with gasoline and set them alight. Men who crawled from the blazing, hellish infernos were gunned down. A few, however, managed to escape and, with the help of friendly Filipinos, make their way across the Sulu Sea in bancas, and told their stories to horrified listeners.

While the Americans viewed this act as one of intense cruelty, the Japanese were, in fact, following an army edict that the prisoners, already disgraced by their very act of surrendering, were not allowed to fall back into American hands. Lapham knew this, and he feared the men in Cabanatuan would soon be targeted for similar elimination, especially as MacArthur's forces drew ever closer. Even Gen. Masaharu Homma, the "Poet General" who loved American movies and whose pro-democratic, pro-Western leanings often got him into trouble with his superiors, would not be able to ignore the order.

That was why Lapham had just ridden thirty miles through Japanese-held territory. This would be a personal appeal, and one he hoped could not be ignored.

★   ★   ★

Following Wismer's directions, Lapham found the 6th Army G2 tent and dismounted. Lapham had radioed ahead, so Krueger's intelligence chief, Col. Horton White, had been expecting the guerrilla leader and was aware of Lapham's concerns. He now greeted Lapham as the major tied his horse, and offered him food. Lapham declined.

He briefed White on the camp, and about the Palawan massacre and his belief that it would be repeated at Cabanatuan as the Japanese grew more desperate.

"Our troops entered the town of Guimba this morning," White said, pointing to a map pinned to a bulletin board. "That still puts the camp twenty-five miles behind Jap lines. What's the opposition?"

"There are about nine thousand of the bastards in and around Cabanatuan City, five miles to the west, and there's a camp here"— Lapham pointed at the map—"along the Cabu River about half a mile to the northeast. The numbers there vary."

"How many Nips inside the camp?" White asked.

"Depends," Lapham replied. "The permanent garrison is about seventy-five men, but Japs are frequently moving along this road that runs to Cabanatuan City, and sometimes troops stop at the camp and bivouac. Right now, there are about two hundred and fifty."

"Tell me about this road," White said, pointing to the line passing in front of the camp.

"It's a major thoroughfare," Lapham said. "Convoys often use it. Look, Colonel, I know this is a difficult undertaking, but it is essential. I'm convinced these men will be killed, and soon, if we don't get them out. The Japs are on edge, and it won't take much to push them into a homicidal rage."

"I agree," White said. "Let's go talk to General Krueger. We have several companies of Sixth Army Rangers here, and this is right up their alley."

"Can they handle the reconnaissance end, too?" Lapham asked.

"They won't have to," White replied. "We have specialists who can do that admirably."

★   ★   ★

Krueger, also aware of the situation, was in full agreement with White, both of the mission's risk and its importance, and consulted his map. Krueger had known of the camp and had been informed about the Palawan affair, and he shared Lapham's fears.

"Our troops should reach Cabanatuan in five days," he said. "Today is the twenty-sixth—that means time is of the essence. We need to get those POWs out of there before January thirtieth, or there might be none to rescue. Arrange a briefing now. I want Mucci, Dove, Nellist, and Rounsaville there."

The summons came that same afternoon. Bill Nellist, Jack Dove, and Tom Rounsaville entered the briefing hut, where they found White and Lapham at the map table. Col. Henry Mucci and Capt. Robert Prince of the Rangers were also present. After introductions, White told Lapham about the success the two Scout teams had had at Cape Oransbari in New Guinea the previous October, in freeing close to seventy hostages from Japanese hands and delivering them to safety. Lapham was suitably impressed.

"That was a cakewalk compared to this one," White told them, then revealed the nature of the mission, just as Lapham had laid it out for him.

"Aside from the fact that you'll be twenty-five miles behind Jap lines, with as many as ten thousand of the rice-eaters within five miles, your problems will include the prisoners themselves. These are generally men considered too ill or weak to be of any value as workers. Another reason the Japs will likely kill them before our forces arrive." White straightened up. "Bill, since Tom was in charge at Oransbari, you will be overall Scout leader. Jack, you will be the contact man, and move with the Rangers. Captain Prince will command the Rangers, but Colonel Mucci will go along as overall commander of the mission. You will be supplied with maps and the latest aerial recon photos."

Mucci, standing ramrod straight, a pipe clenched in his mouth and a pencil-thin mustache lining his lip under a prominent nose, looked at Nellist.

"Lieutenant, this mission is strictly voluntary," he said. "You can decline if you want, and no one will question your guts and dedication. Speak up now."

"If I were in that camp, I'd want someone to come and get me, sir," he replied. "We're in."

"No one gets left behind," Mucci said. "We take out every single man, regardless of how weak. Even if a man is dead, we bring his body back."

Everyone nodded in agreement.

"Colonel Mucci's men will pull out Sunday morning," Horton said. "Bill, that means you and your teams will leave twenty-four hours earlier. Get to the camp, get the info the Rangers will need, and get it back to them."

"I plan to be in position and ready to attack by nineteen thirty on Monday," Mucci said. "That's fifty-three hours from now, so get me as much intelligence as you can."

"Bill knows what to look for," White said. "Are there any questions? If not, go with God."

★   ★   ★

As Mucci returned to his Rangers to make his plans and preparations, the Scouts readied themselves. In addition to his personal weapon, each man would carry extra ammo bandoliers, a .45-caliber automatic with spare clips, a trench knife, and three hand grenades.

Their preparations complete, Nellist, Rounsaville, Dove, and the twelve Scouts climbed into a two-and-a-half-ton truck for the ride to Guimba, the jumping-off point. As the deuce-and-a-half bounced along the dirt roads, the Scouts in the back and Dove riding in the cab with the driver, U.S. fighter planes roared overhead, strafing Japanese positions at the front lines just a few miles away.

The truck rolled to a halt in a grove of trees just outside Guimba, which was a cluster of nipa huts with tin roofs, set randomly along the dirt road. Lapham was already there, and greeted the Scouts as they climbed down from the truck bed. Nellist, Rounsaville, and Dove followed the guerrilla leader to the headquarters hut while the friendly Filipinos served the Scouts a meal of black beans and rice.

"Get some sleep," Nellist told the men. "It's going to be a long night."

They left at nine p.m. under a starry sky lit by a half moon. Dove remained behind as contact, although he would have no radio until the Rangers came up. All messages between himself and Nellist would be relayed by runners, which was deemed safer than possible radio interception.

Kittleson and two guerrillas took the point as the column moved single-file through the night, their destination being Balincarin, which they had to get to by daybreak. This would be a twenty-four-mile forced march, most of it through rice paddies, now caked and bone-dry, making walking difficult due to the hardened caraboa hoof prints. They also traversed bamboo thickets and fields of tall kunai and cogon grass, the latter an inedible plant whose only use was for thatching, and whose leaves, with their silky hairs, made a man's skin itch. Filipinos believed cogon fields were haunted.

When a village was encountered, the column moved around it, giving it wide berth. The last thing they wanted was to rouse the local population. Any tip to the Japanese of the American approach and the mission was off.

As the Scouts moved through the night, at one point wading the knee-deep Talavera River, the only sound was the occasional barking dog in the distance. Nellist fretted about the noise kicked up by the dogs, worried that they might give away his presence. Mucci shared this concern, and as a result, sent word ahead with the guerrillas to have the dogs muzzled, their snouts tied shut, until he had passed. Once or twice Kittleson thought he heard a different noise, and dropped to a knee. The others followed suit. When he was sure all was safe, he rose and signaled the rest to follow.

Nine miles into the march, they were approaching the National Highway. Out in front, in the darkness, was the unmistakable clanking sound of tank treads and trucks. Nellist called a halt.

"Lotta shit up ahead the way it sounds," Kittleson whispered to Nellist.

Nellist nodded.

"Japs use the cover of night to pull their troops back from the Manila area, through Cabanatuan to San Jose," he said. "Go take a look."

As Kittleson, along with the two guerrillas, crawled forward, Nellist and Rounsaville covered their heads with a poncho. Nellist lit his red-lensed flashlight and the officers looked over the map.

Kittleson and the two Filipinos reached the edge of a ravine that overlooked the roadway. Making his way to the edge, Kittleson saw vehicles rolling along the highway, their headlights gleaming through cat's-eye slits. At this point, the highway crossed the ravine on a small, thirty-foot-long wooden bridge. On the floor of the ravine, about eight or ten feet below the bridge, a small stream flowed. What dismayed Kittleson more than the traffic moving along a road they had to cross were the three tanks that stood by the bridge, one on one end and two on the other.

Indicating to one of the Filipinos to remain, he and the other man slithered back from the ravine and returned to the column.

"Those three Fujiyama Flivvers don't look like they're gonna move any time soon," Kittleson concluded.

Nellist nodded, deep in thought.

"How high is the bridge?" he asked. "Can we get under it?"

"We can pass underneath standing up," Kittleson said. "And we should be able to get through. The ground on both sides is thickly overgrown."

Gathering the teams around him, Nellist briefed the Scouts on what lay ahead.

"We'll work our way into the ravine and go under the bridge three or four men at a time," he said. "Once on the other side, keep going about a hundred yards, then stop and wait for the rest."

Reaching the ravine, the column descended and hid themselves in the high vegetation. The three tanks were still on the bridge. Kittleson and two guerrillas led the way, walking, stooped over, at first, and then, as the grass got shorter, dropping to all fours. Overhead, the Japanese tankers smoked and laughed over a shared joke. Under the bridge, Kittleson and the Filipinos stopped as a convoy rumbled across the span, knocking dirt and debris down on their heads. They then moved on, making it to the other side and proceeding into the underbrush.

It took fifteen minutes for Nellist to get all of his men beyond the bridge, and once reassembled, they were off again. The Rizal Road, about seven miles farther on, also carried enemy truck traffic, but it was less heavy and the Scouts were able to leapfrog across it with little difficulty. After crossing the road, Nellist double-timed the column for a mile before calling a halt.

The Scouts arrived in Balincarin, a poor village of ramshackle huts, at daybreak as scheduled. They were greeted by guerrilla leader Juan Pajota, who immediately informed Nellist of a division-strength column of Japanese moving along the National Highway from Cabanatuan City, four miles from the camp, plus the presence of hundreds of men at the Cabu River, just half a mile northeast of the prison compound.

Following a meal of rice and beans, the Scouts moved forward, toward the village of Platero, across the wide but shallow Pampanga River, for their first look at Cabanatuan prison camp. As they lay on their bellies in the grass, what they saw was dismaying. The camp sat in an open plain seven hundred yards away. From their position, which was the closest they could get and still remain safely concealed, all they could see was the wire enclosure, guard towers, and rooftops. The terrain all around was grassy plains and cultivated fields with a sprinkling of nipa huts. Clouds of dust from a convoy passing the camp rose into the air. In the far distance, the silent volcanic cone of Mount Arayat loomed four thousand feet into the sky.

"This is not good," Nellist muttered.

★   ★   ★

Twenty-four hours behind the Scouts, Mucci's column was also on their way to the camp. The column consisted of 121 Rangers, including 107 from Charlie Company under Prince, and a platoon from Fox Company led by Lt. John P. Murphy. On January 29, as the Scouts were approaching the camp, Mucci's men linked up with guerrillas led by Capt. Eduardo Joson, thought by Lapham to be the most capable guerrilla leader in the area, at the village of Lobong, west of Balincarin. Joson had with him about 80 of his fierce guerrilla band. This brought the number of men with Mucci, including guerrillas supplied

by Lapham, to 286 men. This column, bristling with arms and determination, began making its way forward toward the staging area at
Platero, just a mile and a half from the prison compound.

* * *

Nellist, Rounsaville, and their men had spent most of the day and into
the night watching the camp from the tall grass along the Pampanga
River. Some members of the teams also counted noses in the Japanese
camp along the Cabu River. After obtaining what intelligence they
could, the two Scout leaders walked back to Platero, where they found
an anxious Mucci, who had been unable to sleep. At four a.m., Nellist
and Rounsaville sat down with Mucci, Dove, and Prince and relayed
what they had collected so far.

"I'm afraid it's a lot of bad news," Nellist began. "For one thing,
you're going to have to postpone the attack twenty-four hours."

That news jolted Mucci.

"We can't," he said. "The longer we stay here, the greater our
chances of being spotted."

"I know that, sir," Nellist said. "But a Jap convoy of about division
size is passing by the camp. They shut down during the day to avoid
being seen by our planes, but at night they are back on the road and
the place looks like Main Street in Tokyo. Your attack tomorrow night
would run right into them."

Mucci clenched his jaw, his lips tightening on his pipe, as he pon-
dered this setback. Pajota had warned him about the convoy, but he
had discounted the guerrilla leader's claim, preferring intelligence
supplied by the Scouts.

"What's the ground like around the camp?"

"As bad as we were told," Nellist said. "It's a wide-open plain of low
grass and cultivated fields. So far, we haven't been able to get close
enough to see a lot of detail. We can't see inside the camp."

"But you're sure the prisoners are still there?"

"Yes, sir," Nellist replied. "Pajota has assured us they are. They're
too weak and sick to be transported."

"What about Jap troops?" Mucci asked.

"The Dokuko 359 Battalion is bivouacked at the Cabu River, half a mile away to the northeast," he said. "Inside the camp itself, we figure about seventy guards and maybe another one hundred to two hundred transients who stopped for the night. Four tanks went into the camp, none came back out."

Mucci sat quietly for a few moments.

"All right," he said firmly. "We'll reschedule the attack for nineteen thirty on Tuesday. But the info you've supplied me with is not good enough, Lieutenant. I need more, a lot more. I need to know the number of sentries, how many guard towers they have and their location, are there any machine-gun emplacements, where are the prisoners housed, where are the guards housed, are there tanks, how is the fence constructed and does the gate swing in or out. That is vital information. Do you understand?"

"Yes, sir," Nellist acknowledged. "We'll get it."

★ ★ ★

Nellist had made that pledge to Mucci without knowing how he would go about delivering on it. For the rest of the night, the Scouts watched the stream of Japanese vehicles roll by the camp, moving north in the direction of Bongabon. At dawn, as expected, the traffic stopped. The Scouts also watched for any sign that the Japanese were about to kill the prisoners, but Nellist felt that, with just the few guards, and the fact that the main gate remained closed, this seemed unlikely.

Nellist discussed the challenge of gathering more information with Rounsaville.

"There's only one way I can think of," he said, watching a few farmers work the fields between him and the camp. Then he pointed to a solitary nipa hut, mounted on stilts, that sat some two hundred yards from the camp's main gate, just on the other side of the highway. "We need to get into that hut."

"Well, you can't go out there dressed like that," Rounsaville said.

Then he turned to one of his men, Rufo Vaquilar. "Pontiac, see if you can borrow some farmers' clothes."

While the American-born Filipino went about his assignment, Nellist informed Pajota of his plan. The guerrilla leader assured them that word would be gotten to the farmers to ignore the two strangers and added a warning that should there be any betrayal, the guilty person would have more to fear from him than from the Japanese.

A short time later, two farmers slowly walked across the fields, making their way to the lone hut, where, they had been told, farm implements were stored. The two—Nellist and Vaquilar—wore peasant garb, baggy to help conceal the Colt .45 automatics hidden underneath, and large, wide-brimmed straw buri hats. Nellist also had slipped his carbine inside his trouser leg, causing him to walk with a limp that he hoped would not attract attention.

The two men kept about a hundred yards distance between them to avoid the appearance of being together. Nellist, who was taller than the average Filipino, walked stooped and would occasionally stop and bend down, as if inspecting the crops growing around his feet. As promised, the other farmers kept working, not acknowledging the men walking past them.

Reaching the hut, first Nellist, then Vaquilar, they climbed the ladder. Inside, both men collapsed to the floor briefly to rest their taut nerves. They expected at any time to hear warning shouts, but none came. A battered rocking chair stood by an open window that faced the compound just two hundred yards away. Nellist drew the carbine from his trousers and sat in the chair, carefully peeking out the window. His eyes lit up as the entire camp was spread out before him. Beyond the wire he could see weary prisoners shuffling around and could count the number of guards at the gatehouse and in the guard tower at the northeast corner of the camp.

"Yes, Pontiac, there is a God," Nellist beamed.

Referring to an aerial photograph of the camp, Nellist began using his carbine to sight in on various buildings as a means of gauging distances and elevations. By that means, he drew a rough map of the camp in his notebook. When he identified a building, he labeled it with a number on the aerial photo, with the building's description written on a paper overlay.

Pajota helped the Scouts collect more detail. A number of his guerrillas, also dressed as farmers, moved freely around the fields near the camp, observing and making mental notes. Then they meandered into the "tool hut" to report. One young boy mounted on the back of a hulking caraboa rode the beast around the entire perimeter of the camp, noting terrain features and Japanese defensive positions. Vaquilar, meanwhile, left the hut and located some of the Filipino farmers who had worked inside the camp. He questioned them in detail.

From his observations and from reports coming to him from the locals and the guerrillas, Nellist knew that the compound was eight hundred yards deep and six hundred wide. The camp was bisected by a dirt road, with the prisoners billeted on the left of the road and the guards and camp officers to the right. Additional barracks buildings to the rear of the camp behind the prisoners' huts were used to house transient troops. The buildings were mostly constructed of bamboo with thatched roofs. The ground inside the camp sloped upward slightly as one walked from front to back. The main gate was eight feet tall and consisted of two doors constructed of lumber and barbed wire, and secured by a single padlock. When opened, the gates swung either in or out. The compound was surrounded by three rows of barbed wire ten feet high and guarded by two guard towers, one at the northeast corner and the other at the rear of the camp, and four pillboxes, although the pillboxes did not appear to be manned. Nellist saw no sign of the tanks that had rolled in the day before, but he did note a large galvanized metal building that could serve as a garage three hundred yards inside the main gate. On a grimmer note, a large makeshift cemetery was at the camp's southeast corner.

He estimated the camp garrison at 75 men with possibly another 150 transient troops inside, although they might be gone by dark.

About one thirty in the afternoon—Nellist and Vaquilar had been in the hut for some two hours—Vaquilar spotted Gil Cox, Harold Hard, and Franklin Fox crawling toward them. They had taken the circuitous route back to the Pampanga River, then snaked their way across the field undetected. When they reached the bottom of the ladder leading up into the hut, Nellist glared down at them.

"What the hell is this, a convention?" he snarled. "Where are the others?"

"Spread out all over," Fox said.

"Stay there," Nellist ordered. Then he folded up his notes and the map and dropped them down to Fox. "Get that back to Mucci before he blows his cork."

After the Scouts departed, Nellist and Vaquilar hung around to continue their observation. About four p.m., Nellist said it was time to go.

As they prepared to depart, Vaquilar, alarm in his voice, said, "Bill."

Nellist saw Vaquilar peeking out the window and joined him.

A young native girl had approached the main gate to the camp and began talking to the guards. She handed something to one of the Japanese soldiers, causing Nellist, as he later noted, to become "damned concerned" lest she betray them.

"Goddamn it," Nellist cursed. "I thought Pajota warned the civvies to keep the hell away from the camp."

"I'm sure she didn't spot us," Vaquilar said. "Do you think she saw the Rangers?"

"I don't know," Nellist replied.

After a while, the girl left and the Scouts continued watching.

Vaquilar said, "Why don't I go out there and walk around and see if the Nips are wise to anything?"

"OK," Nellist said. "Go ahead, but I can't cover you from here."

"I know," he said.

Vaquilar slipped two pistols under his clothes and left, walking away to the right. When he reached the road, he strolled along the shoulder, passing the camp and the guards within no more than forty feet. As he walked by the guards, he respectfully tipped his straw hat. The guards nodded sullenly in reply. As he acknowledged the guards, Vaquilar used the opportunity to scan the camp with his eyes. All seemed quiet. Twenty minutes later he was back in the hut.

"Everything seems normal," he reported.

"Good. Let's get the hell out of here," Nellist said, and they departed, satisfied that whatever the girl had told the Japanese, it had nothing to do with the impending attack. The two men breathed easier.

What Nellist did not know was that the girl was trying to sell the Japanese fresh fruit, and that she had been sent by Pajota to spy.

Satisfied the Japanese were none the wiser, the two Scouts climbed down the ladder. They walked back along the road, then cut across the fields and soon rejoined Rounsaville and the rest of the men.

★　★　★

That night, in a nipa hut in Platero, Mucci, Prince, Pajota, Joson, Nellist, Rounsaville, Dove, and Prince's platoon leaders, Lts. John Murphy, Melville H. Schmidt, and William J. O'Connell, were gathered around a small table formulating their plan of attack. By the light of an oil lantern, Mucci spread out Nellist's sketch. Mucci immediately noted that the biggest threat to the operation were the Japanese at the Cabu bridge. Pajota said he and his men would tie the enemy down with small-arms fire to prevent them from crossing over the river, while Joson and some more guerrillas would establish a roadblock west of the camp to prevent any help coming from Cabanatuan City.

"We will need thirty minutes to get in there and get the POWs out," Mucci said.

"We understand," Pajota agreed.

The next problem was crossing the seven hundred yards of open field undetected. Even crawling, as they would need to do, there was a high probability of being spotted by Japanese in the guard tower. A diversion was needed, and at Pajota's suggestion a request was radioed back for a plane to fly low over the camp. Pajota had told Mucci that flyovers by U.S. planes irritated the Japanese and drew their undivided attention.

Prince next addressed the actual attack on the compound.

"When we get to this depression near the road," Prince said, "Murphy, I want you to take your platoon and swing left and make your way to the rear gate. O'Connell, Schmidt, your platoons will go through the main gate once we've opened it. When we get inside, O'Connell, your men sweep the camp to the right of the road. That's where the Japs are. Schmidt, your platoon will follow me to the left and free the prisoners. You Scouts can go in with me."

He next assigned the unit's bazooka team to head at the double-quick for the corrugated shed and knock out any tanks that might roll out.

"The main thing is to get the prisoners moving," Prince said. "Herd them, shove them, carry them, I don't care. But we have to get them back to the Pampanga River, where the Filipinos will have caraboa carts waiting to carry the weakest.

"Murphy, you start the show," Prince ordered. "At nineteen thirty, you fire a single shot. That's the signal. When we've cleared out all of the POWs, I will fire a red flare. That means the raid is over, and everyone should be pulling back."

"Remember, all of the prisoners go," Mucci said. "No one is left behind."

★   ★   ★

As the sun rose on the morning of January 30, the Rangers breakfasted on coffee, eggs, and fruit supplied by Platero villagers. Ahead of them, the Scouts downed K rations. Nellist and Rounsaville had returned from Platero and briefed their men on the plan and their role in it. Then, like the Rangers, they sat and waited.

Throughout the day, the Scouts kept an eye on the camp, watching for any unusual activity, but all remained quiet.

With the sinking of the sun late that afternoon, Prince and his men, less Mucci and Dove, who remained in Platero, joined the Scouts. And as the evening deepened, 121 Rangers and 13 Alamo Scouts were crawling across the field, nose to boot heel. Initially, the grass was tall, affording adequate concealment, but the closer the men drew to the road, the shorter the grass. Prince signaled a halt, and everyone stopped.

Where the hell was the flyover?

As if on signal, at about six thirty p.m., a Northrup P-61 Black Widow from the 547th Night Fighter Squadron came roaring out of the sky and skimmed over the camp. Out in the field, the attackers could hear the prisoners cheer as the twin-tailed night fighter, named *Hard to Get* and flown by twenty-six-year-old Kenneth Schreiber, buzzed overhead, its twin Wasp engines resounding across the landscape. All eyes in the camp, Allied and Japanese, were pointed skyward, some in joy, others in anger as the aircraft made several low passes overhead, often turning and twisting and climbing and diving.

With the Japanese guards focused on the aerial acrobatics over-head, Prince signaled forward, and everyone resumed crawling.

The plane made several passes, during which Schreiber could see the Rangers crawling across the field, before flying off into the rapidly darkening sky.

As the Rangers approached the camp, a bell began tolling from somewhere inside the wire. The attackers froze where they were and waited, expecting that at any moment the field would be swept by searchlights. But nothing happened. Prince later learned that the bell was rung by a navy POW who insisted on sounding the watch. The men crawled on.

The last two hundred yards of field were the worst. The grass was lowest here, and though it was pitch dark now, a full moon would soon be rising from behind the Sierra Madres and would bathe the landscape in its eerie glow. Time was of the essence.

It had taken an hour to crawl across the field, and by the time Prince's men reached the drainage ditch, night had taken over com-pletely and lights burned inside the camp. The attackers were just across the road from the main gate, and twenty yards ahead they could see the glow of the guards' cigarettes. Inside, guards—some dressed only in loincloths in the evening heat—were seen lounging and chatting. Oriental music from an unseen record player or radio filtered through the night. Even the sentries in the towers seemed relaxed.

On reaching the ditch, Murphy's platoon split off to the left. As they made their way around the side of the camp some sound, real or imagined, spooked a guard. He shouted out a challenge, not once but several times, and took a few steps toward the crouching Americans. Cursing to himself, Murphy drew a bead on the man with his carbine, placed his finger on the trigger, and held his breath as he waited. His patience paid off, as the guard, seemingly satisfied that it was his imagination or a passing animal, withdrew.

Murphy's men finally reached their position, but Murphy, nervous at being the one to signal the attack, decided to wait beyond the seven thirty starting time to be sure everyone else was in position. At the front gate, the others waited, nerves as taut as cables, wondering about Murphy's delay. Then, at about seven forty, ten minutes behind schedule, Murphy took aim at a soldier in the camp who was seated on a bench and squeezed off a round. The sound of the carbine in the still night was ear-shattering. The soldier jerked, then toppled to the ground. A sentry in the guard tower yelled something, then gunfire instantly splintered the bamboo wall. The guard spun and dropped from the tower, landing on the roof of a barracks building.

At the sound of the first shot, the Rangers at the front gate opened fire. A sentry by the gatehouse fell dead. Kittleson and Ranger Sgt. Ted Richardson raced forward. Richardson's job was to get the gate open. He smacked it with the butt of his Thompson, but the lock refused to yield. He slipped his .45 automatic from its holster and aimed at the lock. Inside the camp, a Japanese guard fired at Richardson. The bullet struck the pistol and sent it flying. Kittleson, with his Tommy gun, and a BAR man fired on the soldier, who was thrown backward by the impact of the slugs. They then raked the camp as Richardson retrieved his pistol and shot off the lock. As he pushed the gate inward, it snagged on the body of the dead sentry just inside the wire.

"Pull it toward us," Kittleson yelled.

They did and Rangers were soon streaming into the compound.

Bullets buzzed through the air. Rangers and Japanese alike were yelling and some screamed in pain as lead found flesh. Rangers kicked open the doors of the buildings identified as Japanese-occupied, sprayed the inside with their weapons, then tossed in grenades. Flames began to lick the walls of the bamboo structures.

*   *   *

By now the fight had also gotten under way at the Cabu bridge. The rattle of gunfire erupted, followed by a dull boom that rumbled across the landscape as Pajota's guerrillas exploded TNT under the bridge that separated the Japanese from the prison camp.

The bridge remained standing, but was badly holed, preventing tanks from crossing over. However, Japanese troops formed up on the far side and, with a shout of "Banzai," stormed across the damaged span.

Pajota's men were ready for them.

Formed into an inverted V, they poured rifle and machine-gun fire into the screaming mass, driving them back. Outraged, the Japanese charged into the murderous fire again and again, with devastating results, their dead stacking up on the bridge three and four bodies deep.

A Japanese attempt to flank the guerrillas by wading across the river upstream from the bridge was also turned back.

*   *   *

The Rangers raced through the camp, blasting huts and spraying lead at enemy defenders. The Japanese, caught unaware by the sudden attack, had no plan of defense, and their bodies littered the ground.

Through this maelstrom, the Ranger bazooka team ran to their assigned position near the corrugated iron shed. As a loader slid a rocket into the tube, two trucks carrying infantrymen burst out of the garage door on the building and raced for the front gate. The bazooka man, Sergeant Stewart, lined up on the first truck and let fly. The rocket tore into the truck, which erupted in flame. The loader quickly fed in a new round and tapped Stewart on the shoulder to indicate "ready." Stewart, aiming at the second truck, squeezed the trigger. The rocket closed the distance in a heartbeat. It hit the truck, which blew up. The force of the explosion drove it into the first truck, creating a massive pyre of burning junk. Stewart reloaded, turned, and sent a third rocket into the shed itself, which was torn apart with a roar of smoke and fire. The two bazooka men then took up their carbines and began shooting the Japanese, some with flaming clothes, who were jumping from the burning trucks.

★   ★   ★

Lieutenant Schmidt and his men had by now made it into the prisoner quarters and began herding POWs toward the gate. Frightened and thinking the Japanese were killing them, many refused to go and some even tried to hide or resist.

"Get to the front gate," a Ranger yelled. "You're being rescued."

Off to the side, the Rangers heard a man yell "Banzai" and turned to see a lone guard charging them. A few rounds from a carbine cut him down.

All of the prisoners were emaciated and weak, and a number had to be helped out of the camp. Some were carried on the backs of Rangers. Cpl. Jim Herrick, a Ranger, carried one man who died one hundred feet short of the gate, his frail health giving out even as liberation loomed.

"I'm not putting him down," Kittleson heard him say. "No one gets left behind."

A Japanese mortar began to fire, dropping rounds among the raiders and prisoners alike. The detonation of the first round sent metal shards flying, one of which caught Rounsaville in the buttocks. He grunted with pain and fell.

"I got him," Nellist shouted, and ran to his friend.

Rolling Rounsaville over, he cut away the bloody trousers with his knife and saw a jagged piece of steel protruding from the flesh.

"The medic isn't here," he said. "I'll operate on you."

"Oh, great," Rounsaville moaned, then winced as Nellist dug out the offending metal with a pliers.

"Goddamn it, Bill," Rounsaville said through waves of pain. "You're all thumbs."

"Hey," Nellist said and grinned. "Just think how proud you'll be when they pin that Purple Heart on your ass."

He patched the wound with a bandage and said, "Now get to the river."

Shrapnel from another mortar round hit Alamo Scout Alfred Alfonso in the gut. He rolled in pain, his hands clutching his bloody midsection. A Ranger was hit by the same round and a medic raced over and began treating both men. He stabilized them and had them sent to the rear, Alfonso carried on a stretcher.

As it launched a third round, Nellist and others spotted the mortar and opened fire, silencing the gun. However, the last round seriously wounded the Rangers' only physician, Capt. James Fisher. Grievously injured, he was carried to the rear.

To Kittleson, it looked as if "the gates of hell had been thrown open" as these human skeletons, backlit by burning buildings, shuffled toward him, trancelike.

Not far from Kittleson, Ranger corporal Roy Sweezy, one of Murphy's squad leaders, was shot down. He was dead by the time his buddy, Cpl. Francis Schilli, got to his side. Schilli administered last rites with his canteen, then hoisted the body up onto his back and carried him out.

No one is left behind.

By the front gate, Scout Sgt. Harold Hard saw one prisoner, literally skin and bones, who seemed about to collapse. He reached out and took the man by the arm, horrified that his fingers and thumb reached the entire way around the skinny limb. He gently led the man rearward.

Kittleson helped another man toward the river. As he did, the man told him how the Japanese had made them work the fields, even when sick, and beat them if they looked up from the ground.

Many of the prisoners wore the tattered remains of uniforms, but some were clad only in white underwear. This drew sporadic Japanese fire, so Kittleson told the men to remove the underpants, which they did, continuing the trip naked until they reached the river and were out of range.

At the river, as promised by Pajota, twenty-five caraboa carts were waiting. The weakest and those who had to be carried were gently loaded onto the carts, lying on the grassy bedding of rice straw, until the carts were filled to capacity with five or six men apiece. Then, as a red flare fired by Prince arced up into the sky to signal the end of the raid, the caravan, which included 516 prisoners, headed for Balincarin.

The Scouts, meanwhile, covered the withdrawal by setting up a defensive perimeter, laying out their ammo clips and grenades in case they were needed. Waiting there in the dark, the river to their front, the Scouts, less Rounsaville and Alfonso, who were being treated by medics at Platero, watched the glow of the fires from the camp.

★   ★   ★

Back in the camp, one man remained. Edwin Cherry, an aging British soldier who had been captured at the fall of Singapore in 1942 and sent along with other British prisoners to the Philippines as a slave laborer, had been in the latrine, stricken with severe dysentery, when the raid went down. Almost stone deaf, he had never heard the battle raging outside. When he emerged, he walked back to his hut, aware of the dead Japanese littering the ground and the burning buildings in the guard area, but not knowing what to do. He stepped inside his barracks and he lay down on his bunk.

★   ★   ★

About an hour after the raid, Jack Dove joined the Nellist team, walking up from Balincarin.

"Any sign of the Nips?" he asked Nellist.

"Nope. All's quiet."

"Good," Dove said. "A British POW told me we missed a guy. Some old Brit whose elevator doesn't go all the way to the top. I'm going to try to find him."

With that, Dove was moving quickly across the river and the field beyond. Arriving at the camp, he located Cherry, roused the man, and brought him back.

No one is left behind.

After about a two-hour wait, Nellist and his men pulled back toward Platero. The caravan's path was easy to follow, with ruts from the cart wheels and human and animal footprints. Local natives were busily shoveling dirt over the tracks in hopes of avoiding Japanese retaliation.

At the village, the Scouts found about one hundred of the sickest men lounging around the huts. Natives directed Nellist to the hut being used as a hospital. Pushing aside the blanket that covered the doorway to prevent light from escaping, Nellist found Alfonso and Rounsaville lying to one side. On a makeshift operating table, Doc Fisher was being worked on by a local physician, Dr. Carlos Layug, and two former POWs, Dr. Merle Mussleman and Dr. Herbert Ott, the latter an army veterinarian. POW Chaplain Hugh Kennedy stood nearby. Also watching the proceedings was Maj. Stephen Sitter, a Ranger who volunteered to remain behind.

"You guys OK?" Nellist asked Rounsaville.

"Yeah," Rounsaville said. "I'm fine and Al here will be OK, too."

"How's he?" Nellist asked Rounsaville, nodding toward the table. Rounsaville just shook his head.

Nellist went back outside.

Around one a.m. Dr. Mussleman and Chaplain Kennedy joined him.

"How's the patient?" Nellist asked. "We've got to get out of here before the Japs find us. The longer we stay, the more the danger."

"I've done all I can for him," Mussleman said. "It won't matter if we move him or not."

"He's in God's hands now," Kennedy added.

Nellist turned to Kittleson.

"Kit," he said. "Get something we can use as a stretcher."

Kittleson nodded, and with the help of some other Scouts located the fanciest house in town, which sported a heavy wooden Spanish door. Gently, Fisher was laid on the door, which took six men to carry, and the little column began the three-mile trek to Balincarin.

The trip took about an hour. When they arrived, Mucci's column had moved on, but a radio was left behind for the Scouts. Sitter suggested he contact 6th Army HQ for a plane to fly in and evacuate Fisher. Nellist agreed, and the call was made. A plane would arrive around dawn. All through the night, Filipino men, women, and children, with shovels, axes, and by hand, chopped out a landing strip. Meanwhile, a Scout provided Fisher with blood for a much-needed transfusion.

The landing strip was finished an hour before dawn, but the plane did not arrive. And it might not have mattered if it had, for Fisher rose up on his elbows and said weakly, "Good luck on the way out." Then he lay back down and died.

The body was respectfully wrapped in canvas and placed in a hastily dug grave. Kennedy provided the eulogy and led the prayer, something he had grown proficient at after four years behind barbed wire. Then the Americans were off.

The trek would be easier. With the help of the civilians, Andy Smith had rustled up several more caraboa carts, so the sickest could ride back.

The sun was up by now, so Nellist led the column toward American lines, keeping them as close as possible to the edge of the forest, or in low-lying drainage areas, to cut down the chance of detection. Once, Kittleson and Sabas Asis, at the point, signaled everyone to get down. A Japanese patrol was moving left to right across their front, through a grassy field. The enemy eventually disappeared into the forest, and after a brief wait the pathetic column resumed its march.

By noon, the caravan was about ten miles from American lines. The Scouts tried to cheer the suffering men.

"It'll be steak and ice cream for supper this evening, then a clean bed and a pretty nurse," Smith told the men. "Both at the same time if you're real lucky."

That brought a smile to men who had had little to grin about since 1942.

As the column approached a fork in the trail they found the pathway blocked by about twelve Filipino guerrillas. The men were members of the People's Army to Fight the Japanese, known simply as Hukbalahaps, under the overall command of Luis Taruc, whose communist ideology often put him at odds with both the Japanese and the Allies. On a number of occasions the Huks, as they were dubbed by the GIs, skirmished with Lapham's guerrillas and had even shot the American's executive officer. The Huks also had no qualms about plundering native villages, and torturing or murdering those who resisted.

The group that now blocked Nellist's way was led by a squat man wearing jeans and a cast-off U.S. Marine blouse. The scar on his face, the Garand in his hands, and the crisscrossed bandoliers of .30-cal ammo over his shoulders made him look especially fierce.

"This is Hukbalahap land," he said, gesturing menacingly with the Garand. "You cannot pass."

Nellist glared at Scarface. To either side of him, Kittleson and Cox tightened the grips on their Tommy guns.

"Let us through, you little sonofabitch," Nellist snarled. "We're the goddamned U.S. Army and we're going through, so get the hell out of the way."

The Huk leader gave Nellist a hard stare and did not budge. Kittleson cocked his Tommy gun and tilted the barrel toward Scarface.

"Move aside, Bill," Kittleson said. "I'll cut 'em all to hell."

Scarface glanced at Kittleson, then back at Nellist, an uneasy look coming into his eyes. He shifted his gaze to Cox, who also had his Thompson pointing at him. No one moved and tensions kept rising. Then Scarface, realizing that if gunfire erupted he'd be the first to die, angrily stepped aside. Nellist gestured for the column to move forward. As it did, Cox and Kittleson remained stationary, guarding its passage through the Huks. When all of the men had passed, Kittleson gave Scarface a mock salute, then he and Cox followed the group, keeping a wary eye on the Huks until they were out of sight.

About an hour later, Nellist's caravan reached American lines at Talavera.

★ ★ ★

On February 5, Jack Dove returned to Cabanatuan, now in American hands following the 6th Army's advance. Wandering through the now-abandoned camp, he sifted through the wreckage of the buildings with Lt. Charles Hall of 6th Army G2, looking for intelligence documents, maps, and other items. In one prisoner hut, Dove found makeshift death certificates kept by prison doctors. They were written on the backs of milk can labels and hidden. Dove filled a sack with documents.

Dove returned again three days later, this time with money. All of the farmers who lent their caraboa carts received five pesos.

★ ★ ★

Back home, word of the raid at Cabanatuan was big news and filled the front pages of newspapers everywhere. GIs had freed 516 prisoners—489 Americans, 23 British, 2 Norwegians, 1 Dutch, and 1 Filipino—and gotten them all out safely, although 2 died of heart attacks on the trek to freedom.

As Americans read the reports, a new name came to their attention: Alamo Scouts.

So much excitement was generated by the raid that twelve Rangers, including Prince, and two Scouts, Harold Hard and Gil Cox, were returned to the United States to take part in a nationwide bond drive. Prince and Hard made an appearance on NBC's popular radio program *We the People*, where, after Kate Smith sang "God Bless America," they performed a dramatization of the raid.

On March 7, the men were in Washington, D.C. Whisked to the White House, they were ushered to the Oval Office, where they were greeted by FDR. With the president was Lt. Gen. Joseph "Vinegar Joe"

Stillwell, whose own exploits in the China-Burma-India theater were legendary, and crooner Bing Crosby.

Without rising from his chair, the president said, "I want to shake hands with everyone. You men did a fine job."

The tour ended in Minneapolis on April 22, and after a thirty-day leave, the men returned to their units.

"I was damned glad to get back," Cox recalled later.

And the war went on.

CHAPTER 14

"If I Don't Make It, It's Up to You."

Rescue at Los Baños, February 23, 1945

Terry Santos was one of the more than 50 percent of graduates from the Alamo Scout Training Center who did not serve on a team. For some, it was because they had simply not been selected. For others, it was at the request of their former commanding officers, who were reluctant to part with their best-trained men. In the case of Santos, it was at his request.

Santos enlisted in the army in his native San Francisco in January 1942. After completing his basic training at Camp Roberts, California, the twenty-year-old went to his first sergeant and requested permission to volunteer for the air corps. His sergeant put a hand on his shoulder and said, "Son, you'll live and die in the infantry."

"Thanks a lot," Santos thought.

A short time later the eager recruit was back with another request. Responding to a poster on the bulletin board seeking volunteers for the U.S. Airborne Forces, Santos thought, "What the hell. If I can't fly all the way, I'll fly part of the way."

He made the request to his first sergeant, who asked, "Are you nuts?"

"No, Sergeant," Santos replied. "I just want to try something different."

After trying without success to talk Santos out of it, the sergeant said, "It doesn't make sense that anyone would want to leap out of a perfectly good airplane."

"It's something I need to do," Santos replied.

"OK," the sergeant said. "If that's the way you feel."

Getting the OK to volunteer was just the first hurdle Santos had to clear. The next was, at 128 pounds, he was 2 pounds under the required minimum weight for the airborne.

"I lost weight during training, sir," Santos told the doctor during the physical.

The doctor stared at Santos, then said, "Do you really want to go that badly?"

"Yes, sir, I do," Santos replied.

"OK," the doctor said. "I'll put you down at one hundred and thirty. But when you get to the training camp, you'd better weigh a hundred and thirty."

"I will, sir," Santos answered.

About a week later, Santos, assigned to the fledgling 11th Airborne Division, stepped down from the train at the small terminal in Toccoa, Georgia, a rural hamlet tucked away in the Blue Mountains. There, he and some other airborne candidates climbed into the rear of a deuce-and-a-half truck for the trip out Highway 13, past the Toccoa Casket Company, to the airborne training camp. After stowing his duffel bag in one of the barracks, Santos reported for the check-in physical. There, not only did he find that he had not kept his promise to gain the needed two pounds, but had actually lost two more. Santos quickly came up with an explanation.

"You know, you're supposed to weigh one thirty," the doctor said. "You weigh one twenty-six."

"I must've lost weight on the train, sir," Santos said. "The food was terrible and I had no appetite and it took me a week to get here."

The doctor looked at him quizzically, then said, "All right."

Since there was no organized class currently going through training at Camp Toccoa, Santos took on the job of keeping himself fit. Looming twelve hundred feet above the camp was Mount Currahee, a Cherokee Indian term for "Stands Alone." Every morning, Santos jogged the winding dirt road that wended its way "three miles up and three miles down" the mountain.

Santos was at Toccoa just two weeks when he saw another flyer calling for volunteers; this one, he recalled, was for "a special unit." Rather than wait for the 11th Airborne to train and be activated, Santos volunteered and was transferred. The "special unit" turned out to be the Office of Strategic Services, or OSS. Training at Fort Benning, Georgia, was as tough as Santos had expected, and included qualifying parachute training—four night jumps and one day jump, the opposite of the airborne.

Upon graduation, the men were offered commissions as second lieutenants. Santos turned it down.

"As an officer, you have no latitude," he explained in 2007. "As an enlisted man, I had all sorts of latitude. I could tell them to go shove it if I wanted to."

He instead wore corporal stripes, although he was considered by the OSS to be a sergeant.

His transport to the war in January 1943 was an old converted four-stack, World War I–vintage destroyer, an aging hulk with open gun mounts instead of turrets. When Santos boarded the ship at San Francisco's Treasure Island with five of his buddies from OSS training, the ship's skipper insisted the five lieutenants go to the officers' quarters, while Santos rode with the enlisted men.

"If he goes down, we go down," one of Santos's friends told the skipper.

But the argument was futile, and the ship captain won.

Bound for the China-Burma-India theater, the first stop for Santos and his OSS team was Noumea, on New Caledonia. After a brief stay, they were off for Australia, but the ship was diverted to New Guinea. Their stay there was even briefer. Informed that OSS teams were on the ship, MacArthur sent a staff officer to meet them. MacArthur strongly mistrusted the OSS and its ties to the Joint Chiefs of Staff, and he wanted none of them within his command area. He wished to maintain absolute control over all the intelligence-gathering work done within his sphere of influence.

"Those of you who wish to remain with the OSS and go on to the CBI will remain on the ship," the officer said. "If you don't want to go on, you may transfer to the 6th Army."

Three, including Santos, opted to remain, and, soon catching wind of the Alamo Scouts, all three volunteered.

"I volunteered to see if I'd be accepted, because the requirements were quite stringent," Santos said years later.

The only one of the three selected, Santos joined the ASTC's fourth class with Bill Nellist and Tom Rounsaville.

Santos excelled at the rugged conditioning, and his ASTC team was the only one in almost two years of training to get into a firefight with an enemy patrol during their pregraduation reconnaissance exercise, killing several Japanese soldiers.

Upon his graduation, Santos heard that his former unit, the 11th Airborne, was put on alert for a combat jump. Eager for action, Santos went to see Red Williams, commander of the Alamo Scouts, and requested to be returned to the airborne forces.

"You're a first-rate Scout," Williams said. "Why do you want to go back to the Eleventh?"

"I think they're in for a big airborne operation, and I want to be part of it," Santos replied.

"I hate to lose you, but if that's your wish, OK," Williams said, and released Santos.

He returned to the 11th Airborne, but the "big operation" never materialized, and, with his recon training, he was assigned to the newly formed Provisional 11th Airborne Reconnaissance Platoon, twenty-six privates and three noncoms under the command of Lt. George Skau.

In the military, "provisional" means the unit did not technically exist. The Alamo Scouts, for example, were a provisional branch of the 6th Army, its members being carried on company rosters as being on "detached duty."

Similar to the Scouts, the recon platoon was the brainchild of the division commander, Maj. Gen. Joseph Swing. Like Krueger, he wanted a small, highly trained, all-volunteer unit that he could deploy as he wished, no questions asked, as he deemed necessary, without explanations. Thus the platoon was not an authorized part of the 11th Airborne. On paper, the men were assigned to other duties within the division, when, in point of fact, they were the division's ghosts or "snoopers," men who were there, yet were not.

★   ★   ★

Allied intelligence had known about the Japanese internment camp near Los Baños for quite some time. The camp, located forty miles south of Manila, just beyond Luzon's largest lake, Laguna de Bay, and twenty-four miles behind enemy lines, held some twenty-one hundred prisoners, almost all civilians.

Ever since the Americans stormed ashore at Lingayen Gulf and Nasugbu, Batangas, on January 9 and January 31, respectively, to retake Luzon in a two-prong assualt, the Imperial Japanese Army was being relentlessly pushed back. Subsequently, the Japanese high command was becoming increasingly desperate, and news began filtering down to Allied commanders that the Japanese had begun killing innocent civilians and prisoners of war as they retreated.

MacArthur was deeply concerned about the plight of thousands of prisoners in various camps on Luzon. Aside from the horrific conditions under which most were held, there was the fear that they would be murdered by their captors. By February 1945, several POW rescues had been carried out, including Cabanatuan, and at the University of Santo Tomas and Bilibid Prison, these last two during the height of the battle of Manila.

Now it was the turn of Los Baños.

The camp was located on the Philippine Agricultural College and Forestry Campus, now called the University of the Philippines at Los Baños. The sixty-acre tract was tucked between the foothills of Mount Makiling and the northern edge of Los Baños facing Laguna de Bay.

Surrounded by barbed-wire fences, the camp was a cluster of

barracks and huts. Inside were 2,146 captives, including 1,527 Americans, 329 British, 133 Australians, 89 Dutch, 30 Norwegians, 22 Poles, 16 Italians, and 1 Nicaraguan. There were also 12 U.S. Navy nurses and a few servicemen, but the balance of the internees were businessmen, teachers, bankers, and missionaries.

The job of rescuing the hostages was handed to General Swing on February 3. At that time, however, the airborne troops were locked in combat at Manila with the Japanese, who were stubbornly defending the former U.S. bases at Nichols Field and Fort McKinley, just south of the city. Swing ordered his staff to come up with a plan and refine it, so it could be implemented at the earliest possible time.

The unit selected to conduct the mission, the 1st Battalion, 511th Airborne Regimental Combat Team under Maj. Henry Burgess, was pulled off the so-called Genko Line—a system of Japanese-occupied pillboxes and antitank fortifications—on February 18 and sent to the Parañaque district to rest and refit. Two days later, they were ordered to prepare for the raid. The aid of local guerrillas was also enlisted.

The Joint U.S. Army–guerrilla plan that was devised consisted of four phases. Phase One called for the 11th Airborne's Provisional Reconnaissance Platoon, together with some twenty Filipino guerrillas, to row native bancas across Laguna de Bay two nights before the raid. There, just prior to the attack, Skau's five recon teams under lead scout Terry Santos and Sgts. Martin Squires, Cliff Town, Leonard Hahn, and Robert Angus would deploy. Hahn's team, using colored smoke grenades, would mark the landing beach on the lakeshore, as well as the drop zone for the paratroopers. As the C-47s carrying the airborne troops arrived, the other recon teams were to attack the five Japanese defensive positions outside the camp, taking them out and killing the enemy guards.

Phase Two involved airborne troops of B Company, led by Lt. John Ringler and supported by Lt. Walter Hettinger's Machine Gun Platoon, parachuting onto the drop zone, linking up with guerrillas and the recon teams, and assaulting the camp.

In Phase Three, the rest of 1st Battalion, riding across Laguna de Bay on fifty-four amtracs of the 672nd Amphibian Tractor Battalion under Lt. Col. Joseph W. Gibbs, would come ashore at the landing beach marked by Hahn and his recon team, and travel the two miles overland to the camp, arriving as the attack was under way. The internees would be loaded onto the tracked vehicles and taken back across the lake to safety.

The fourth and final phase called for the 188th Glider Infantry Regiment, minus one battalion, along with Company C of the 637th Tank Destroyer Battalion and elements of the 472nd and 675th Field Artillery Battalions, to move forward on Highway 1 to act as a diversionary force and to engage the Japanese 8th "Tiger" Division. This would facilitate the escape by protecting the internees' flanks.

Casualties were expected to be high, but all agreed it was a risk that had to be taken.

★   ★   ★

On February 10, recovered from his wounds following Cabanatuan, Alamo Scout Tom Rounsaville was sent to the Los Baños area, setting up radio networks around the barrio of Pila on the southeast shore of Laguna de Bay. His job was to report on Japanese escape routes from Manila. Along with Lieutenant Skau—the two were friends from Rounsaville's 11th Airborne days—he organized guerrilla activity in the area and fed intelligence concerning Los Baños to the 11th Airborne's G2 officer, Lt. Col. Henry Muller. They also observed the internee camp and estimated Japanese strength at 250 men.

Two days later, on February 12, a nineteen-year-old Greek-Filipino named Freddy Zervoulakas slipped out of the camp and made contact with the guerrillas. Told that a rescue attempt was being mounted, he was sent back to the camp to spread the word. The internee committee decided that it would be best for the prisoners to do nothing, lest they alert the guards.

In the meantime, Skau and Santos, who spoke Tagalog and was the platoon's ranking NCO, had already reconnoitered the camp; for Skau, this was his second trip. This time he planned to locate a landing zone for the amtracs as well as a drop zone for the paratroopers. Initially, Skau suggested taking the entire platoon, but Santos thought otherwise.

"I think it'd be foolish to take the whole platoon," Santos told him. "We'd make too much noise. I think the two of us can do it alone."

Climbing into a banca, the two men paddled across the wide lake. The trip took nearly five hours because the Americans had to steer in a wide arc around Alamba Island, where the Japanese had a patrol boat base, blocking the direct route to Los Baños.

Arriving near the village of Nanhaya, about ten miles from Los Baños, Skau and Santos, led by Filipino guides intimately familiar with the terrain, began their overland trek. The walk took about another four hours, passing through rice paddies and jungle. As they drew near, the first order of business was to locate a landing zone for the amtracs. After a brief search, and with the guide's help, they discovered a clear strip of beach at Mayondon Point near the barrio of San Antonio, close to the road that led directly to the prison compound two miles to the east. Marking the location on a map, they headed for Los Baños, not so much to observe the camp as to find a drop zone for the paratroopers. A suitable field was found nine hundred yards east of the camp.

"This should work," Skau told Santos. "It's not too far, yet not close enough to make the Japs panic and open fire on the internees. Let's get back to HQ."

★   ★   ★

Santos and Skau had no sooner returned than a civilian engineer named Pete Miles escaped from Los Baños. In talking with the 11th Airborne's Lieutenant Colonel Muller, Miles revealed details of the guards' daily routine that could prove valuable to the troops making the assualt.

"Every morning at about quarter 'til seven, the Japs do half an hour's worth of calisthenics," Miles said. "Their arms are stacked and they are dressed only in loincloths."

If true, this meant an assualt at that time could minimize the danger to the internees and GIs alike. But it had to be confirmed. Muller called for Skau.

"Muller told me, 'I'm assigning this to the recon platoon to verify,'" Skau told Santos.

"Like hell he is," Santos replied. "He's assigning it to the two of us."

That night they again made the long journey, first by banca, then by foot, to Los Baños. They waited until morning and confirmed Miles's information.

★ ★ ★

The assault on the camp was slated for seven a.m. on Friday, February 23. On the night of February 21–22, the recon platoon, down to twenty-two men instead of the usual thirty-two because of casualties and illness following its operations on Luzon, was broken into five assault teams. Loaded onto three bancas, they pushed off from shore for the long voyage across Laguna de Bay. The guerrillas, alerted by the Bamboo Telegraph, a series of runners and native drums, would be waiting for them when they arrived at Nanhaya.

The first banca, the HQ boat, held Skau and five men. Santos and five more men rode the second boat, with the rest of the platoon, ten men, aboard the third and largest banca. The bancas, piloted by natives, traveled individually, to arouse less suspicion. Despite the moonless night, however, a Japanese patrol boat spotted Santos's craft. Santos heard its engine some distance off, and then saw the craft as it cruised toward them from out of the gloom. Santos made his way to where the helmsman stood.

"If you don't tell them what I told you to say before we left shore, you'll be the first man I'll kill," he said menacingly. "And speak only in Tagalog."

Then he turned to the other recon men.

"Stay low," Santos said. "If they try to board us, I'll fire the first shot."

He pointed to one of the two men with the .30-caliber grease guns.

"You aim for the deck and cut down everyone you see," he said, then looked at the other submachine gunner. "You aim for the boat's waterline. If that doesn't stop them, we'll all cut loose and throw grenades."

As the patrol boat pulled close, its commander shouted out a challenge. At Santos's direction, the Filipino helmsman explained that he had been out fishing late because he had struck a good catch. Santos heaved a sigh of relief when the Japanese officer accepted the explanation, and steered his boat away. Shooting it out with the Japanese might have scrubbed the entire mission.

The rest of the trip was uneventful and Santos's banca reached Nanhaya and linked up with Skau and his men. The guerrillas of the 45th Hunters-ROTC Regiment were there, too. Then they waited for the third banca. At dawn they were still waiting, and as the sun climbed into the sky, heralding the start of another hot, oppressive day, there was still no sign of the large boat.

"If they don't show up," Skau told Santos, "we still go, only we break up into smaller units and take the same targets."

At last the third boat made its appearance. It had broken a rudder shortly after departure and had to turn back for repairs. The men on board were parched and sweat-soaked after the cruise across the lake under the broiling sun.

"OK, we're back to Plan A," Skau said. "Let's go."

Each assault team, including guerrillas, contained about twelve men, but as Skau led his column on the long four-hour march to Los Baños, many of the Filipinos melted away. Later, Santos discovered that the guerrillas expected the Americans to do the fighting, while they planned to be the first liberators into the compound.

As they neared the camp, Hahn's squad was detached to mark the landing beach for the amtracs. The rest continued on.

About a quarter mile from the compound, the recon platoon came across a Japanese outpost, a windowless shack open on one end. Cautiously and in complete silence, Santos made his way to the OP and peeked inside. A Japanese sentry was seated, propped against one wall, his rifle and a field phone by his side. The man was sound asleep.

Santos realized this soldier would be the "easiest kill in the world," but if his headquarters called him and he did not respond, they'd be out to check on him. So Terry Santos slinked back to the group, and they gave the OP a wide berth as they moved on.

After reaching their attack position, the group split up and headed for their objectives. Santos and his three men, Vince Call, Larry Botkin, and Barclay "Mick" McFadden, were assigned to knock out two pillboxes guarding the camp, bamboo-reinforced gun emplacements side by side, with machine guns jutting out from them. Between the pillboxes and the jungle were about seventy yards of uneven but relatively open ground, with minimal cover.

Inside the camp, all seemed quiet. The men could see prisoners milling about but, from their position, not the guards going through their morning calisthenics.

As seven a.m. approached, the drone of planes could be heard overhead as the nine C-47s carrying B Company roared toward the camp. At three minutes before seven, as Santos and his team reached the bank of Boot Creek, just outside the camp, a Japanese sentry hunting among the bushes near where Santos and his men were hiding fired at an animal. Mistaking the shot for the signal, a guerrilla, wielding a machete, leaped from the underbrush and hacked the man to death.

With no choice but to attack early even though they were not quite in position, Santos and his men opened fire on the pillbox. The Japanese responded, and pandemonium broke out as lead slugs split the morning air. The machine guns in the pillboxes raked the Americans' location. Slugs from the first burst hit Call in the shoulder and grazed Botkin's face. Both men were down. Santos, his Garand smoking, turned to McFadden.

"Mick, stay with the wounded," he said. "I'm taking the pillboxes. If I don't make it, it's up to you."

Flat on his belly, Santos snaked his way forward, knowing the closer he got to the enemy the safer he was, since the Japanese could only depress the barrels of the machine guns so far. He slinked from cover to cover, taking advantage of uneven terrain features as bullets tore up the ground around him. When he got to within range, Santos took a phosphorous grenade from his belt, yanked the pin, and tossed it. He followed the Willie Peter with a fragmentation grenade. The deadly combination blew both gun pits apart. But Santos was not out of jeopardy yet. Another machine gun located on a slight knoll near a large tree to his left opened up on him. Taken by surprise by this unreported strongpoint, Santos hugged the ground close. Then, as before, he began to slowly make his way in the gun's direction. Drawing as close as he dared, Santos tossed a Willie Peter, again followed by a fragmentation grenade. The fiery explosion silenced the gun. Then, from the smoldering position emerged a Japanese soldier, his clothes afire from the phosphorous grenade, staggering and screaming in a gruesome dance of death. Santos leveled his Garand, which he always kept loaded with armor-piercing rounds, and, without aiming, fired. At close range, the devastating, high-powered, steel-jacketed AP bullet hit the screaming soldier, whose upper torso literally exploded at the impact.

"Jesus Christ," Santos muttered in awe.

As Santos dealt with his objectives, Sergeant Town's squad raked several guardhouses along the perimeter with weapons fire. A Japanese patrol charged him, and his men chopped them down with a vicious fusillade. The guerrillas, meanwhile, had reemerged, overrunning part of the camp. They battled Japanese guards at the rear of the compound, while at the front gate Lieutenant Skau's team fought their way into the camp, exchanging fire with the guards.

By now the paratroopers of Lieutenant Ringler's B Company were arriving. Carried from their starting point at the recently recaptured Nichols Field on C-47s of the 75th Troop Carrier Squadron, their flight had been unmolested by either enemy fighters or antiaircraft guns. Arriving over the well-marked DZ, the troopers hastily leaped from the Skytrains at just five hundred feet and drifted toward the battle.

As the troopers bore in on the camp, the rest of the recon platoon had already burst into the compound, where they encountered the guards, many still in loincloths, from their exercise period, scrambling for their weapons. The recon men opened a devastating fire, mowing down the guards in heaps, and sending the rest fleeing into the jungle.

The shooting was over in less than twenty minutes and Santos yelled for McFadden to bring the wounded men forward. As he did, the amtracs began rumbling into the camp.

The next problem was getting the internees onto the vehicles. Many refused to go without their personal possessions, and some wanted to drag extra clothes and other articles with them. The order was given to torch the barracks buildings, cruelly, but out of necessity, burning out the prisoners and forcing their evacuation.

As each of the fifty-four amtracs was loaded with internees—only about half, primarily the sickest, along with women, children, nuns, and twelve U.S. Navy nurses, could be taken on the first trip—the armored vehicle drove back to the lake and chugged across the water.

After the last amtrac had departed, the GIs herded the rest of the people toward the lakeshore to await their return. As they neared the beachhead, the distant rumble of tracked vehicles could be heard. Fearing it might be approaching Japanese reinforcements, panic swept the internees as the Americans yelled for them to "scatter and take cover." All sighed with relief as the first of the returning amtracs rolled around a bend in the road.

Time was of the essence. While the Americans had killed many of the Japanese garrison, another ten thousand men were less than ten miles away, and might even now have been alerted and were racing toward Los Baños.

Even as the GIs were loading internees into the amtracs, gunfire was heard in the distance, off to the north. The fire was part of the 188th Glider Infantry Regiment's diversion. Elements of the diversionary force had rolled out Highway 1 and attacked Japanese positions just across the San Juan River. Heavy fighting took place around Lechería Hills, some of it hand-to-hand, and troopers J. C. Doiron and Virgil McMurtry were killed, as were two guerrillas, Pfc. Atanacio Castillo and Pfc. Anselmo Soler. Despite the losses, by mid-morning the troopers had cleared the area and were marching toward Los Baños, thus cutting the road between the Japanese Tiger Division and the internment camp. From his position on high ground, the commander, Colonel Soule, the expedition leader, could see the amtracs loading the internees and heading across the lake like water bugs. When the last vehicle had cleared, he ordered a defensive withdrawal back across the San Juan River.

At lakeside, a Japanese machine gun, which had somehow reached the LZ, opened fire on an amtrac, its 7.62mm slugs bouncing off the vehicle's steel sides. Cpl. Dwight Clark of the 672nd Amphibian Tractor Battalion, manning the amtrac's .50-caliber machine gun, spotted the enemy position inside a wooden hut and opened fire. The heavy lead slugs tore the shack apart and silenced the gun before it could inflict any casualties.

Santos and the recon platoon boarded the last amtrac to leave Los Baños. His four-man team had suffered the only American casualties among the men who had raided the camp. The number of Japanese killed was not known, although it was probably between eighty and one hundred. No internees were killed or injured.

The raid at Los Baños had freed 2,147 internees, including Lois Kathleen McCoy, who had been delivered three days earlier in the prison infirmary by U.S. Navy nurse Dorothy Danner and was now being carried to safety by her mother, Mildred, an American schoolteacher who had been working in Manila, and her father, Oscar, who had been the Philippines representative of Republic Steel of Ohio.

Santos was awarded a Silver Star for his actions during the operation, the first of two he would win.

One objective was left unaccomplished. Los Baños's supply officer, Lt. Sadaaki Konishi, had been especially brutal to the internees. Orders had gone out to capture the man if at all possible, but despite rumors that he had been killed, he had, in fact, managed to escape into the jungle.

However, sometime later he was observed working as a Filipino laborer by a former Los Baños internee. The internee notified the local police, who jailed Konishi. After the war, he was tried for war crimes and sentenced to prison.

★   ★   ★

The raid at Los Baños, one of the most successful rescues in American military history, went almost unnoticed by the public back home in the States. That was because on the very same day, February 23, 1945, hundreds of miles to the north on the stinking, steaming volcanic island of Iwo Jima, five U.S. Marines and a navy corpsman raised a flag atop an extinct volcano called Mount Suribachi. That image, captured by Associated Press photographer Joe Rosenthal, became a powerful symbol of the war effort in the Pacific.

The photograph ran on front pages of newspapers across the United States, eventually to become the impetus for the war's most successful bond drive.

Meanwhile, news of the rescue of twenty-one hundred civilians in the Philippines was buried deep inside the same issues—in some papers, as far back as page five.

CHAPTER 15

"I Wouldn't Trade the Whole Damned Jap Army for One Alamo Scout."

Final Operations, January–July 1945

From the moment American troops stormed ashore on Luzon in January until August, when Yamashita and what was left of his army had been pushed back into mountainous pockets of resistance, the Alamo Scouts had more than enough work to occupy them. Teams led by Herman Chanley, Jack Dove, John McGowen, Bill Nellist, Tom Rounsaville, Wilbur Littlefield, George Thompson, Woodrow Hobbs, and Bob Sumner were constantly in the field, their missions often overlapping. In addition, new teams led by Robert S. Shirkey, George Derr, Henry Adkins, and Wilmot B. Ouzts, as well as scratch teams under Vance Q. Williams, John G. Fisher, John A. Roberts, Henry R. Chalko, James Farrow, and Joe Moon, were organized for impromptu assignments.

Combined, these men paved the way for MacArthur's troops as they carved away at the Japanese defenses.

As January dragged into February, the battle for Luzon intensified. Fighting at Manila had been especially ferocious as Adm. Sanji Iwabuchi, in defiance of General Yamashita's wishes, ordered his sixteen thousand men to stand fast and defend the city. Fighting in and around

Manila lasted from February 4 to March 4, and devastated large sections of the once-exotic city, especially in the Intramuros district, the Walled City, an old Spanish fortress near the port, where many government buildings stood.

When the fighting ended, nearly all of Iwabuchi's men were dead, and so were as many as 100,000 Filipino civilians, caught in the murderous cross fire.

But even before the fight at Manila had begun, Alamo Scout teams were out in advance of the troops, monitoring Japanese moves and defenses.

On January 22, three days after Nellist's men returned from spotting the Japanese big guns blocking the advance on Manila, Woodrow Hobbs's team landed north of the Bataan Peninsula. Their job was to observe Highway 5, the main coastal road, leading from the town of Gapan south to Manila. This included monitoring the roads feeding onto Highway 5, as well as enemy activity in the surrounding barrios and foothills.

By this point in the war, changes had taken place on some of the teams, due to men being recalled by their units or leaving the Scouts for other reasons. Hobbs's team, for this mission, included Sgt. John Phillips and Irv Ray, both formerly of the Dove Team. Ray had been awarded a battlefield promotion to second lieutenant. Also with Hobbs was Ray Wangrud, formerly of the Reynolds Team, John Hidalgo of the Littlefield Team, and Bob Ross of the Lutz Team.

This homogenous group of Scouts had just the day before returned from an aborted mission to check on Japanese activity between San Miguel and Subic Bay on the northern end of Bataan. It was to have been a very dangerous mission in an area crawling with enemy troops, but the team wanted to go, and were disappointed at the order—it came directly from MacArthur—canceling it.

Now—it was January 23—they traveled by C-47 from 6th Army HQ to Lingayen, a forty-minute flight, escorted by four P-38 Lightning fighters. From there the team was flown, one by one, in L-5 scout planes to a small airstrip at the town of Akle, ten miles south of Sibul Springs. At Akle they were met by Captain Cabangbang, a Filipino officer attached to the Allied Intelligence Bureau, and Captain Santos of the BMA Guerrilla Division.

A command post and radio relay station was established at Akle, and the Hobbs Team remained there for two days. Then Hobbs, accompanied by Wangrud and Hidalgo, traveled north to Sibul Springs, while Ray and Phillips headed south to Angat. Ross was dispatched to Novaliches, eight miles northeast of Manila. Guerrillas escorted the Scouts.

From these locations, the Scouts sent back a steady stream of intelligence on supply dumps, troop movements, and defenses. Throughout the American advance on Manila, the Scout team moved ahead of them, maintaining contact with frontline units.

During this time, Hobbs's men often had a chance to socialize with Littlefield and his team, who had been out since January 14, watching enemy troop movements along Highways 3 and 13.

On February 12, their mission over, the Hobbs Team reassembled at Novaliches and entered the smoking ruins of Manila with the U.S. forces.

★   ★   ★

As fighting in Manila subsided, Philippine-born Scout leader Rafael Ileto's team spent the ten days between February 17 and February 27 organizing guerrilla units in the Pantabangan-Caranglan area, and set up road watches between Guimba and Gapan on Highways 15 and 5, to the north of Cabanatuan City.

On February 28, they were out again, this time bound for Camarines Norte province aboard a PBY Catalina. It was the start of a seventy-one-day mission, the longest ever for an Alamo Scout team.

The seaplane landed just offshore, and Ileto was met by Maj. Bernard L. Anderson, a guerrilla leader and army air force officer who had been in the jungles since the fall of the Philippines.

Anderson supplied the team with a thirty-foot sailboat, and the next day the Scouts were gliding across the deep blue water toward Cabalete Island. They were diverted, however, to the town of Perez on

Alabat Island. A guerrilla leader, Captain Areta, greeted them there, and the Scouts set up a radio station and organized the movements of Areta and his four hundred men. Working with Thompson's team near Mauban via radio, the Scouts monitored Japanese troop movement and coastal activity. On March 26, the team coordinated an airdrop by two C-47s. The planes droned over the barrio of Bagasbas, dropping 250 '03 Springfields, 50 Thompson submachine guns, ammo, rice, salt, flour, cigarettes, money, and medical supplies.

★   ★   ★

The Littlefield Team returned from their twenty-four-day Tarlac mission on February 7 and were back out the next day. Boarding L-5 recon planes, they were flown one by one to the town of Malolos, where they landed on a crude airstrip hacked out by natives, who, between them, had just one pick and one shovel. While they did not know it yet, the men would be in the field for sixty-eight days.

For this mission, Littlefield would have with him Lee Hall, a graduate of the ASTC's first class and formerly of the Barnes Team; Ben Mones, an American-Filipino radio operator from San Francisco who had accompanied Littlefield on several other missions; and Zeke McConnell. The mission was to set up watch stations and an intelligence network along Highway 5 from Malina north to Malolos.

Originally, Littlefield was to take with him an American captain, but he refused. He knew the officer and considered him "kill crazy." The man had three Japanese skulls mounted on his jeep's bumper, and Littlefield suspected he wanted to go along just so he could kill more of the enemy.

Littlefield and his men passed through the 1st U.S. Cavalry lines at dawn on February 7 after first coordinating their movements with U.S. artillery so they would not get American shells dropped on their heads.

About a mile from American lines, they spotted a farmhouse in a clearing inhabited by an aging farmer and a girl of about twelve, whom Littlefield learned was the man's granddaughter. A small village lay beyond in the distance. There were no Japanese to be seen, yet as they watched, three U.S. planes roared in and began strafing the town, dropping hundred-pound bombs from under their wings.

When the planes departed, Littlefield and his men moved forward. The farmer and girl were rattled by the nearby air raid, but unharmed, and Littlefield tried to convince them to leave by either going into the jungle or to American lines, but they refused. Littlefield knew that, stuck between the lines as they were, the two were in extreme danger, and tried again to get them to leave. He warned that the Japanese may come back.

"No," the old man said. "My home. Stay here."

As an American artillery barrage began to walk its way across the landscape, Littlefield decided it was time "to get the hell out." He hurried his men across the rice fields and to the town, where he found a number of the inhabitants had been wounded by the navy planes. There was no sign of the Japanese. Fortunately, some American deuce-and-a-half trucks came rattling along the road passing through the village and Littlefield flagged them down. He got the most seriously wounded villagers put on board the trucks. The farmer and his grand-daughter still refused to leave their farm. Littlefield later learned that the Japanese did return to the area, accused them of spying for the Americans, and beheaded both.

The wounded villagers, meanwhile, were taken to the American hospital at the University of Santo Thomas, where, as they lay recuperating, the hospital came under Japanese artillery fire. The injured villagers were again moved out of harm's way.

Littlefield's lengthy mission continued. As the team drew near the village that Mones originally hailed from, Littlefield granted him a two-week furlough to visit family, even though he had no authority to do so.

"I made it sound official," he said years later.

Near the end of the sixty-eight days, Littlefield was staggered by a severe bout of dysentery, and it happened at the worst possible time. Alerted of the Scouts' presence, a large body of Japanese troops were on their trail. Littlefield, his guts churning, could not keep up with the men as they slogged through the jungle on their way toward the American lines. He emptied his bowels thirty-two times in one day, mostly passing blood.

"It was terrible," Littlefield recalled. "I was sick as a dog."

Consequently, the men slowed to his pace. Finally, Littlefield ordered them to move on without him.

"The Japs are about an hour behind us," he told them. "I'm slowing you down and I won't sacrifice all of you for my sake. Get moving. I'll be coming along."

Naturally, the team was hesitant to leave Littlefield, or any member, behind.

"I said go, goddamn it," Littlefield ordered.

They departed. Once out of sight, though, Zeke McConnell dropped back and hid behind a tree, keeping an eye on Littlefield. After a great deal of struggle, Littlefield reached McConnell's position and the Cherokee stepped out.

"What the hell are you doing here, Zeke?" Littlefield said, somewhat startled. "I told you to keep going."

McConnell smiled.

"You didn't think I'd leave you behind to take care of all those Japs alone, did ya?" he said.

With that, he accompanied his friend to safety.

★   ★   ★

On February 17, Herm Chanley, who had been on the Hobbs Team originally but was given a team of his own the previous December, landed near the coastal town of Baler. Chanley's job was to perform a reconnaissance of Casiguran Sound to see if it would provide an adequate anchorage for ships of the 7th Fleet.

Once ashore, Chanley's team, consisting of Staff Sgts. Glendale Watson and Allen H. Throgmorton, Sgts. Juan D. Pacis and Juan E. Berganio, and Pfcs. Bobby G. Walters and Nicholas C. Enriquez, contacted the 103rd and 205th guerrilla squadrons. Chanley and his men quickly discovered that the weaker unit, the 103rd under Lieutenant

Ilipio, with five hundred men and just fifteen miscellaneous weapons, was extremely valuable in helping the Scouts accomplish their mission, while the 205th under Captain Bautista, with five hundred men and fifty-two weapons, proved unreliable.

After learning that the one hundred Japanese who had been in the Baler area had been forced to leave due to incessant harassment from the guerrillas, Chanley and his men relocated, conducting reconnaissance excursions around the barrio of Dinadiawan and the Dilalongan River, with the aid of agents from the Allied Intelligence Bureau, who now joined them.

Picked up by a destroyer on March 1, the team was back onshore the next day, this time accompanied by four naval officers, two AIB agents, and nine guerrillas. Hacking their way through the jungle in three groups, with Chanley and eleven men in the center, Throgmorton and four guerrillas guarding the left flank and Watson and five guerrillas on the right, they proceeded to a Japanese airfield two miles south of the Dilalongan River to see if it was usable. They found the runway overgrown with razor-sharp kunai grass, and the navy men were unhappy with it, so the search continued. A new, more satisfactory site was located a mile farther on, and the men returned to the beach, where an LCVP picked them up.

★   ★   ★

Even before Manila fell, MacArthur began making plans for his return to that tadpole-shaped rock in Manila Bay, Corregidor. Here, even more than Bataan, was the burning source of his humiliation thirty-two months earlier. It was a sore his pride could not endure.

The problem was, intelligence sources estimated that as many as 5,670 Japanese troops, including 800 Japanese civilians, mostly men who escaped from the fighting on the mainland, were defending the island. The 1st Battalion of the 503rd Parachute Infantry Regiment along with the 3rd Battalion of the 34th Infantry Division were being prepped for the initial assault, but first more information was needed.

To get that, 6th Army HQ tapped the Sumner Team, temporarily under John McGowen, after Sumner came down with jaundice.

On January 26, as Nellist and Rounsaville were preparing to push off for Cabanatuan, McGowen and his men boarded a PT boat in Subic Bay and headed across the dark water into Manila Bay and toward Corregidor. Manila, aflame from the raging fight, burned in the distance, the glow from the fires lighting up the entire horizon. Tracers arced through the night sky, and the dull boom of artillery like a drumbeat out of Hell rolled across the bay.

As the PT closed on the island, its radar picked up echoes of two Japanese destroyers. They spooked the PT skipper, who stopped his boat.

"This is as far as I dare go," he told McGowen. "You'll have to go the rest of the way on your own."

"It's seven goddamned miles," McGowen fumed. "We can't take rubber boats that distance."

"That's your decision," the skipper said. "But I go no farther."

Angrily, McGowen, who hated leaving a job undone, polled his men.

"We decided to get the hell out of there," Bill Blaise later wrote. "It would have been suicide."

It was the first and last mission the Scouts ever aborted on their own.

★   ★   ★

On February 8 McGowen, again at the head of the Sumner Team, with Lawrence Coleman, Bill Blaise, Bob Shullaw, Harry Weiland, Ed Renhols, and Paul Jones, accompanied by Filipino Sgt. Vincent Quipo of the Philippine Message Center, were back in the bush.

This time their mission was to establish a radio station on the coast of Zambales province, which borders Bataan to the north. Traveling by native bancas, they landed at Loclocbelete, a barrio near the city of Palauig, a few miles north of the airfield at Iba. Setting up the radio in a house, the team began patrolling north along the National Highway from Santa Cruz, checking out roads and bridges, as well as Iba Field, which they found to be usable.

Although they saw no Japanese, they were informed by guerrillas of the Montalla command that as many as one thousand of the enemy were in the area, mostly operating in small foraging groups three miles east of Santa Cruz. The guerrillas also said between three thousand and six thousand Japanese were strung out over a two-mile stretch east of Botolan along the Capiz Trail.

The team continued patrolling the area for the next week, before being recalled by 6th Army headquarters.

★   ★   ★

After Cabanatuan, Nellist and his team did a stint bodyguarding MacArthur and his staff on Bataan. On February 19, Nellist and his men, with Sergeant Quipo, just back from the McGowen expedition, boarded a Mariner seaplane in Lingayen Gulf and were flown to Magallanes on southwest Luzon. There they were to contact the Escudero guerrilla group, a large but poorly equipped unit under the Sorosogon province governor Escudero. It was 6th Army HQ's belief that if the guerrillas could be resupplied, they would be of great use in the upcoming invasion of Ligaspi in March, so the team boarded native bancas for the trip to the town of Casiguran. Things got off to a bad start. While the team was unloading the generator that powered the SCR-694 radio, it fell overboard and was lost.

Out of communication, Nellist led his men on foot toward Escudero's headquarters at San Juan. There, Nellist requested use of the guerrillas' radio to ask that a new generator be airdropped. Escudero agreed, provided they also drop ammo for his men. The drop was done, after which Nellist instructed Escudero to meet him at the village of Bulan, where they would link up with the Lapus guerrilla band. Nellist was unaware that Lapus and Escudero were adversaries.

Arriving at Bulan on February 23, the Scouts conducted reconnaissance forays and captured one Japanese soldier and several Formosan laborers. They also took depth soundings of the water and analyzed beach conditions. Six days later, Escudero, with about two hundred men, and Lapus, with about sixty guerrillas, both arrived in camp, and the air of hostility between the two men could have been cut with a knife. Nellist headed off trouble by stepping in to act as mediator. Neither Escudero nor Lapus would serve under one or the other, but both agreed to take orders from Nellist. A potentially violent confrontation was avoided.

On March 9, Nellist assumed authority over all the guerrillas in the area, about one thousand men in all. It was a precarious command, since the guerrillas came from various organizations and fiercely bickered among themselves. As a means of separating them, Nellist assigned each group to a specific sector. Each was also given a radio, enabling them to communicate through the Guerrilla Net Control, a network that had been established on Luzon. Since the guerrillas were not professionally trained soldiers, adept at conducting major assaults, Nellist instructed them to snipe at the enemy and harass their patrols and outposts. At this they excelled, and the Japanese withdrew to an area ten miles west of Legaspi known as Little Bataan.

Nellist continued to monitor this far-from-homogenous outfit, establishing a much-needed military policy and stern discipline.

One unit, the Orubia group, pulled out of the defense line and returned to Nellist's HQ, saying they were going home to rest. Nellist could not allow that, for fear others would do the same. Instead, he lined the men up, disarmed them, and told them to leave without their weapons and not return. The guns were dispersed among other guerrillas.

Of particular trouble was a guerrilla leader named Zabat, who ran an oppressive administration in his sector, which sometimes included robbery and murder. He levied excessive taxes on the people, 20 percent on sharecroppers and landowners. Nellist ordered Zabat to cease these activities, and he did. For a short while. Then he started again, reinstating his taxes and placing an additional 20 percent tax on gross revenues from cabarets, cockfights, and gambling houses. Nellist again ordered him to stop, threatening to cut off his supply of American arms and ammo. That finally worked, and Nellist came to realize that controlling their flow of support was a means of keeping the guerrillas in line.

In addition to guerrilla units, Nellist also organized a civilian spy ring. He quickly found that the best agents were elderly Filipino women, who would go village to village selling eggs, chickens, and produce, all the while pinpointing fuel dumps, artillery supplies, and other possible military targets.

In Legaspi, the women discovered that the most important Japanese installations were in buildings with red tile roofs, and one woman located ammunition storage tunnels. They uncovered so many targets that 6th Army simply ordered saturation bombing on the entire area.

The invasion of Legaspi was set for April 1, and for two weeks prior to that Nellist was in direct contact with the invasion task force, sending them daily reports on enemy movements. Once the troops were ashore, Nellist and his team linked up with the task force HQ and coordinated guerrilla operations.

★   ★   ★

Meanwhile, Tom Rounsaville, after Cabanatuan and Los Baños, had established a command post at the barrio of Pila in order to monitor enemy traffic at Laguna de Bay. Joining Rounsaville's Team was Pfc. Leroy Donnette, replacing Frank Fox, who returned to his original unit. Donnette was the only member of an Alamo Scout team to never have gone through the ASTC program. Donnette had been "overhead personnel," assisting the Scouts in training exercises, until Nellist invited him to join the team.

On March 2, Bill Littlefield—still on the mission that would end with his bout of dysentery—linked up with Rounsaville at the town of Pila. Together they set up OPs to keep an eye on four square miles of area around Laguna de Bay. Assisting them were forty-eight Chinese communists of the Wai Chi guerrilla group, fierce and well-disciplined fighters, Littlefield recalled.

Between March 2 and March 25, Rounsaville established a network of radio stations connecting Pila, Mount Atimba, Nagcarlan, Dyapp, and Tayabas. This network allowed Rounsaville to coordinate guerrilla activities with the U.S. 7th Cavalry Regiment. Nellist oversaw this network until April 6, when it was turned over to the 1st Cavalry Division, and the Alamo Scout team departed.

★ ★ ★

Littlefield continued to operate in Pila. The town was held by one thousand guerrillas from five different groups, including Squadron 48, all communist Hukbalahaps. Littlefield and his men were quite comfortable in Pila. Shown nothing but hospitality by the villagers, the men slept in a large modern home. Villagers cooked for them, and the house had a refrigerator that made its own ice cubes. There were electric lights and even a bidet.

"I'd never seen one before," Littlefield said in 2007.

The only problem was with the electricity. Power came from a generating plant fifteen to twenty kilometers away, and when the Japanese, who had electricity in their bivouac area as well, occupied the plant, they shut off the service to Pila. When guerrillas recaptured the plant, they shut down power to the Japanese. Control of the plant seesawed back and forth, but neither side destroyed the useful facility.

The provincial capital of San Fernando soon fell to the guerrillas, and Littlefield and his men relocated there and arranged for ammo drops for the Filipinos. This drop included bazookas, which the guerrillas had never seen. Over the next two days, Littlefield received frequent requests from the guerrillas for more bazooka rockets. Wondering what the hell was going on and where all this ammo was going, he trekked up to the guerrillas' line to investigate.

It was a difficult trip, over felled trees used as roadblocks and across rice fields. When he reached the front, Littlefield mounted some high ground and indicated that the Squadron 48 guerrilla leader join him. The leader, Alfredo Amdavid, a name he had assumed in order to protect his family in Manila, did so nervously. A Japanese shell whistled overhead and both men quickly scooted down the hill and into a ditch. They stayed there as a few more shells came screaming in. When he raised his head, Littlefield saw a Japanese soldier jump out from cover about a hundred yards away and take off running. Suddenly there was a loud whoosh as a guerrilla fired a bazooka rocket at the man. The Filipinos were using the bazooka to fire at individual soldiers.

Littlefield put a halt to the practice.

★   ★   ★

While Littlefield and Nellist were working with guerrillas around Laguna de Bay, George Thompson and his men went south by sailboat to Santa Lucia, arriving March 9. After establishing a command post at the town, they moved inland to Mauban and discovered some two hundred Japanese. After reporting the enemy presence, they arranged for an airdrop of arms and ammunition to resupply the men of General Vera's Southern Luzon guerrilla group. With the aid of the guerrillas, Thompson and his men set up an intelligence-gathering network among the local population and blocked major roadways to hamper Japanese vehicular movements.

★   ★   ★

In New Guinea, General Krueger had vetoed the idea of sending his Alamo Scouts into the field to capture Japanese general Hatazo Adachi, commander of the 18th Army, saying, "I wouldn't trade the whole damned Jap army for one Alamo Scout."

Now, his ideas had changed.

For weeks, 6th Army G2 had been trying to discover the whereabouts of Adm. Nobutake Kondo and Maj. Gen. Rikichi Tsukada, who jointly commanded the enemy troops in the Zambales Mountains area. Tsukada commanded army forces out of Fort Stotsenburg, while Kondo, who in 1942 led the Aleutians diversionary force during the Midway operation, led the naval forces from the naval air station at San Marcelino.

Red Sumner, recovered from jaundice and back with the team, was at Iba with his men when he was summoned to the briefing tent. He was told that U.S. forces would be attacking east, over the Zambales, to push out the Japanese and put Clark Field and Fort Stotsenburg back under the American flag.

"It'll be no easy job," Sumner was told by Col. Horton White. "The terrain is horrible, double canopy jungle and tough to navigate. In our favor, though, is that the Nips are disorganized and out of food. They are dying of starvation and lack of medical supplies. If our move is successful, we can cut 'em off and let 'em wither on the vine completely."

White lit a cigarette and continued.

"But that's not your concern," he said. "We believe General Tsukada and Admiral Kondo are hiding out in the Zambales. We'd like to get our hands on them. It'd be a big feather in our cap, and might force a lot of Japs to surrender."

Setting out on March 28, Sumner's first big hurdle was not the enemy but a regimental commander named Lt. Col. Harry Mangold. Mangold's job was to seal off the Japanese escape route from Bataan to the Zambales. He was unfazed by Sumner's mission and said he had warned his men that he'd court-martial anyone who took a Japanese prisoner. Meanwhile, the 6th Army's psychological warfare section had published surrender leaflets that were being dropped by the thousands over enemy ground.

"These leaflets are having an effect, sir," Sumner told Mangold. "Some Nips are starting to come in, and the more we capture, the more they tell us during interrogation and the more of our guys who won't get shot. Will you countermand your order to shoot any Jap trying to surrender?"

Mangold stared at Sumner.

"You get the hell out of my area and stay out, Lieutenant," he snarled.

"With all due respect, sir, my commanding officer is General Krueger, and I will check in with him," Sumner replied, then saluted and left.

He radioed 6th Army HQ and got White, who passed him along to Krueger.

"You have my authorization to go over Mangold's head," Krueger said. "Report to his division commander in person, and I will be sending the colonel a personal message."

That was the last problem Sumner had with Mangold.

Sumner and his men spent the next several weeks combing the mountains for the enemy flag officers, questioning natives and Japanese POWs alike. From what they learned, their quarry was on the move, and the Scouts seemed to be just a few days behind them.

On April 30, in the Bucao River–Mount Botolan area, the Scouts got into a hot skirmish with a small group of Japanese consisting of a naval petty officer and four seamen. One man was captured, while the rest were killed or fled. The prisoner told Sumner, through an interpreter, that Admiral Kondo had been killed by junior officers during a mutiny. The information proved untrue. Two days later, Sumner was told by Negrito tribesmen that a number of sick and starving Japanese were ahead in the village of Pinatubo. The Scouts entered the village with caution, weapons at the ready. The village consisted of four nipa huts. Inside each, amid the stench of decaying flesh, were seven to ten dead enemy soldiers, clouds of flies buzzing around them. None were the officers he sought.

May 2 found the team patrolling near the village of Paluig. Eighteen Japanese were spotted coming toward the Scouts, so Sumner spread the men out in an ambush. When the enemy soldiers arrived, the team opened fire. In the short but deadly fusillade that followed, fifteen were killed and three captured.

Since Japanese soldiers were not expected to be taken prisoner, they had never been warned not to talk if they were, so the three POWs chatted freely. From them, Sumner learned that the officers he was chasing had traveled north along the coast to Baguio, where they were to rejoin Yamashita's command. A second patrol that day from Masinloc to Santa Cruz resulted in another firefight. Eight Japanese were killed, and the Scouts took from them a bundle of documents and maps.

Then, on May 7, during a routine communications check, Sumner received a radio message that the Germans had surrendered in Europe. The news didn't do much for the spirits of the men still engaged in a hot war on the other side of the world.

"A lot of good that does us out here in the jungle chasing Nips," Sumner told his men.

The longer the chase for the two flag officers went on, the more it seemed a pointless exercise to Sumner. All the search was uncovering were small clumps of Japanese soldiers, either dying of starvation or disease, or already dead. He finally radioed back that he felt there was no way he would catch up to the enemy commanders, and was told to end the mission.

What Sumner had accomplished, though, was to supply weapons and equipment to a number of guerrilla bands, including one led by Manual Roxas, who, in 1946, became the first president of the independent Republic of the Philippines. Sumner was also forever convinced that his getting Mangold to allow for the taking of POWs saved many American lives.

★ ★ ★

While Sumner was not successful in capturing Tsukada and Kondo, that did not dampen Krueger's newfound excitement at possibly making top Japanese commanders POWs.

General Yamashita had been holding off the Americans in northwestern Luzon for four months, or about the same length of time the Americans had defended Bataan exactly three years earlier. The Cagayan Valley, which the Tiger of Malaya was defending so stubbornly, was a major food supply area for the island and the only practical American approach route. Protected on the east by the Sierra Madre mountains, the Cordillera Central Range to the west, and the Palai, Carabello, and Mamparang mountains to the south, it was a formidable position.

On May 13, the Americans finally punched through the Japanese line at Balete Pass and pushed north, but the Alamo Scouts were already there ahead of them. Between April 30 and June 30, when the 6th Army ceased operations on Luzon, the Scouts would conduct twenty missions in this region.

Tom Rounsaville did the first one. His job was to find and capture Yamashita.

On April 13, with Sergeants Alfonso, Vaquilar, Laquier, Donnette, and Gadung, the latter a Filipino radio operator, Rounsaville boarded a C-47 for the town of Tuao. There he contacted Col. Don Blackburn's 11th Guerrilla Infantry unit. Word had come down that Yamashita had been sighted in the area. Rounsaville interrogated a pair of Japanese POWs, who told him the general had his HQ at Bayombong, but a trip there, armed with photos of Yamashita to show to civilians, proved fruitless.

Returning to Tuao, Rounsaville next questioned an American civilian who had escaped from the Japanese.

"He's hiding out in a cave at Madupapa," the man said. "He's guarded by about three thousand troops."

Moving to Madupapa, the Scouts found the area crawling with Japanese, and spotted six men carrying a field-grade officer on an elaborate chair. But the officer was not Yamashita.

The next excursion was to the barrio of Calapangan on the west bank of the Cayagan River, where a guerrilla who had escaped the Japanese said his guard mentioned that he had seen Yamashita riding in a civilian car. However, he said, Yamashita had since moved to Tuguegarao, where he boarded a plane bound for Japan.

This rumor turned out to be true, and the mission was over. However, during his sixteen-day manhunt, Rounsaville was able to confirm the presence of nine thousand Japanese in the Aparri region, south to the Paret River, with the heaviest concentration being between Lallo and Gattaran. There were another three thousand at Tuguegarao, three hundred to four hundred at Aparri and Buguey, and four hundred to six hundred at the Paret River. He also pinpointed a number of enemy defensive positions and rescued two downed pilots. However, both were dangerously ill, and even an emergency airdrop of intravenous glucose did not save them. He had both men buried and their graves marked. Their personal items he later handed over to their squadron chaplain.

★   ★   ★

Not all Alamo Scout teams spent April and May hunting Japanese generals.

Traveling in a large banca powered by Filipino oarsmen, Bill Littlefield and his team left Guinayangan on April 18, bound for Mantubig in Camarines Sur province, on Luzon's southern tip. His mission was to locate a landing area for a battalion of men from the 1st Cavalry Division.

It was a long trip and the boats stopped four times for food and water. It took them two days to reach their goal, with rowers being recruited from fishing villages every ten or twenty miles. When they arrived at Camarines Sur, the Scouts found out from the natives that the enemy had abandoned the entire district. Searching for the best landing spot, they scouted along the coast. At Mantubig, Littlefield liked what he saw and radioed the coordinates back to 1st Cav headquarters. Then he settled down to wait.

It just so happened that there was a wedding in the village that day, and the Scouts were allowed to join the festivities. They ate rice and sun-dried fish and attended the wedding ceremony. Afterward, the natives threw a party for the Scouts, and Littlefield, in the spirit of fun, decided to play a joke on the incoming 1st Cav boys. That night, as the Higgins boats rolled ashore and dropped ramps, the alighting Americans, weapons ready for a possible fight, were greeted by children holding hand-painted signs proclaiming LITTLEFIELD FOR MAYOR.

Temporarily attached to the 1st Cav during the drive on Manila, Littlefield was sent on a reconnaissance mission in advance of the troops. The expedition was pointless, Littlefield thought, not to mention suicidal. From his position on the U.S. front line, he could easily see Japanese off in the distance, "swarming like ants."

"I want a driver and an armored car," he said.

The vehicle was sent up, and Littlefield climbed in beside the driver.

"Get me closer," he said. "I need to see what I'm up against."

The car moved forward and soon came under heavy small-arms fire. Bullets rattled off the steel sides like pebbles. Littlefield had seen enough. The reconnaissance was scratched.

★ ★ ★

In late March, Jack Dove and his team, Sgt. James Farrow, 1st Sgt. Fredirico Balambao, and Sgt. Peter Vischansky, left Lingayen Gulf and landed in the area of Labayat. They were assigned to monitor Japanese troop movement along the Labayat-Famy Road and identify enemy escape routes for soldiers fleeing the area south to Mauban.

During the mission, which was also a combat patrol—a rarity for the Scouts—the team was diverted to an offshore spit of land called Fuga Island to bring out some downed American airmen. They discovered the fliers all dead. They had been used for bayonet practice. Outraged, the Scouts ambushed a Japanese defensive position, and in a short, hot skirmish, killed several of the enemy.

On April 23, while reconnoitering the west side of the Umiray River near the village of Blate, Dove and his men, along with escorting guerrillas, got into a six-hour fight with about two hundred Japanese troops. Amazingly, the Scouts and guerrillas suffered no casualties, and the enemy retreated to the north. Continuing to the town of Maroraqui, they ran into fifty enemy soldiers, and in the fight that followed, three Japanese were killed. The rest retreated to the southeast. The following day, Dove and his band met the same large body of Japanese they had fought forty-eight hours earlier. A four-hour battle ensued, leaving six enemy soldiers dead and one taken prisoner.

This off-and-on contact lasted for two weeks. During that time, at least eighteen Japanese were killed, and three were captured.

★ ★ ★

The Nellist Team's final mission started badly when the C-47 the men were riding in crash-landed on the airstrip at Manaoag in Isabela province on May 18. The men were shaken but otherwise unharmed, and immediately created a command post at the town. The next day, Nellist, Kittleson, Siason, and a Filipino radioman, Sgt. Agapito C. Apano, hiked through the jungle to the junction of the Cagayan and Magat rivers, twenty miles south of Ilagan, and set up another radio post and a spy network of local Filipinos. The rest of the team, Wismer, Asis, and Smith, performed a similar task from Ilagan, north to Cabagan.

A severe rainstorm broke over the men on the night of May 23. Nellist, Kittleson, Siason, and Apano came across an old wooden tobacco shed and slipped inside for shelter. As they sat huddled in the dark, the heavy rain drumming on the roof, a new sound reached their ears: the sloshing of many shoes in the mud. Risking a peek through cracks in the plank walls of the shed, they held their breath as a company of Japanese slogged by, so close Nellist could have reached out and touched them. Rain cascaded down their bodies and Nellist prayed they would not try to seek refuge in the shed. They didn't, and were shortly gone from sight.

Wismer, Asis, and Smith, meanwhile, met with Kiang Chi Kien of the committee of Overseas Affairs of the Republic of China. Kien offered to use his local contacts to set up an intelligence network on the east side of the Cagayan River, near Highway 5. Wismer agreed, and was soon getting reliable reports to pass along to 6th Army HQ. Wismer was also asked by the commander of the 14th Guerrilla Infantry, an American named Major Damian, to call in an air strike on Japanese crossing the Siffu River heading into Barocboc. On May 25, thirty-two B-25 Mitchell bombers plastered the barrios of Vira, Santa Cruz, Callang, and Simimbahan, where the Japanese garrisons were stationed.

On May 29, Nellist and his group crossed the Magat River and entered the headquarters of the 7th Guerrilla Infantry. The guerrillas turned over four prisoners, three Taiwanese and one Japanese from the 32nd Ship Regiment. They also agreed to supply the Americans with two guides to take the Scouts to the town of San Mariano. There, the mayor told Nellist that Japanese were present in large numbers between San Mariano and Palanan. With that information in hand, the men began heading back, riding in a caraboa cart on the raised roads that separated individual rice paddies. A guerrilla led the Japanese prisoner by a rope that was tied around the man's waist. His hands were also bound.

The group stopped for a break on the southern slope of the road, hiding the cart out of sight. As they rested, a Japanese patrol was spotted approaching along the same road. The men lay flat in the tall grass, hoping the enemy would walk on by, when, to everyone's dismay, the enemy decided to take a break on the opposite side of the road. Nellist watched a Japanese soldier, not fifteen feet away, light a cigarette. Nellist was concerned that the prisoner would cry out to his comrades, but that fear went away when he saw that Kittleson had a firm grip on the man's throat.

The enemy patrol soon rose and moved on without incident.

The Nellist Team reunited at Manaoag on June 2, and the Scout leader decided it was time to interrogate his prisoner. With the help of a twelve-year-old Filipino girl who spoke Japanese, he questioned the man, but without success. The soldier refused to talk.

"Kit," Nellist said, "bring him out in back of the hut."

Kittleson did so. The Japanese soldier watched as Nellist slid his .45 from a shoulder holster and laid it on a table. "Mark out a grave, Kit, and then have him dig."

The Japanese soldier was soon babbling out all he knew.

While at Manaoag, Nellist called for an airdrop to resupply the guerrillas, requesting weapons, mines, bazookas, shoes, and socks. When the drop was made twelve days later, the bundles contained Thompson submachine guns with clips that did not fit, no mines, no bazookas, no socks, and shoes too big to fit the Filipinos.

Immediately following the airdrop, Nellist again split his team in two parts. He and Kittleson fed information to the HQ of the 37th Infantry Division on enemy troop strengths, while Wismer and his group moved farther into the hills. Wismer set up his radio station in a schoolhouse, where it was destroyed when American bombers leveled the building. Nellist now had to contact Wismer by dropping handwritten notes from an L-5 scout plane.

On June 22, the Nellist Team was ordered to return to American lines. While complying, Nellist, Kittleson, and Siason came across six guerrillas of the 7th Guerrilla Command Post, who were planning to attack a shack containing fifteen Japanese soldiers. To support them, Nellist and Kittleson set up the guerrillas' .30-caliber machine gun and fired on the hut. The Japanese spotted them and returned fire. One of their first shots ricocheted and struck Nellist in the right thigh. The American's wounding unnerved four of the guerrillas, who turned and fled. The other two remained and helped the Scouts make a stretcher so they could carry Nellist out. Nellist was taken to the 43rd Field Hospital. His war was over.

★   ★   ★

On May 15, Red Sumner left the Alamo Scouts to work for 6th Army Intelligence. His team, veterans of many tense missions, was taken over by Lt. Chester B. Vickery, who would lead them on their final two assignments before Scout operations ceased entirely.

On June 2, Lt. George Derr led his brand-new team, consisting of Pfc. William E. Teague, Sgts. Thomas J. Kolas and Charles J. Stewart, and Pvt. Robert D. Hamlin, into the Bontoc area for a ten-day intelligence-gathering mission. On this foray into enemy territory, Derr nearly hit the jackpot. On June 21, he and his men discovered General Yamashita at his headquarters near Banaue. Derr tried to make his way closer, but could not. Yamashita had eighteen hundred men at his headquarters camp. Derr wisely decided to pull back.

Another new team, led by Lt. Robert Shirkey, and containing Sgt. Richard G. Andrews, Pfc. Clyde S. Townsend, Staff Sgt. Clinton R. Tucker, and Sgts. Michael Zwer and Martin Grimes, reconnoitered Casiguran Bay on Luzon's east coast. On his second mission to Palanan Bay, Shirkey headed up a mini–task force consisting of two gunboats, two LCIs, and two hundred guerrillas. On June 12, the gunboats bombarded the beach while Shirkey's force landed and fought with enemy patrols. The next day he and his men came across an eight-man Japanese patrol resting by a stream. Four men were sunbathing nude. Creeping to within twenty yards, Shirkey rose, leveled a BAR, and opened fire. Six Japanese were killed. The other two tried to escape but were captured.

Operating sixty-five miles behind enemy lines, Shirkey, too, was looking for Yamashita, but was ordered out after it was confirmed that Yamashita had fled the islands and was back in Japan.

★　★　★

On July 1, 1945, the 6th Army turned control of the Luzon operation over to the 8th Army and began planning for its next big venture, the invasion of Japan itself.

Since landing on Luzon in January, the 6th Army had engaged and defeated the Shimbu and Kembu groups in the west and south, and had pushed Yamashita's Shobu Group back into the mountainous northeastern corner of Luzon. In the process, 214,000 Japanese troops had died.

The Alamo Scouts performed forty-three missions. They had aided in rescuing more than five hundred Allied POWs and coordinated guerrilla activities throughout Luzon. Although they didn't know it yet, for most of the teams, the war was over. The few Scout teams still in the field were turned over to 8th Army control. The 8th Army's commander, Lt. Gen. Robert Eichelberger, renamed them the Octagon Scouts, after his army's code name. Irate, Krueger got on the phone to Eichelberger and raised hell, and the name Octagon soon vanished.

Among these final Scout missions, the Vickery Team, formerly the Sumner Team, set up roadblocks on highways north of Aparri and worked with guerrillas until July 7, when they were ordered out.

Bill Littlefield's last mission started on July 1. Accompanying Littlefield was Allen Throgmorton, Oliver Roesler, radioman Bob Shullaw, Zeke McConnell, Ben Mones, and one other man.

Sent to the village of Sadanga, Littlefield and his men lived among the Igorotes, an indigenous tribe much like the Indians back in America. A fierce people who lived high in the mountains, they loathed the Japanese, severing the heads of those they killed in order to save the jawbone. These grisly reminders of their kill would be laid out on the ground, while the warriors performed a native dance around them.

Shortly before Littlefield's arrival, a twenty-five-man Japanese patrol arrived in the village. A group of Igorote boys between the ages of ten and twelve befriended the Japanese, built them a fire, and helped prepare their food. That night when the soldiers slept, the boys killed them all, beheaded them, and collected the jawbones.

Likewise, Filipinos from below did not go to the mountain people alone or unarmed.

Luckily, the Igorotes liked the Americans and were scrupulously honest. If the Scouts left camp and forgot anything, a runner was sent from the village to return it.

Even so, Americans were not immune from violations of Igorote law. Littlefield and his men discovered the skeletal remains of two Americans who had not surrendered to the Japanese in 1942 and sought refuge with the mountain tribe. One of the men had a sexual affair with a married Igorote woman. For that transgression, her husband and his friends killed him. The other American was killed because he witnessed the murder. Igorotes feared arrest and being brought to the lowlands, for there they often contracted diseases like malaria, unknown in the mountains, and died.

Littlefield collected the dead Americans' dog tags and arranged for the remains to be recovered by Graves Registration.

According to Igorote tradition, when two children, male and female, reached puberty, they left home and lived in a common hut called the Ulu. When a girl got pregnant, she and the boy were considered married.

The adult women, arms tattooed, were bare from the waist up, and some were very attractive. This social quirk amused the Scouts. Often they radioed Lee Hall, formerly of the Barnes Team but now commissioned and leading a team of his own, who was also among the Igorotes about twenty-five miles away, and talked about the bare-breasted women. This practice earned them an angry "Get the hell off the air, you bastards," from the air force, which shared the same frequency. It seemed the references to the women's breasts were distracting the airmen.

*   *   *

The final three Alamo Scout combat missions of World War II were all carried out by Jack Dove.

On July 16 he and his team boarded two PT boats of Squadron 28 for a fifteen-mile trip to Ibahos Island, the last island of the Philippine chain before reaching Formosa, arriving that afternoon. Their assignment was to reconnoiter Ibahos, Sabtang, and Batan islands, and see if they could find a suitable location for an airstrip. The American high command still considered invading Formosa.

Unfortunately, a storm rolled in and prevented the recon, but Dove managed to locate three civilians who informed him that Ibahos was unoccupied, but on Sabtang and Batan there were one thousand head of cattle that the Japanese kept for food. Dove was also told there were twenty-three Japanese soldiers on Sabtang, controlling civilian traffic and monitoring the collection of food in the islands.

Dove and his men went ashore at Ibahos and conducted a brief reconnaissance. When it came time to leave, however, the sea was so rough that Dove radioed the PT boat to pick them up on the island's leeward side, and the team carried their rubber boat across the island.

Six days later they were back, this time on Batan Island. Dove and his men were to gather more information on the Japanese garrison. Contacting a civilian agent on the island, the enemy troops were identified as members of the 61st Imperial Mortar Brigade under the overall command of Maj. Gen. Hikotaro Tajima, who commanded all Japanese forces in the Batanes and Babuyan islands. While reconnoitering the island, Dove and his team pinpointed numerous defensive positions, including twenty-seven 75mm and two 47mm howitzers.

The final mission came on July 28, when Dove's team was sent to

Fuga Island to discover enemy troop strength. Coming ashore on the island's north coast at three a.m., they contacted local fishermen, who pointed out where two Japanese soldiers were sleeping. In a quick ambush, Dove captured the men. Through interrogation, plus information gathered from other civilians, Dove estimated enemy strength at 550 to 600 men with three 75mm howitzers. But many of the men were suffering from dysentery, malaria, and malnutrition, negating their combat value.

While on Fuga, Dove and his team brought back thirty-nine civilians—two PT boats were needed—including the family of Alfonso Sycip, the president of the Philippine branch of the Bank of China. Sycip fled to Fuga in 1942, thinking it was safer than staying in Manila. He and his family had been held by the Japanese, and were half starved.

Dove's arrival back at Claveria on July 30 brought an end to the Alamo Scouts' wartime operations.

CHAPTER 16

"It Would Have Been Near Suicide."

Japan and Deactivation, August–September 1945

Operation Olympic, the first phase of the plan—code-named Downfall—to conquer the home islands of Japan, was slated to kick off on November 1, 1945. Olympic called for a feint at the island of Shikoku by one American corps, while three other corps stormed ashore on the southernmost island of Kyushu. Some 767,000 men, including Krueger's 6th Army, would be involved, as would many veterans of the now-ended war in Europe.

The Japanese knew the invasion was coming, too. All across the land, the military was gearing up the population for a do-or-die fight. More than five thousand planes were being prepared for kamikaze attacks, as were hundreds of suicide boats. Along Japan's coasts, civilians worked side by side with the army to prepare coastal fortifications. Four million civil servants and 2.5 million soldiers, many brought back from Manchuria and Korea, were told they were being given the "divine chance" to save the nation. And in fields, parks, and school yards everywhere, old men, women, and children armed with bamboo spears were learning how to attack and kill the American invaders. To overcome their crude armaments, the government convinced them that their "strength in the citadel of the spirit" would lead them to prevail.

The national slogan became "100 million die together."

The Americans also knew what they were facing, and it was a grim reality indeed. At a strategy meeting at the White House in Washington, D.C., Chief of Staff George C. Marshall warned that losses would be "frightful." With Olympic set for November 1 and Coronet, the invasion of the main island of Honshu, expected to start in March 1946, half a million American deaths were not out of the question. Many times more would be wounded.

The thought of those horrendous casualties left Secretary of War Henry L. Stimson pale and weak.

★ ★ ★

Up until now, the Alamo Scouts had been fortunate. After more than one hundred missions, many fraught with extreme danger, they had never lost a man killed in action. But as the invasion of Japan loomed, that luck seemed certain to change.

Six Alamo Scout teams were preparing to go ashore in southern Kyushu in advance of the American invasion, and what they were in for was relayed to Bill Littlefield a few years after the war when he ran into Red Sumner. Sumner had gone into Japan with the occupation forces in 1945, and had the chance to tour the area the Scouts were to have reconnoitered.

"They would never have been able to get us back out," he told Littlefield. "There was barbed wire strung on the beaches and in the water, and soldiers with dogs patrolled constantly."

Zeke McConnell was far gloomier. Speaking after the war, the Cherokee Indian said, "Our perfect record wouldn't have lasted if we would have had to go to Japan. We would have lost a lot of men. It would have been near suicide."

Not every Scout was as fatalistic.

Conrad Vineyard had been recruited from Company F of the 164th Infantry, which he had just joined as a replacement, fresh from the States. But word of his swimming prowess had gotten around, and Scout Martin Grimes and one other man approached Vineyard. Taking him aside and sitting under a tree, Grimes filled Vineyard in on the Scouts, "really opening up," Vineyard recalled.

"How many men were in your squad when you joined it?" Grimes asked.

"Two," Vineyard replied.

"How many men are in a squad?"

"Anywhere from twelve to eighteen."

"What do you think happened to the rest?"

"Well, I guess they didn't make it."

"We've never lost a man in action," Grimes stated.

That impressed Vineyard, as did the promise of first-class accommodations and food. He agreed. His orders were cut and two days later he was on his way to the ASTC at Subic Bay in Luzon.

A member of the ASTC's ninth class, Vineyard and others were all eager to get into the field, and did not consider the danger they were facing.

"We felt we were invincible, that we were the master of all situations and that nothing would happen to us," he said in 2007. "We believed we were smart enough to take care of ourselves. We all just wanted to go in and get the job done."

★   ★   ★

Jack Dove got a preview of what was in store for the Scouts when he paid a call on an old friend, Maj. John Lahmer, at Lahmer's Philippine CP at San Fernando. The Scout leader found Lahmer, a project officer for Operation Olympic, working on a six-foot-by-six-foot color contoured relief map laid out on a table. The map clearly showed the beach landing zones.

"Do you want to see where you're going to land, Jack?" Lahmer asked. "Pull up a chair."

Dove sat and Lahmer proceeded to go through the plan, pointing out terrain features, the coastal cliffs and narrow beaches. He told Dove of estimated enemy troop strengths and defenses, and the times American reinforcements would be arriving, plus other details, all of which, Dove later confessed, "scared the piss out of me."

The Scouts would be put ashore several days before the main landings to reconnoiter the beaches. They would go in at night, carried close to shore by submarines. The Scouts were to bring back prisoners if possible for interrogation.

"It's going to be tough," Lahmer said.

"Tough, hell," Dove replied. "Our chances are practically nil."

One Scout had an even darker forecast when he heard the assignment.

Pvt. Carl Bertoch of the Adkins Team, which was to land on Kyushu and look for sites where American prisoners were thought to be held, recalled that the men did not consider it a suicide mission. But neither did they expect to make it back.

Whether that, indeed, would have come to pass would never be tested. On August 6, 1945, the B-29 bomber *Enola Gay*, with Col. Paul Tibbets at the controls, dropped an atomic bomb, leveling the city of Hiroshima. On Sunday, August 9, another B-29, *Bock's Car*, dropped a second bomb on the port city of Nagasaki. Three days later, the Japanese capitulated. The next day—Thursday—a message was received by the Alamo Scout teams to cease all hostilities against the Japanese and return immediately to the ASTC at Subic Bay on Luzon.

★   ★   ★

The first peacetime mission of the Alamo Scouts commenced on September 14, when a team led by Lt. George Derr boarded a ship in Manila, accompanied by General Krueger and his staff. The ship was bound for Japan. After a stopover at Okinawa to pick up General "Vinegar Joe" Stillwell at 10th Army headquarters, the ship continued on. It docked at Wakayama on September 19, and Krueger immediately established 6th Army HQ. A day later, Krueger watched the arrival of men from the 5th Marine Division, and witnessed the Japanese signing over to the marines the Sasebo Naval Air Base.

On September 24, Krueger and his party, including Derr's team, traveled to Nagasaki to view the ruined remains of the city. Staff Sgt. Clinton Tucker, a member of Derr's Team, recalled seeing steel girders twisted by the intense heat, and saw where buildings had been swept away, leaving just their concrete foundations. The blast area, Tucker remembered, was "saucer-shaped," and extended beyond the city and up into the adjoining hills, where it burned thousands of trees and mowed down countless more like blades of grass before a scythe.

Krueger's party stopped by a torpedo factory, or at least what had been one. The factory's metal lathes and other machinery had melted and washed down gutters into culverts, where the molten steel rehardened.

The few civilians they encountered walked in a dazed fashion, as if just awakening from a bad dream. Makeshift military hospitals were filled to overflowing with victims, many horribly burned, and the most badly injured were evacuated to American hospital ships.

Leaving the devastation that had been Nagasaki, Krueger and his entourage arrived in Kyoto on September 28, where he set up his headquarters in the government offices in the Daiken building. For his living quarters, he commandeered for himself and his staff rooms at the Miyako Hotel outside of the city.

★　★　★

While Derr's men guarded Krueger, eight Scouts from the Adkins and Grimes teams, traveling in two jeeps, went in search of Japanese armaments. The Japanese had been told to collect their weapons and deposit them at a central location, after which infantry units came along and, under Scout supervision, destroyed the guns, usually by lining them up and cutting them in half with acetylene torches.

The Adkins Team, in particular Sgt. William E. McCommons, was also assigned the task of sifting through almost five hundred samurai swords to select the best ones to be given as souvenirs to Krueger and his top staff. For this, McCommons enlisted the aid of a Japanese general, who helped him pick out the six swords of highest quality. These were passed along to 6th Army HQ. He then had the general select the next best sword, which McCommons kept for himself.

★ ★ ★

The end of World War II found Bill Littlefield in California. He had been given a forty-five-day furlough on the guarantee that he would return to duty in the southwest Pacific. He agreed.

"I'd have done anything to get back to the U.S., even for a little bit," he later recalled.

But now the war was over, and his orders to return to duty never came through.

For Conrad Vineyard, the war's end came even before he had a chance to ply his Alamo Scout skills. His class never graduated from the ASTC, and Vineyard himself was returned to the Americal Division, from which he had been selected for Scout training weeks earlier.

His return happened so fast, he had to leave some of his possessions behind, specifically, his uniform with his new Alamo Scout patch, a round red, white, and blue patch designed in 1944 by medic Harry Golden, which bore the likeness of an Indian superimposed over the façade of the Alamo. He had sent his uniform to be dry-cleaned.

"Can I go pick up my uniform at the dry cleaner?" he had requested when news of his return was handed to him.

"No," was the terse reply. "Your orders say you leave immediately."

He never saw his Alamo Scout clothes again.

Vineyard ended up being sent to Japan with his division, coming ashore at Yokohama. He recalled the people were "very gracious" and they traded eggs for cigarettes. This was a far cry from the hostile reception he expected and the possible trap he and other GIs were warned about by their officers.

★　★　★

Terry Santos had been fighting on Okinawa since early June. The 11th Airborne had been dispatched to the island as reinforcements to fill some of the gap left by heavy American casualties. There, amid the bloody fighting at Naha, his friend and commander, Red Skau, had been killed.

Now the fighting was over, and Santos, who during the course of the war had won two Silver Stars, two Bronze Stars with the V for Valor, and a Purple Heart, was called into his regimental commander's tent.

"Santos," the officer said. "You have more than the required eighty-five points to be sent home, but I'd like you to go with us to Japan, to be one of the first Americans to set foot on Jap soil."

"Are you crazy?" Santos said. "I've been waiting for this chance to go home since I joined the army."

The officer tried again to change Santos's mind, but without success.

"Well," he said. "There's nothing I can do to stop you."

"I know there's not," Santos replied.

Terry Santos arrived in San Francisco on October 8, two days before his twenty-fourth birthday.

★　★　★

A lot of the Alamo Scouts were in Santos's position. Two days before Krueger left for Manila, word went out to the 154 Alamo Scouts, staff, and overhead personnel that any man with the needed eighty-five points who wanted to go home could do so. The rest would join Krueger in Japan, or could opt to return to their original units for separation or reassignment. Scouts who wished to go to Japan were reassigned to the 6th Ranger Battalion, while those who were being sent home would await transport in the Philippines.

On October 10, Red Sumner hauled down the Alamo Scout flag for the last time, and officially closed the Scout training camp.

"I took down the flag and shut off the lights," he later said.

During the twenty-one months since John McGowen's first mission to Los Negros, the Alamo Scouts had conducted 106 more, for a total of 108. They had killed an estimated five hundred enemy soldiers and had taken sixty more prisoner. But more important, they had provided Krueger and, by extension, MacArthur with much-needed and accurate intelligence that paved the way for victory in the Southwest Pacific.

The experience they gleaned was valuable, so much so that after the war's end, the Defense Department conducted interviews with the Scouts and incorporated their techniques and training into new textbooks for amphibious warfare, especially in regards to scouting, patrolling, intelligence collecting, raiding, and guerrilla operations. These firsthand experiences were later taught to fledgling officers at West Point and the Infantry School at Fort Benning, as well as other military training centers.

But while the army lauded the activities and skill of the Scouts, unlike other elite units, such as the Devil's Brigade or Merrill's Marauders, it was not until 1988 that the Alamo Scouts, now reaching retirement age, were granted the right to wear the Special Forces shoulder tab. At that time, they were recognized as the army's first Long Range Surveillance Unit at a service at the John F. Kennedy Special Warfare Center and School, in Fort Bragg, North Carolina.

On March 13, 2008, a plaque honoring the Alamo Scouts was dedicated at the National Museum of the Pacific War in Fredericksburg, Texas. Fifty people attended, mostly family members. Only four of the aging Scouts, Terry Santos, Bob Buschur, Jack Geiger, and team leader William Barnes, made it to the ceremony.

The reason for this delay in recognition was because, until the late 1980s, Alamo Scout missions were considered classified. The men, as they were discharged, were basically told to go home, resume their lives, and shut up about what they did during the war.

Why their missions were classified was never explained, but the abrupt disbanding of the unit without any form of recognition, not even a pat on the back and a "well done," left a bitter taste in the mouths of many of the men.

Through the Years

The Alamo Scouts officially disbanded in Kyoto, Japan, in November 1945, almost two years after Krueger first selected Col. Frederick Bradshaw to organize and train the elite fighting unit.

Now the war was over, and for many, that meant a return to home and family, trying to pick up their lives where they left off. Others, forged by the army in time of war, made the military a career.

General Krueger retired to San Antonio in 1946 and bought his first home. There he wrote a book entitled *From Down Under to Nippon: The Story of the 6th Army in World War II*, which was published in 1953. His life, however, was far from one of peaceful retirement. In 1947 his son James was dismissed from the army for conduct unbecoming an officer, and in 1952 his daughter Grace was convicted of stabbing her army husband to death while he slept. She was tried by court-martial and sentenced to life with hard labor. She was released in 1955 when the U.S. Supreme Court ruled that military trials of civilians were unconstitutional. In 1962 Krueger Middle School was founded in San Antonio. Krueger died at Valley Forge, Pennsylvania, on August 20, 1967, and was buried in Arlington National Cemetery. He was eighty-six years old.

Col. Frederick Bradshaw hoped to return to his beloved Jackson, Mississippi, and resume his law career and, maybe, make a run at state government. That dream was cut short in 1946 when he died at his home from a massive heart attack.

Bradshaw's executive officer and heir as Alamo Scout commander, Homer Williams, retired from the army in 1950. He died in a car crash in 1993.

Mayo Stuntz, the Scouts' ingenious supply officer, retired from the army in 1945 as a lieutenant colonel. Afterward, he joined the Central Intelligence Agency, from which he retired in 1975. He lives in Virginia and has coauthored books on local history.

Scout Lewis Hochstrasser left the army in 1945 and worked as a feature writer for the *Wall Street Journal* for many years before becoming a publicist for the Signal Oil Company. He wrote the first unit history, an unpublished manuscript entitled *They Were First: The Story of the Alamo Scouts.* He died at his home in California in 1996 at the age of eighty-two.

Robert "Red" Sumner made the army a career, never considering any other path. While in Tokyo with 6th Army HQ, he met an army nurse named Dorothy during a blind date. After the date, Dorothy told her friends she would not be seeing him again because the young officer was "too full of himself." In 1947, they were married at Fort Bragg and would eventually have five children. Later, Sumner continued his college education, which the war had interrupted, and earned his bachelor's degree.

Always active and with a love of the outdoors, Sumner refused to play golf, saying it was a game for "old men."

In 1980, Sumner was instrumental in the formation of the Alamo Scout Association, and served as its director for many years. Under him, the group grew to over sixty members.

Red Sumner died at his home in Tampa, Florida, on August 3, 2004.

Philippine-born Rafael Ileto stayed in the army. He rose to the rank of lieutenant general and served as ambassador to Iran, and, later,

Minister of National Defense under President Ferdinand Marcos. Ileto died in November 2003.

Robert T. Schermerhorn lived in Pomona Park, Florida, where he worked in the home construction industry. He never had any contact with his fellow Alamo Scouts until the current Alamo Scout Association executive director Russ Blaise called him in November of 2003. Schermerhorn died on May 22, 2005.

John Geiger became a rigging contractor for his family-owned business in Newark, New Jersey. He met and married his wife, Betty, and they had nine children. The Geigers have been married for sixty years and still reside in New Jersey.

Aubrey "Lee" Hall, the first Scout to receive a battlefield commission, remained in the army. Demoted back to sergeant after the war, he eventually retired as a master sergeant. He lived with his wife, Maude, in Hawaii until his death on July 19, 2008.

John McGowen, who led the first Alamo Scout mission and became the "old man" of the unit, left the army in November 1945. He worked for a year on banana plantations in Panama and Costa Rica, and was an assistant professor of economics at Texas Christian University for a year. For the next thirty years, he worked for a U.S.-based oil company, spending time in Saudi Arabia and elsewhere in the Middle East. Married shortly after the war, and with two children, his first wife died. He met his second wife, Christine, an Englishwoman, in Crete in 1977 and they married in 1979. They resided in England.

McGowen had no contact with any of his wartime comrades until he attended a Scout reunion around 1980.

He died on October 31, 1991, and was buried by his father's side in Hartley, Texas.

Hollywood-handsome John Dove remained in the army, retiring as a full colonel. During his career he served in Germany and Saudi Arabia and did one tour of duty in Vietnam in 1967–68. He died at his California home on September 23, 1995.

Wilbur Littlefield returned to Los Angeles and graduated from law school. He hung out his own shingle for a time, then took a job as a

Los Angeles County public defender. He eventually became head of the department with some seven hundred attorneys working under him. He married shortly after the war, and his wife, Vera, died in 1998. Retired now, Littlefield still lives in Los Angeles.

Irvin Ray left the army and tried different career paths. With his brother Stanley, who was also color-blind, he tried his hand at house painting. They abandoned this idea when, on a job, it was discovered they were using two different colors.

Ray joined the National Guard in 1947 and was called up during the Korean War, but was not sent overseas. He later transferred to the Air Force Reserve, and retired from the Reserves in 1983 as a major general. Ray married his wife, Terry, whom he had known since high school, in 1949. The Rays had three children, and when their son Michael completed his ROTC training for the National Guard, his dad pinned on his new lieutenant bars.

Irv Ray died on April 24, 2004, while Michael was serving in Iraq; Michael did not make it back for the funeral.

William Blaise was discharged from the army on October 3, 1945, and reenlisted the next day. He was assigned to Company A, 703rd Military Police Battalion and did military burial details at Arlington National Cemetery, where his job was to help carry the caskets to grave sites and fold the flag. In 1946 he married Elaine Haas and they had two sons.

Blaise left the army on February 28, 1947, and moved to Merrick, Long Island. There he took a job as assistant paint foreman for Plant 3 of Grumman Aerospace in Bethpage. During the Apollo moon mission days, Blaise helped work on the lunar modules. He retired in 1980 and moved to Port Richey, Florida. Bill Blaise died on July 26, 1997.

Medic Dominck Cicippio left the Scouts in February 1945 and returned to his unit. That April he was shot through the leg by a Japanese sniper. Infection set in and he nearly lost the leg. Both he and the leg recovered, and he returned to Norristown, Pennsylvania, and took a job with Valley Forge Sheet Metal. He met Rose Chiccarine and they married in 1950 and had two sons. The younger, Jimmy, contracted leukemia and died in 1980. Cicippio used his medic skills to help his son through his final days. Cicippio died on March 16, 2004.

Scout team leader Robert Shirkey went to law school and became a lawyer in 1950. Recalled during the Korean War, he served with the 5th Regimental Combat Team. Discharged in 1952, he resumed his law career, but remained in the Reserves. He retired in 1984 as commanding general of the 89th Reserve Command, making him the last remaining general officer to have fought against the Japanese. He lives in Missouri.

William F. Barnes served as head coach of the UCLA Bruins from 1958 until 1966, and is a member of the Tennessee Sports Hall of Fame. He lives in Los Angeles.

Terry Santos attended college under the GI Bill at San Francisco State University. He became a hydraulic engineer. Retired, he remains active with the Alamo Scouts Association and still lives in his native San Francisco.

William Lutz became a Methodist minister after the war and has since lost contact with the Scouts.

Oliver Roesler returned to college and became a logging engineer. His neck wound earned him a 10 percent disability, and the thirteen dollars a month he got from that helped pay his tuition. With his two brothers and his father, he started a lumber company. He still lives near Seattle and enjoys salmon fishing. He said he is not sure he'd join the Scouts again, but said, "I wouldn't trade the experience for anything."

He still carries the shrapnel in his neck.

William E. Nellist, a man who was not big on taking orders, remained in the army for a while. On three occasions the CIA tried to recruit him, but he said no, worried that it would interfere with his hunting and fishing. Instead, when he left the army, he became a plumber, saying he did not want a desk job. Nellist and his wife, Jane, had two sons. He died on September 5, 1997.

Thomas Rounsaville spent thirty-two years in the army, serving in the Korean and Vietnam wars. In 1965 he commanded the ground forces that freed white captives being held by rebels in the Congo. Rounsaville retired in 1973 as a colonel, and died on April 16, 1999.

Galen Kittleson also stayed in the army, joining the Special Forces in 1961 with the rank of command sergeant major. In 1970, at the age of forty-five, Kittleson was in Vietnam, where he was part of the raid at Son Tay to free American prisoners in North Vietnam. That action, plus another POW rescue mission later, made him the only man in U.S. military history to take part in four POW raids in two wars. He retired to Iowa, and died on May 4, 2006.

Andy Smith, Kit's buddy, played minor league baseball for the Chicago White Sox, the Cleveland Indians, and the St. Louis Browns. Recalled for both the Korean and Vietnam wars, he served in both conflicts as a case officer for army intelligence. Later in life, Smith taught at several different schools for the Department of Defense, including the U.S. Army Intelligence Center and School at Fort Huachuca, Arizona. He retired in 1975 as a master sergeant and died on January 18, 2000.

Conrad Vineyard returned to California. After college, he married and had two daughters. Vineyard worked as a civil engineer and researcher, mostly in Golden, Colorado. After his wife died, he remarried, and today he and Priscilla live in Colorado.

He had lost all contact with the Alamo Scouts until discovering their Web site a few years ago. He has been an active member of the Alamo Scouts Association ever since.

Robert Buschur ended the war as a private, although he was considered an "acting platoon sergeant." Sent to Korea after the end of World War II, he remained there until December 1945, then returned to Ohio. There he married Rita and they had twelve children. They still live on their farm, and in 2007 he attended his first Alamo Scout reunion.

Harold Hard, a witty man who never said an unkind word about anyone, his daughter recalled, returned home, where he married his wife, Marie. They had three children. Hard died in December 1995, just shy of his fiftieth wedding anniversary.

Zeke McConnell had been asked to go to Japan after the war, but with more than eighty-five points, he declined and returned to his family in Washington. He went to work as a painter at the Cushman Indian Hospital, where, in 1946, he met and married Mae Ladinne Duffy. They had five children. McConnell later worked for the City of Seattle in the maintenance department, and was active in the local Boy Scouts as a scoutmaster. An exceptional archer, he enjoyed giving bow and arrow demonstrations with his son, Lester. McConnell retired in 1980 and kept up a lifelong friendship with Bill Littlefield.

In January 2007, Littlefield hurried from Los Angeles to be at the bedside of his desperately ill friend. McConnell died on February 4, 2007.

William McCommons, whose job was to select samurai swords for General Krueger and his staff, returned to college. Prior to the war he had attended the University of Illinois on a scholarship, studying geology. He volunteered to clean test tubes in the laboratory at Halliburton. He did that for a month before he was drafted. After the war, Halliburton gave him five years' back salary and a new job. He bought his own business, a small oil company, in the 1950s. He married, had four children, and spent twenty-six years as a scoutmaster for the Boy Scouts. McCommons died in 1998.

George Thompson came home and earned his law degree. He was later elected to the Missouri Supreme Court. The Alamo Scout team leader died on October 17, 2005.

Australian Raymond "Moose" Watson, an Alamo Scout instructor and head of the New Guinea "Police Boys," stayed in the army and was promoted to major. In 1947 he was appointed a Member of the British Empire, allowing him to use the prestigious M.B.E. after his name. Watson died in Australia on July 27, 1998.

"Baby" Lois McCoy, now Lois Bourinskie, who was carried out of Los Baños at age three days, graduated from the Providence College of Nursing in Oakland, California, in 1966 and worked at Southwest Washington Medical Center in Vancouver, Washington, as a registered nurse. Widowed more than twenty years ago, she still lives there, painting watercolors and acrylics.

*   *   *

While the Alamo Scouts never captured the Japanese commanders they sought in the Philippines, American military authorities eventually did.

Generals Yamashita and Adachi were among a number of Japanese civilian and military leaders placed on trial for war crimes.

Adachi was convicted for issuing orders that encouraged the execution of Allied airmen and in connection with the maltreatment and arbitrary executions of other prisoners by men under his command, and sentenced to life in prison. While imprisoned at Rabaul on September 10, 1947, he used a rusty paring knife to commit ritualistic hara-kiri.

Yamashita, the Tiger of Malaya, was tried for crimes committed by men under his command, but to which there was no direct evidence linking his complicity. His being tried for "command responsibility" became known as the Yamashita Standard, although critics of MacArthur claimed the only crime Yamashita committed was defeating the egotistical American general.

Yamashita was found guilty and hanged on February 23, 1946.

APPENDIX A

Alamo Scout Team Rosters

McGowen Team: John R. C. McGowen, Paul A. Gomez, John P. Lagoud, Walter A. McDonald, Caesar Ramirez, John A. Roberts

Barnes Team: William F. Barnes, Louis J. Belson, Warren J. Boes, Aubrey Hall, John O. Pitcairn, Bobby G. Walters, Robert W. Teeples

Thompson Team: George S. Thompson, Jack E. Benson, Joseph A. Johnson, Theodore T. Largo, Anthony Ortiz, Joshua Sunn, Glenn L. Heryford (last mission addition)

Sombar Team: Michael J. Sombar, James R. Crokett, Ora M. Davis, Charles F. Harkins, Virgil F. Howell, David M. Milda

Dove Team: John M. Dove, Alton P. Bauer, Denny M. Chapman, John G. Fisher, Irvin C. Ray, John E. Phillips

Hobbs Team: Woodrow E. Hobbs, Gordon H. Butler, Herman S. Chanley, Edgar G. Hatcher, Vern R. Miller, Joe Moon

Reynolds Team: Gean H. Reynolds, William C. Gerstenberger, Lucian

A. Jamison, Winfred E. McAdoo, Leonard J. Scott, William R. Watson, Ray W. Wangrud

Sumner Team: Robert S. Sumner, William F. Blaise, Lawrence E. Coleman, Paul B. Jones, Edward J. Renhols, Robert T. Schermerhorn, Harry D. Weiland

Farkas Team: Arpad Farkas, Raymond Aguilar, Jack C. Bunt, Jack C. Greenly, Charley D. Hill, Harold L. Sparks

Littlefield Team: Wilbur F. Littlefield, Samuel L. Armstrong, Alva C. Branson, John E. Hidalgo, Zeke McConnell, Elmer E. Niemela, Allen H. Throgmorton, Paul G. Bemish

Lutz Team: William B. Lutz, John J. Geiger, Clifford A. Gonyea, Oliver J. Roesler, Bob Ross, Robert E. Shullaw

Nellist Team: William E. Nellist, Sabas A. Asis, Gilbert Cox, Galen C. Kittleson, Thomas A. Siason, Andy E. Smith, Wilbert C. Wismer

Rounsaville Team: Tom J. Rounsaville, Alfred Alfonso, Franklin Fox, Harold N. Hard, Francis H. Laquier, Rufo V. Vaquilar, Leroy Donnette

Ileto Team: Raphael M. Ileto, James Farrow, Pete Vischansky, Paul E. Draper, Estanislao Bacat, Fredirico Balambao

Ouzts Team: Wilmot B. Ouzts, Donald E. Brown, Harvey L. Hines, Edward W. Walsh, Elijah H. York, Fred J. Knaggs

Derr Team: George A. Derr, Robert D. Hamlin, Tommy J. Kolas, Stewart J. Minzer, Charles J. Stewart, William E. Teague

Shirkey Team: Robert L. Shirkey, Richard G. Andrews, Donald D. Grimes, Clyde S. Townsend, Clinton R. Tucker, Michael Zwer (Donald D. Grimes took over elements of the team.)

Hall Team: Aubrey L. Hall, Norman S. Boschert, Curtis Broussard, Clifford S. Henrickson, Joseph F. Novella, William G. Swain (Team was formed but never went on a mission.)

Grimes Team: Willis (Martin) Grimes, Paul F. Adams, Arnold R. Bethell, Kenneth A. Cameron, John R. Long, Cruz C. Vega

Adkins Team: Henry L. Adkins, Carl A. Bertoch, Kenneth A. Cameron, William E. McCommons, Lyle C. Wooten

Chanley Team: Herman S. Chanley, Juan E. Berganio, Nicholas C. Enriquez, Juan D. Pacis, Allen H. Throgmorton, Glendale Watson

Note: Due to various reasons, the composition of Alamo Scout teams changed throughout the war. Men other than those listed also performed operational missions as part of "scratch teams."

APPENDIX B

Glossary of Terms

ASTC: Alamo Scout Training Camp

amtrac: landing vehicle with tank treads, able to also operate on land

CBI: China-Burma-India theater of operations

CP: command post

Deuce-and-a-half: army truck capable of carrying two and a half tons

Fujiyama Flivver: Japanese tank

G2: intelligence officer

HQ: headquarters

LCI: landing craft (infantry)

LCM: landing craft (mechanized)

LST: landing ship, tank

LCVP: landing craft, vehicle, personnel

M1: infantry weapon, usually refers to the Garand rifle

M1A1: carbine with folding wire stock, generally issued to paratroopers

OP: observation post

OSS: Office of Strategic Services, forerunner to the Central Intelligence Agency

RCT: regimental combat team

Willie Peter: phosphorous grenade

XO: executive officer

SELECTED BIBLIOGRAPHY

Bowers, Pat. "Darkness Was Their Ally." *Alamo Scouts Newsletter*, vol. 5, no. 10, May 1993.

Busch, Briton Cooper. *Bunker Hill to Bastogne: Elite Forces and American Society*. Dulles, Va.: Potomac Books, 2006.

Johnson, Frank D. *United States PT Boats of World War II in Action*. Poole, UK: Blandford Press Ltd., 1980.

Manchester, William. *American Caesar: Douglas MacArthur, 1880–1964*. Boston: Little, Brown and Co., 1978.

Sasser, Charles W. *Raider*. New York: St. Martin's, 2002.

Sides, Hampton. *Ghost Soldiers: The Forgotten Epic Story of World War II's Most Dramatic Mission*. New York: Doubleday, 2001.

White, W. L. *They Were Expendable*. New York: Harcourt, Brace and Company, 1942.

Zedric, Lance Q. *Silent Warriors of World War II: The Alamo Scouts Behind the Japanese Lines*. Ventura, Calif.: Pathfinder Publishing, 1995.

ACKNOWLEDGMENTS

There are many people I need to thank for their help in creating this book.

First and foremost is Russ Blaise, executive director of the Alamo Scouts Association and son of the late Sgt. William F. Blaise. Russ was enthusiastic over the project from the beginning, and agreed to publish a letter from me to the surviving Alamo Scouts and their families in the association's newsletter, outlining my project and requesting their help. My letter was greeted by an outpouring of offers for assistance.

Russ next helped me procure phone numbers and addresses, so I could speak directly with the men or their surviving spouses or children. He also read the manuscript and gave me pointers and suggestions. And last, Russ was invaluable in gathering most of the photos that appear in this book.

Thanks must also go to Lance Q. Zedric, whose groundbreaking book *Silent Warriors of World War II: The Alamo Scouts Behind the Japanese Lines* proved an invaluable source and springboard for launching me into this project. Lance had the wonderful good fortune to write his book while many of the Scouts now gone were still alive, and the book he created will be the pathway future historians of the Alamo Scouts will have to follow.

His continued work, along with that of Russ Blaise, of preserving the history and memory of the Alamo Scouts is a vital task.

Despite the help of Russ and Lance, this work would have been infinitely more difficult without the help of the entire Alamo Scouts family. The intimate interviews with Scouts Terry Santos, Lee Hall, Jack Geiger, Oliver Roesler, Bill Littlefield, Conrad Vineyard, and Bob Buschur, as well as a letter from Robert Teeples, helped me bring the human element into the work.

Geiger and Roesler, surviving members of the Lutz Team, were especially helpful in my piecing together that team's missions.

The same is true for the men who no longer have a voice to speak with. My interviews with Terry Ray, the widow of Irv Ray, and her daughter Karen Mathews, the family of Harold Hard, Jane and Linda Nellist, Les McConnell, Russ Blaise, Christine McGowen, Michael Thompson, Jim McCommons, and Bob Cicippio provided me with insight into these men.

Of special note is Ann Sumner, the daughter of Alamo Scout team leader Robert Sumner; she, in cooperation with Russ Blaise and Lance Zedric, provided me with her late father's wonderful and insightful memoirs.

The maps in this book, which go far in helping tell the story of the Alamo Scouts, were created by my colleague Dan Morris, artist for Lancaster's *Intelligencer Journal* newspaper.

Last, my thanks to my agent, Dave Robie, for giving me the push I needed to look for a World War II subject to write about, and—of course—to my wife, Barbara, and daughter Sarah, for their patience with me as I researched and wrote yet another book.

INDEX

ABOUT THE AUTHOR

Larry Alexander, a journalist and columnist for the *Intelligencer Journal* newspaper in Lancaster, Pennsylvania, for more than a decade, has won numerous awards for excellence in journalism. He is the author of the national bestseller *Biggest Brother: The Life of Major Dick Winters, the Man Who Led the Band of Brothers.*

In the fall of 2008, Larry Alexander, author of *Biggest Brother*
and *Shadows in the Jungle,* embarked on the journey of a
lifetime. With his friend Forrest Guth, a World War II veteran
and an original member of the Band of Brothers, he set out to
rediscover the incredible legacy of Easy Company.

Read on for a special sneak preview of
In the Footsteps of the Band of Brothers,
coming in hardcover from NAL Caliber in May 2010.

Just outside the village near where the D-14 meets the D-913, or Sonnier Road, leading toward the coast, the Americans came under German machine-gun fire from a tree line about 350 yards on the battalion's right. The dirt road was somewhat sunken here, and Dick Winters told me how he used this opportunity to sit against the road embankment, protected from the enemy bullets, to take a welcome break. Colonel Strayer ordered D Company to do a reconnaissance of the field, a job carried out by Lt. John Kelly, who, Malarkey recalled, looked like "a boxer whose face was all beat up," who possibly had "taken one too many blows, not the kind of guy you want telling you to go on a do-or-die mission to capture guns that were sure to be well protected by soldiers who'd been preparing for months."

Winters said Kelly inexpertly deployed his men and tried a frontal probe with prior reconnaissance to assess the situation. Pinned down, he and his men finally worked their way back to the battalion. That was when Strayer called on Winters. Lt. George Lavenson, Strayer's aide, found Winters where he had been relaxing and told him, "Strayer wants you up front." Winters found Strayer and Clarence Hester talking with a harried Lieutenant Kelly. Winters stood silently near the small group. Hester soon turned to him.

"There's fire along that hedgerow there," Hester said without pre-amble. "Take care of it."

Hester then turned and walked away without any further instructions.

★   ★   ★

Paul Woodadge led Forrest and me into Le Grand Chemin on the afternoon of our second day in Normandy. The village is much as it was in 1944, a cluster of buildings bisected by the D14 roadway, now paved. We didn't stop at Le Grand Chemin, but rather pulled off onto a small siding just south of the village. There on June 14, 2008, a group of Easy Company veterans and friends, led by Frank Slegers and Marco Kilian—who would be our contacts in Belgium later in our trip—had erected one of four E Company monuments that mark the Band of Brothers' European battlefields. These monuments, several made of brick and concrete, tell the story of what the company did and list the names of the men killed in the fighting, etched into highly polished black granite slabs.

We stopped at the Brecourt Manor marker and got out of the van. The marker relates how Winters and his dozen men attacked and destroyed a German artillery position, just as recounted in Ambrose's book and in the miniseries. But while it recounts the story of the Brecourt Manor fight, it also muddies the water. For on a separate pedestal next to the monument is etched a map drawn by Michel de Vallavieille sometime after the war, and endorsed by Winters, that features a major discrepancy from the accepted story of the fight. I will delve into this later in this chapter.

Like the Meehan marker, this one does not sit by the actual site. The field Winters and his men crossed and the line where the German guns stood are several hundred yards and one tree line away, on private property still owned by Charles de Vallavieille, Michel's son. It is extremely difficult to see the actual field from the marker, but Paul told me we had an appointment with Messr. de Vallavieille the next day, and would walk the field then.

★   ★   ★

Winters did not have to wait for an appointment from the de Valla-vieille family to see Brecourt Manor. His appointment came directly from Colonel Strayer: Take out those guns.

Winters told me a number of times how he hated to charge into a situation without having the opportunity to assess the risk to himself and his men. To that end, on a number of occasions he undertook dangerous but, he deemed, necessary one-man reconnaissance missions. And so he did here, cautiously moving along a hedgerow to within sight of the German position. The enemy was located, not in a trench as depicted in the miniseries, but a treelined ditch about four hundred yards long, separating two fields. The trench in the film, with its walls of woven vines, is as Winters told me, "What happens when you let an Englishman design the set. It looks like something out of World War I." Unlike the somewhat exposed position depicted in the miniseries, here in this heavy growth of trees and brush along the ditch, the guns were perfectly camouflaged, which is why aerial photos never revealed them.

At Brecourt, the Germans had placed four 105 mm guns, which the Americans at first mistook for 88s. (The excellent German 88 mm gun was so feared and respected by the GIs that throughout the war, almost every enemy gun they came up against was called "an 88," regardless of its actual caliber.) The position was manned by about fifty Germans of the Sixth Battery, Ninetieth Regiment, and protected by several machine guns. The enemy guns had been rolled into the ditch until their wheels rested against the earthen wall, with three of the guns facing Utah Beach three miles away, while the fourth faced left, toward the causeway a few hundred yards off.

But is that the way they really were? Or were all four guns on line to defend the beach? The accepted history of the fight tells us one gun was turned, but there is one convincing piece of evidence that suggests otherwise.

So which is correct? Possibly both.

★ ★ ★

Until I visited Brecourt with Paul Woodadge, I was blissfully unaware of any discrepancies in the fight on this field. Our appointment with Charles de Vallavieille was on November 6, our last full day in Normandy. As was so often the case on this journey, the day was overcast with a slight off-and-on drizzle. At the Brecourt monument we had visited earlier, we turned right from the roadway onto the long lane that leads to the manor house. Charles de Vallavieille greeted us, and led us into the quadrangle courtyard and into the kitchen of the big stone house. We sat around the large table where, in years past, Dick Winters, Walter Gordon, Don Malarkey and, yes, Forrest Guth, had sat before me with Charles' uncle, Louis. Messr. de Vallavieille greeted Forrest like an old friend of the family, which, indeed, he was. The de Vallavieille family has always had the utmost respect for the men of Easy Company, despite the fact that it was a paratrooper who—the man's identity is not known—shot and wounded Charles' father, Michel, who was then twenty-one. It is believed the soldier assumed the family to be collaborators since the German guns were on their land.

Messr. de Vallavieille presented Forrest with a gold medal on a red, white and blue ribbon, which he hung around my friend's neck, over his bright yellow *Band of Brothers* jacket, a gift in 2001 to all the Easy Company veterans from HBO. The medal proclaimed Forrest to be a "citizen of honor" in St. Marie du Mont. This shows how the family feels about these men, for on the day Winters attacked the Germans here on this ground, Forrest, Gordon and the others were still at Marmion Farm.

As Forrest and Messr. de Vallavieille chatted, Paul and I left for the battlefield. Entering through an iron gate, we walked the soggy field by the tree line that had once concealed the quartet of 105s. It is a tangle of trees, brambles and other vegetation, running for about three hundred yards before it intersects another hedgerow coming in perpendicular from the left. This marks the famous "L" in the German "trench." Out in front and slightly to the right of the German position, barely visible through the trees, lies Le Grand Chemin and the roadway leading to the beach. To the left, and running across the fields toward the village, are two hedgerows, one of which was used by Winters and half of the men in their approach to the guns, and the other used by Compton and the rest of the patrol. Behind where we stood, across the broad field, is another tree line where enemy machine guns were positioned.

Picking our way across the muddy field, Paul and I stopped at the "L" in the German line, and he began explaining some of the variations in the Brecourt story.

The known facts are that, after his one-man reconnaissance, Winters returned to the village and briefed his men, which consisted of sergeants Lipton, Toye and Guarnere, corporals Malarkey and Robert "Popeye" Wynn, and privates Mike Ranney, Cleveland O. Petty, Joseph D. Liebgott, Walter Hendrix and John Plesha Jr. Guarnere, who asked Winters how many Germans they were up against. Winters had no idea.

Pvt. Gerald Lorraine, of Service Company and one of Colonel Sink's drivers, was standing nearby and asked to accompany the lieutenant and his men. Winters, knowing he needed additional firepower, agreed.

Winters had explained to me that his plan called for "a double envelopment," with Compton, Lipton, Toye, Lorraine, Popeye and Ranney moving along one of two thick hedgerows that led toward the German line, while he took the rest of the men along the second. This would prevent both groups from being pinned down and rendered immobile. Once there, Winters told his two machine-gun crews, Petty and Liebgott on one, and Hendrix and Plesha on the second, to position themselves to lay down an effective base of fire to cover the rest when they attacked. Compton was to get his men in close and lob grenades on one of the German machine-gun emplacements guarding the artillery and Lipton was to make sure he had the TNT he was carrying in a musette bag, to be able to blow up the guns once they were captured. He then sent Lipton and Ranney out to watch the German left flank.

"Speed is everything," Winters told his men. "We've got to hit them hard and fast, and get into that trench before they can react. Then we'll concentrate on the first gun, take it, then attack the rest one by one."

He ordered the men to drop everything except their ammo and follow him.

Malarkey liked the plan and later called Winters "a thinker."

"He'd been given a situation and he could, in about the time it took the rest of us to do an equipment check, figure out a plan of attack," he wrote.

He said Winters later told him that he had put Compton, Guarnere and him in the same group because they "instinctively understood the intricacies of battle."

"That meant a lot to me," he said.

★ ★ ★

The attack unfolded pretty much the way Ambrose outlined it in his book, and as I did in *Biggest Brother*, with my account coming directly from Winters. At his signal, Liebgott opened fire with his machine gun, its .30 caliber slugs raking the German position. The rest of the men joined in, providing cover fire for Compton and his group.

The enemy machine guns responded, and Germans in the trench opened up with their Mauser rifles. A German helmet poked up above the trench. Winters aimed his M1 and squeezed off a round. The helmet dropped out of sight. He later found a pool of blood at the spot but no sign of the German.

Compton, Guarnere and Malarkey slipped grenades from their web gear, yanked out the pins and hurled the "pineapples" at the machine gun. Seeing that, Winters yelled, "Come on! Follow me!" He leaped to his feet and ran forward, the others close behind. The exploding grenades knocked out the MG-42 and its crew, but bullets from Germans in the trench and machine guns in the distant tree line buzzed around the Americans like hornets, kicking up dirt devils at their feet as they charged.

Compton and his men ran forward, getting into the German earthworks. Compton saw two Germans in the end of the trench running perpendicular to the hedgerow.

"I figured I could take out the two Germans easily enough first," he said and ran toward them along the trench. Closing the distance, he stopped and raised his Tommy gun, the one he had been given earlier in the day by the injured McMillan, and squeezed the trigger. Nothing happened. Frantically he yanked the cocking lever and tried again. Nothing. The weapon's firing pin had been broken in McMillan's landing. The Germans heard Compton and wheeled in his direction, looks of surprise and horror on their faces. Then suddenly Guarnere, who was behind Compton, brushed by him and opened fire. One German went down right away; the other turned and ran. Compton tossed a grenade that burst over the fleeing man's head, killing him. Compton later said throwing the grenade was not something he had thought about, but rather was an automatic reaction.

"That was my first kill," he wrote. "I have no idea who he was, what he did outside the war, or if he had a wife or family. You just don't think. A man is trying to kill you, and you either kill him first or be killed waiting to assess the situation."

By now Winters and the others had also reached the trench. Diving behind the earthen wall for cover, Wynn yelped as a bullet struck him in the buttocks. Writhing on the bottom of the ditch and bleeding into his ripped trousers, he kept apologizing to Winters.

"I'm sorry, sir. I goofed," he cried. "I messed up. I'm sorry, Lieutenant."

A German potato-masher grenade thrown from the nearby artillery position landed almost at Toye's feet.

"Grenade!" Winters yelled.

Men dove in all directions. Toye flopped over backward as the grenade went off, shattering the stock of his M1. Recalling that moment, Guarnere later said Toye's rifle took the brunt of the blast: "Otherwise he'd be singing soprano." The Americans tossed grenades back. As they exploded, Lorraine, Guarnere and Winters stormed the gun position, weapons blazing. Three Germans leaped from the trench and ran toward their comrades in the opposite tree line.

With a quick attack, Winters and his men took the first German gun. But where was that gun? Was it at a forty-five-degree angle to the other three, firing at the causeway, as is the accepted version of the fight? Or was it on-line with the others, aimed at Utah Beach? Arguments can be made for both cases.

*   *   *

Brecourt, Paul Woodadge told me, is the part of the tour he dreads most because of the conflicting accounts surrounding it, especially in recent years as more veterans tell their stories.

"It was so easy a few years ago when you had just one version, the one in Ambrose's book," he said. "But now you've got Dick's version, and Guarnere's version and Malarkey's version and Compton's version. This is an absolute minefield of varying accounts."

Some of those differences involve the route of the attack and who came in from where. There is also some question as to the location of what is called Lipton's tree. As the attack began, Lipton climbed a young tree to get a better vantage point, foolishly exposing himself to enemy fire. It was the kind of error a rookie makes his first time in combat. Luckily, Lipton survived to learn from his mistake.

Paul pointed to a tree he assumes to be the one. It is about the right size for a tree that has stood for more than sixty years, and is about thirty yards west of the "L" in the German line. Pointing to the trunk of a felled tree, Paul said some students of the battle think that was Lipton's perch, but Paul feels that, since we know Lipton climbed a young tree, the diameter of this trunk makes the tree too old. Plus, in my own assessment, it is right by the "L" in the German line, making its position too close to the enemy line. From that distance, it is unlikely Lipton could have climbed it unseen. And once the Germans knew he was there, no trained soldier could have missed hitting him.

But the biggest question mark is the exact location of the first gun on the German left. As mentioned earlier in this chapter, the Brecourt monument commemorating the fight includes a pedestal, on which is etched a map detailing the battle that occurred here. That map that, as previously mentioned, was drawn by Michel de Vallavieille who lived on the land, and was endorsed by Winters as being accurate, shows all four guns pointing at the beach.

However, a sketch drawn by Winters for me in 2001 supports the first gun being pointed away from the beach, toward the causeway, and there are aerial photos that seem to support that claim showing, not the guns, but disturbed areas where the guns might have been placed.

Still, Woodadge leans very heavily toward the first map showing all four guns on line. He bases his judgment on time—the first map was drawn shortly after the actual fight—and military logic.

"Personally, I think all four guns were on a straight line," Paul said. "Dick says there was one on the corner here, in an L shape. I don't go along with that. These guns were placed here before the invasion to defend the beach. So it makes no sense to have one gun pointing toward the road. There was nothing there to shoot at."

Another who wrote about the fight, Carwood Lipton, is also not clear on the position of the first gun. Lipton wrote, "A frontal attack against those positions by thirteen men could not succeed, but Lieutenant Winters confidently outlined to us his plan to deceive and defeat the German forces and to destroy the guns. His plan was to concentrate a double envelopment attack on one gun, the one on the German left flank, and after capturing it to hit the other guns, one by one, on their open left flanks."

By "the one on the German left flank," did he mean one was turned to protect the left flank of the position? Or was he simply referring to the gun on the extreme left of the German line, since he goes on to say they would "hit the other guns, one by one, on their open left flanks"?

It could be taken either way.

Lipton went on to say, "These guns were sited to put artillery fire on the full expanse of Utah Beach, where the U.S. Fourth Division was coming ashore from landing craft. They had forward observers along the beach to direct the fire. The capture and destruction of the guns was a major factor in the success of the Utah landings and in the almost complete lack of casualties in that Division during its landing."

Again, by that did he mean all four guns were on line since they "were sited to put artillery fire on the full expanse of Utah Beach"?

Woodadge places great weight on the earlier map because its authors lived just a few hundred yards away.

"They drew the map that shows the guns on a line here, and my logic is they were the ones who were sitting here for years after the war," Paul said. "They would have known where the guns were. Dick, Don, Bill...they were only here for a few hours, then moved off."

Woodadge also feels time and publicity have clouded the facts.

"The TV version has supplanted the real memories. It's fresher and more vivid," he told me. "If I saw a documentary about my old school, that would be fresher in my brain than my own memories would be."

Having now spoken to Paul, with his assumptions based on logic and that map, and Winters, who endorsed the original map, but now says one gun was turned and who was an actual participant in the fight, I would dare muddy the water here with my own conjecture. A compromise, if you will.

Both might be correct.

Before June 6, this gun position was likely set up with all four guns on a row. That makes sense and is simple military logic, to put maximum firepower on the beach, since the goal of Field Marshal Erwin Rommel, who oversaw the defenses, was to stop the invasion at the water's edge.

Up until June 6, the position was guarded by a number of machine guns, protecting both the front and flanks of the battery. The airdrop in the early hours of D-Day changed that. One of the airborne drop zones was just inland of the battery's position.

"There's twelve hundred men landing on that drop zone," Paul said, pointing to the south. "The Germans would have heard the noise. There would have been patrols and gunfire."

At that time, Paul told us, the German commander of the battery shifted some of his machine guns from the battery's front, to the tree line across the field to his rear. After dawn, with the sound of battle to his rear intensifying and with American infantry now storming ashore on Utah Beach out in front of him, the battery commander quite likely realized that the paratroopers were attempting to seize the causeway and hold it for the ground forces. Thus he turned his left flank gun in that direction as a preventive measure. Later, Michel de Vallavieilles drew his map, he based it on guns original positions, not taking into account the change, and Winters did not correct them.

Again, that is my own conjecture. As Paul Woodadge told me, "you tell it the best you can with the information you have, throw in all the variables and let the reader draw his own conclusions."

"Anyone who wants to write the definitive history of Brecourt, they get my absolute good luck and well done," he said.

Woodadge admits that, despite his research, he has more questions than answers.

"I wasn't here," he told me. "The only thing I can use is logic. I cannot come up with a reason why they'd have a gun pointing up there. But everybody says it. Dick says it. Buck stood here and swore blind there was a gun there, so I don't know. What do you do?"

What you do is what Paul plans to do—more research. With the blessing of the de Vallavieille family, he and his staff intend to conduct an examination of the ground with metal detectors that will penetrate three meters into the earth in order to make a thorough examination of the site.

"We're going to use a huge scale map and put this into three-meter grids or something, and we're going to systematically survey each square to see what remnants of metal and shrapnel there is in the ground," Paul said, his voice sounding excited at the prospect. "We'll do the whole gun line and we're hoping that it will pick up four obvious disturbed areas where we can then put a probe in and see if we can find where the guns were because right now it's all based on opinion."

The key to the site is the exact location of that first gun, whether on the flank or on line. After that, he said, the exact positions of the other three should be simple. While Bill Guarnere said the guns were a hundred yards apart, Paul said German artillery pieces were generally sixty to ninty yards apart and Guarnere's statement was an approximation.

"That's someone saying, 'Bill, how far apart to you reckon the guns were?' and him saying, 'About a hundred yards,'" Paul said.

Paul understands the frustration in the minds of visitors he brings here hoping to learn about the fight, only to be confronted with more questions.

"I've brought many groups here and I can sense their disappointment because it's one of the few places where I can't just say, 'Yeah, it happened here,'" he said.

That will, hopefully, soon end.